AGGRESSIVE BEHAVIOR
Assessment and Intervention

Pergamon Titles of Related Interest

Apter/Goldstein   YOUTH VIOLENCE: Programs and Prospects
Center for Research on Aggression   PREVENTION AND
CONTROL OF AGGRESSION
Feindler/Ecton   ADOLESCENT ANGER CONTROL:
Cognitive-Behavioral Techniques
Goldstein/Carr/Davidson/Wehr   IN RESPONSE TO AGGRESSION:
Methods of Control and Prosocial Alternatives
Goldstein/Segall   AGGRESSION IN GLOBAL PERSPECTIVE

Related Journals
(free sample copies available on request)

CHILD ABUSE AND NEGLECT
CLINICAL PSYCHOLOGY REVIEW
JOURNAL OF ANXIETY DISORDERS

PSYCHOLOGY PRACTITIONER GUIDEBOOKS

EDITORS

Arnold P. Goldstein, Syracuse University
Leonard Krasner, Stanford University & SUNY at Stony Brook
Sol L. Garfield, Washington University

AGGRESSIVE BEHAVIOR
Assessment and Intervention

ARNOLD P. GOLDSTEIN
HAROLD R. KELLER
Center for Research on Aggression
Syracuse University

PERGAMON PRESS

NEW YORK · OXFORD · BEIJING · FRANKFURT
SÃO PAULO · SYDNEY · TOKYO · TORONTO

U.S.A.	Pergamon Press, Maxwell House, Fairview Park, Elmsford, New York 10523, U.S.A.
U.K.	Pergamon Press, Headington Hill Hall, Oxford OX3 0BW, England
PEOPLE'S REPUBLIC OF CHINA	Pergamon Press, Room 4037, Qianmen Hotel, Beijing, People's Republic of China
FEDERAL REPUBLIC OF GERMANY	Pergamon Press, Hammerweg 6, D-6242 Kronberg, Federal Republic of Germany
BRAZIL	Pergamon Editora, Rua Eça de Queiros, 346, CEP 04011, Paraiso, São Paulo, Brazil
AUSTRALIA	Pergamon Press Australia, P.O. Box 544, Potts Point, N.S.W. 2011, Australia
JAPAN	Pergamon Press, 8th Floor, Matsuoka Central Building, 1-7-1 Nishishinjuku, Shinjuku-ku, Tokyo 160, Japan
CANADA	Pergamon Press Canada, Suite No. 271, 253 College Street, Toronto, Ontario, Canada M5T 1R5

First edition 1987

Library of Congress Cataloging in Publication Data

Goldstein, Arnold P.
Aggressive behavior
(Psychology practitioner guidebooks)
Includes index
1. Aggressiveness (Psychology)   2. Behavior
therapy   I. Keller, Harold   II. Title   III. Series
[DNLM: 1. Aggression   2. Behavior Therapy
BF 575.A3   G6238a]
RC569.5.A34G65   1987   616.85'82   87-6987

British Library Cataloguing in Publication Data

Goldstein, Arnold P.
Aggressive behavior: assessment and
intervention. — (Psychology
practitioner guidebooks).
1. Aggressiveness (Psychology)
I. Title.   II. Keller, Harold.   III. Series.
155.2'32   BF575.A3
ISBN 0–08–034320–1 Hardcover
ISBN 0–08–034319–8 Flexicover

Printed in Great Britain by A. Wheaton & Co. Ltd., Exeter

To six valued colleagues and very special friends—Doug Biklen, Bob Bogdan, Barry Glick, Ken Heller, Peter Knoblock and Mark Sherman.

APG

To three special friends and valued colleagues from whom I have learned a great deal—Jane Conoley, Arnie Goldstein, and Renée Tapasak.

HRK

Contents

Part I
Introduction

Chapter 1

The Aggressive Behavior Sequence

Throughout this book we have conceptualized any act of overt aggression segmentally, as most typically consisting of a specific sequence of covert and observable events or steps. To the extent that this sequential conceptualization is accurate, one is provided with a tandem series of assessment tasks and intervention opportunities. Techniques of aggression control and reduction may profitably be utilized at each step in this aggressive behavior sequence, with different steps requiring different intervention techniques. Table 1.1 displays this perspective.

Following conceptualization of aggression, one is confronted with a set of assessment tasks to address these covert and overt events. The overall assessment concern is one of determining where and how best to intervene within this sequence. The chapters, in part II of this book, Assessment and Evaluation, provide a thorough presentation and evaluation of these assessment tasks. Because of developmental differences, the assessment tasks for children, adolescents and adults are considered separately. At each level, we will consider specific measures and processes, applicability, research support, and interrelationships among measures as they relate to the basic decision task of where and how to intervene, as well as to other important assessment concerns in the area of aggression. Chapter 3 addresses two other important assessment concerns: identification of individuals at risk for becoming aggressive or returning to aggressive behavior (upon removal from incarceration or other restrictive settings) and evaluation of intervention efficacy. When addressing evaluation of intervention efficacy, we will include a presentation of how the practitioner may design assessment and treatment strategies to make meaningful evaluations as to the efficacy of efforts to change, reduce, and prevent aggressive behavior.

Table 1.1. Behavior Modification Interventions of Value in the
Aggressive Behavior Sequence

Step	Intervention
1. Arousal-heightening interpretation of external stimulus	Anger control training
2. Heightened affective arousal	Relaxation training
3. Malcommunication	Communication training
	Negotiation training
	Contracting
4. Mismanagement of contingencies	Contingency management training
5. Prosocial skill deficiencies	Prosocial skill training
6. Prosocial value deficiencies	Prosocial values training

The chapters provide an in-depth presentation and evaluation of several intervention opportunities. In each instance, we will consider the constituent procedure, range of applicability, research support, and relation to the other interventions which constitute the full sequence of techniques that are of apparent value in the modification of aggressive behavior.

An aggressive act begins, in this view, with a stimulus event and its interpretation as aversive by an individual. This "trigger", accompanied or followed by kinesthetic and other physiological cues which idiosyncratically signal "anger" to the person, result in heightened levels of affective arousal. These two initial stages of the aggressive behavior sequence may be effectively self-managed, respectively, via anger control training aimed at anger-arousing self-statements (chapter 4), and relaxation training (chapter 5) in direct response to the physiological cues of anger arousal. Both procedures, therefore, seek to short-circuit the aggressive behavior sequence via interventions early in its development, both designed to diminish the affective underpinnings of subsequent overt aggression.

However, aggression is most typically a dyadic event, with the aggressor and aggressee reversing roles and spiraling upward in escalating conflict. To be effective, aggression reduction efforts must include not only means for aiding the target person in efforts to reduce his/her own anger level, but also in how to do likewise vis à vis the other party to the conflict. A series of calming techniques (chapter 5) will be considered for this purpose. Armed with such techniques, individuals are better prepared to lower the anger arousal level of their incipient combatants, and move on to more constructive means for conflict reduction. Chapter 6, dealing with communication, negotiation and contracting training, begins to provide these means. In effect, having begun to control undesirable behaviors, the individual can proceed to master desirable alternative responses which are focused on communication processes. Other reliable means exist for accelerating desirable behaviors and decelerating undesirable ones. Chapter 7 presents the array of contingency management procedures which have been effectively employed for such purposes. Means for both providing and withdrawing contingent reinforcement, as well as for providing aversive contingencies, will be examined. These several contingency management approaches to aggressive behavior each assume that desirable, prosocial alternative behaviors exist in the individual's behavioral repertoire, but are rarely expressed overtly. A rather different perspective on prosocial behavior, following from a behavior deficit model, holds quite the contrary that prosocial behaviors may be rarely expressed by an individual because he/she literally does not know how to do so. Such behaviors, in this view, are weak or lacking in the person's repertoire and must be taught quite directly. Prosocial skill training (chapter 8) will be examined for this purpose.

However, a person may be competent in controlling his/her anger, reducing others' anger, communicating effectively with others, and so forth, but may still *choose* to behave in an aggressive manner. To intervene in a truly comprehensive manner vis à vis the aggressive behavior sequence, underlying values may also have to be altered, especially those values which concern regard for the needs and perspective of others. Moral education is designed explicitly for this purpose, and is considered in chapter 9.

Part II

Assessment and Evaluation

Chapter 2
Assessment of Aggression

Assessment of aggression requires a multilevel approach. At a theoretical level, conceptual approaches to understanding aggression range from biologically based theories such as Freud's psychoanalytic theory (1920/1955, 1933/1964) and ethological theory (e.g., Lorenz, 1966; Tinbergen, 1968) to drive theories (e.g., Berkowitz, 1962, 1974; Dollard, Doob, Miller, Mowrer & Sears, 1939; Miller, 1941) and social learning theories (e.g., Bandura, 1973, 1977; Baron, 1977). Just as with personality theory in general, theoretical considerations of aggression have largely moved away from exclusively person-oriented models to person–situation interaction models. These more recently developed models incorporate person-oriented variables along with situational and task variables, as well as the potential interactions among these sets of variables. This more complex, interactional model is, in our view, central to the goal of adequate measurement of aggression. Following our conceptualization of aggression (outlined in chapter 1), one is confronted with a broad set of assessment tasks in order to address the covert and overt events comprising the aggressive behavior sequence. The overall assessment concern is one of determining where and how best to intervene within this sequence.

Clearly, we are arguing for breadth of assessment as opposed to narrowly focused assessment. Given the complexity of aggressive behavior and its concomitants, assessment that is too narrowly focused runs the risk of missing important information and thus leads to misdirected intervention. For example, assessment of children's aggressive behavior must also address family characteristics and interaction patterns (Kazdin & Frame, 1983; Loeber & Schmaling, 1985b), children's stealing (Loeber & Schmaling, 1985a), and the possible co-occurrence of withdrawn behavior, which is a behavioral combination particularly resistant to intervention (Ledingham, 1981; Ledingham & Schwartzman, 1984; Loeber & Schmaling, 1985a).

9

Considerable amounts of research have focused upon the linkage between person-oriented variables and aggressive behavior. Relationships between personality measures and test signals of a disposition to aggress have been shown, but with little direct linkage to the actual occurrence of aggressive behavior by a given individual. Numerous trait measures of aggression have been developed (e.g., Buss & Durkee, 1957; Cook & Medley, 1954; Genshaft, 1980; Posey & Hess, 1985; Robertson & Milner, 1985; Rosenzweig, 1976; Spielberger, Jacobs, Russell & Crane, 1983). Edmunds and Kendrick (1980) reviewed a wide variety of paper-and-pencil measures, along with numerous laboratory tasks designed to assess individual differences in disposition to aggression. They concluded that these measures of disposition generally lacked evidence for predictive validity to actual observed aggressive behavior, particularly by the individual being observed. Given the general lack of support for trait measures of aggression and the more specific lack of support with respect to individual predictive or treatment validity, we will not address the various trait measures except as they help us understand the individual and the aggressive behavior sequence as proposed in this book.

While the amount of research is growing, considerably less is known about the linkage between settings and aggressive behavior, or about person–setting linkages. Theory and research in ecological psychology can be helpful in these areas (Apter, 1982; Apter & Propper, 1986). In addition to person-oriented and setting variables, changing life tasks as one develops (which is related to diverse settings within which we interact and to developmental person-oriented variables), might fruitfully be viewed as an additional and separate set of variables pertinent to a multidimensional picture of aggression. Changing tasks demands as we assume new roles (e.g., spouse, parent, worker, being unemployed) can interact with other person-oriented variables (e.g., coping skills) and with setting variables (e.g., available social supports, presence of a difficult child) to result in the inhibition or disinhibition of aggressive behavior. These task–behavior and person–setting–task–behavior linkages need to be examined conceptually and empirically. Any assessment system for understanding aggression, for deciding upon appropriate interventions, and for evaluating the efficacy of intervention strategies must take into account this diverse set of person-oriented, setting, task, and behavioral variables, and their interaction.

Cone's (1978) taxonomy of behavioral assessment, based upon a person–setting interactional model, provides a useful framework for describing the kind of assessment needed in this area. He presents a three-dimensional taxonomy consisting of behavioral contents, methods, and universes of generalization. Behavioral contents refers to motoric (publicly observable acts), cognitive (private events including thoughts, images, reported feelings), and physiological events. All levels of these behavioral contents are represented in our conceptualization of the aggressive behavior sequence. Methods of behavioral assessment are ordered along a continuum of directness. That is, methods are ordered with respect to the extent that they measure the pertinent behavior at the time and place of its natural occurrence. At the most indirect end of the continuum, assessment methods include interviews, self-reports, and ratings by others (about past events), and self, analogue, and naturalistic observation at the most direct end. The third dimension, universes of generalization, refers to the domains across which we wish to generalize about a given phenomenon. Specific universes of generalization include scorer generalization (interrater reliability), item generalization (referring to how representative a set of stimuli or responses is to a universe of similar situations or responses), generalization across time (stability of a given phenomenon), setting generalization (to determine the degree of setting specificity or generality of a particular set of behaviors), and dimensions of generalization (referring to the comparability of data on two or more different behaviors, which allow us to understand response classes or response clusters).

Consideration of all three of these dimensions is essential to an optimal assessment of aggression and to the measurement of intervention efficacy. While our most immediate concern might be with observable motoric acts of aggression, cognitive and physiological concomitants of aggressive behavior—the other two facets of Cone's (1978) behavioral contents dimension—cannot be ignored. These cognitive and physiological concomitants may be antecedent to, concurrent with, and/or consequent to aggressive acts. For example, one's cognitive attributions concerning the behaviors and intentions of others in a particular setting may serve as an inhibitor or disinhibitor of aggression. With respect to Cone's second dimension, measurement methods in the area of aggression, it should be noted that a major concern with the validity of the commonly used rating scales (self or other) is the degree of behavioral and temporal specificity of the items. In addition, social desirability and other response bias and motivational aspects are pertinent considerations to the use of rating scales of aggression. While analogue observation (at the other end of the methods dimension) is a procedure in which an assessor arranges conditions to maximize the likelihood of aggressive behavior in order to observe its relationship to other variables of interest, its usefulness is limited by the extent to which the results are related to aggressive behavior outside the assessment setting (method and setting generality).

The most frequently used laboratory analogue procedures for measuring aggression have been questioned on these external validity grounds (Bornstein, Hamilton & McFall, 1981; Edmunds & Kendrick, 1980). Such procedures include providing subjects an opportunity to aggress verbally and directly against another individual (e.g., Wheeler & Caggiula, 1966), allowing physical attack on inanimate objects (e.g., Bandura, Ross & Ross, 1963), allowing direct physical aggression against others (though with padded swords and other similar "harmless" objects; e.g., Diener, Dinnen & Endressen, 1975), and leading subjects to believe through deception that they can cause physical injury to another through use of a shock device when in fact harm is impossible (e.g., Berkowitz, 1962; Buss, 1961; Taylor, 1967). The lack of method generality associated with most of these traditional psychological measures of aggression was an important consideration that lead away from strictly person-oriented models of aggression and toward person–setting models. Naturalistic observation often has the problem of reactivity to the presence of an observer, given the negative social sanctions for many forms of aggressive behavior. Certainly, direct assessment of aggression in the settings of concern provides the most powerful procedure for determining treatment efficacy. The problem of reactivity can be dealt with at least partially by directly observing behaviors highly correlated with aggression (dimensions generalization). The work of Burgess (1979) in the area of child abuse illustrates this well. He demonstrated through direct observational procedures a clear relationship between particular parenting styles and actual abusive behavior.

The universe of generalization, Cone's third dimension, is pertinent to the evaluation of assessment measures and to the determination of intervention efficacy. Consideration of strategies and procedures for evaluating treatment efficacy will be considered in the next chapter.

Assessment consistent with this three-dimensional framework, therefore, involves use of multiple methods with multiple responses and response levels within multiple settings. Such assessment applied to the understanding of the aggressive behavior sequence allows the convergence of information in the formation, testing, and strengthening of assessment and intervention hypotheses. Convergence of information is particularly relevant in an area such as aggression where the phenomenon is complex and where there are no universally accepted standard assessment measures. In addition, use of this framework allows the evaluation of unanticipated components of problems and the evaluation of unanticipated effects of interventions to prevent or control aggression.

Two other aspects of the assessment process should be emphasized before we examine specific assessment strategies used to address the aggressive behavior sequence. In addition to assessment being broadly based with a multi-method, multi-level approach, assessment of the behavior sequence must take into account developmental issues. Developmental differences in aggression and its antecedents and consequences have been largely ignored. The concomitants of aggression and its covert and overt aspects vary as the individual and those in the individual's environment, develop. To the extent possible, we will discuss assessment strategies as they apply most appropriately to individuals of different developmental levels (most generally children and adults). Indeed, successful application of some intervention strategies will most likely be dependent upon the child having attained minimal developmental levels of cognitive or social functioning, and assessment will need to address those concerns.

Finally, it is important to note that assessment in the area of aggression has not developed to the level where there are a variety of *standardized* assessment instruments from which to select. Existing standardized instruments are not adequate for assessing the unique problems of the individual and his or her environment. Therefore, the assessment of a given client for purposes of determining where and how best to intervene within the aggressive behavior sequence must be individually tailored. Strategies for assessing each component of the aggressive behavior sequence will be described for children and for adults. The individual change agent will need to adapt and use those strategies that address the particular assessment tasks for a given client of a particular developmental level.

ASSESSMENT OF THE AGGRESSIVE BEHAVIOR SEQUENCE

Arousal-Heightening Interpretation of External Stimuli

The basic assessment task for the arousal-heightening interpretation of external stimuli component of the aggressive behavior sequence is to determine what situational events the individual interprets as aversive, thus leading to heightened arousal, and what are the bases for those interpretations. Here, the focus will be upon the cognitive interpretations of those events, not the situational events that trigger anger arousal or the consequent heightened arousal per se, which are examined in the next section (see p. 16). In addition, we need to determine whether the individual has the skills necessary for benefitting from the associated anger control training. Since the primary focus at this stage of the sequence is upon covert cognitive processes, the methods of assessment necessarily involve indirect measures.

The clinical interview is the most frequently employed assessment method, and it is an important part of the assessment task here with both children and adults. When discussing specific recent anger-arousing events or when presenting sets of potentially anger provoking situational events (discussed more thoroughly in the next section, p. 16), the assessor should inquire how the individual did or would interpret those events. Did the person interpret another's actions as an insult, a threat, a challenge or in other ways as intending to harm or denigrate him or her? Does the individual indicate having considered intention in his or her interpretation of the situation? Was the anger and subsequent aggressive behavior done without any specific reason? A child's response to such questions and situations that he or she would direct aggressive behavior against another person without a specific reason is a strong predictor of concurrent overt aggressive behavior as well as later aggressive behavior (Pitkanen-Pulkkinen, 1981). When presented with conflict situations (actual or hypothetical), does the person generate effective problem-solving strategies or aggressive solutions? Is the individual applying a biased heuristic rule (e.g., "all black people are aggressive and will attack me if I don't be tough first")? If dealing with parent–child conflicts involving aggressive behavior, how is the adolescent interpreting the degree of parental control and how satisfied with that control is the adolescent? Dissatisfaction with parental control is an important discriminator between distressed and nondistressed mother–adolescent dyads (Prinz, Foster, Kent & O'Leary, 1979).

In vivo thought sampling (Kendall & Korgeski, 1979) is another indirect method of assessing the individual's functional and dysfunctional cognitions concerning specific situational events that provoke anger arousal and aggressive behavior. There are not any formal measures for getting at aggression-related cognitions in this manner. However, the clinician can develop a simple recording sheet for the client to record their attributions about the events and intentions of others, or their own self-talk (internal triggers) when provoked (e.g., "That s.o.b. is making fun of me," "I'm going to tear his head off"). Such feelings should be recorded as temporally close to the event as possible. We have used such "hassle logs" with incarcerated delinquents (Goldstein & Glick, 1986) and with elementary school-aged children identified as at-risk for becoming aggressive and delinquent. With very young children that have poorly developed writing skills, teachers have modified our hassle logs by having children draw pictures of the events and their affect concerning events.

Another indirect approach to assessing arousal-heightened cognitions is through the use of self-ratings and analogue tasks. Two measures particularly useful with children include the Children's Action Tendency Scale (Deluty, 1979) and the Affect Questionnaire (Garrison & Stolberg, 1983). The Children's Action Tendency Scale (CATS) is designed for children 6–12 years of age. It consists of 30 problem situation items where the child is required to choose between response alternatives—physical aggression, verbal aggression, assertion and submission—in a paired comparison format. The CATS has considerable data supporting its internal consistency, stability, convergent and discriminant validity, and concurrent and predictive validity to directly observed behavior in school settings (Deluty, 1979, 1981, 1983, 1984). The Affect Questionnaire (AQ) measures self-reported affect to a set of 53 emotional situations. The child is read a short story with an emotional theme and is asked how he/she would feel if in that situation. The child is required to make a forced choice by dividing ten tokens among four designated emotions (fear, anger, happiness, and sadness). The anger scale has high stability, between group discriminative validity, and demonstrated sensitivity to change as a result of an affective imagery training program to modify anger (Garrison & Stolberg, 1983). However, predictive validity to directly observed aggressive behavior has not been demonstrated. Both the CATS and AQ reportedly take about 15–20 minutes each to administer.

For adults, the Reaction Inventory (RI) (Evans & Strangeland, 1971) and Anger Inventory (AI) (Novaco, 1975) can both be useful sources of information on arousal-heightening cognitions. They correlate highly with each other (Biaggio, 1980), so only one scale is needed. They both involve the presentation of a broad range of specific stimulus situations designed to provoke anger reactions (90 and 76 items for the AI and RI, respectively). They measure the extent to which a person is willing to admit angry feelings and the degree to which a person becomes angry when provoked (Biaggio, 1980). Data on their respective reliabilities and predictive validities to anger expression are, however, inconsistent (Biaggio, Supplee & Curtis, 1981; Evans & Strangeland, 1971; Novaco, 1975; Selby, 1984).

Finally, with respect to prerequisite skills for benefitting from the anger control training, that is the intervention most directly addressing this component of the aggressive behavior sequence, the change agent will need to make certain that the individual has the cognitive and attending skills to understand and follow the steps in the anger control sequence. Can the individual remember the steps in the anger control sequence, or are memory aids needed for the individual? Language skills are needed for the self-instructional components in the "reminders" step of the training. Anger control training may or may not include the use of imagery, depending upon the client's ability to generate and use controlled imagery. Imaging and its self-controlled use can be assessed through any of a number of strategies cited in Tower and Singer (1981).

Heightened Affective Arousal

The basic assessment task of this component of the aggressive behavior sequence is to determine what situational events lead to heightened arousal, and anger arousal in particular. While hostility and anger arousal in varying situations is the major concern, it has been found that anger is elicited in adults in unpleasant, arousing, and dominance-eliciting situations (Russell & Mehrabian, 1974). Perhaps the most pragmatic approach to this assessment task is through the use of rating scales, either self-ratings or ratings by significant others in the settings of concern. In order to determine the full range of anger–arousal eliciting situations for a given client, it is necessary to sample a broad range of situations. The Rosenzweig Picture-Frustration Study (Rosenzweig, 1976) has the advantage of providing a measure of aggressive verbal behavior in response to frustrating situations at developmental levels from childhood through adolescence and adulthood. However, it has the major disadvantage of providing too few anger provoking situations.

With children, the previously cited CATS (Deluty, 1979) and AQ (Garrison & Stolberg, 1983) are perhaps the most comprehensive and have the strongest psychometric data to support their use for this assessment task. There are other rating scales for children that were developed for specific populations or settings. For example, Vondracek, Stein and Friedrich (1973) developed a nonverbal technique for use with preschoolers. There are 18 picture sequence sets, each with three pictured response alternatives depicting aggression, avoidance and prosocial behavior. Reliability estimates and concurrent validity with teacher ratings of aggression and with observed aggressive behavior were moderate. There are no predictive validity data or any data on the measure's sensitivity to change. Four measures have been developed and used with psychiatric residential child and adolescent populations. These are the Children's Inventory of Anger (Finch & Eastman, 1983; Finch, Saylor & Nelson, 1983; Nelson & Finch, 1978), the Overt Aggression Scale (Yudofsky, Silver, Jackson, Endicott & Williams, 1986), the Buss Durkee Hostility Inventory (Kazdin, Esveldt-Dawson, Unis & Rancurrello, 1983), and the Adolescent Antisocial Behavior Check List (Ostrov, Marohn, Offer, Curtiss & Feczko, 1980). The Overt Aggression

Scale has very mixed psychometric data and no evidence of sensitivity to change. The Children's Inventory of Anger has very high reliability, concurrent validity with ratings by significant others (peers and adults) and with intake behavior, but no evidence of predictive validity or sensitivity to change. The Adolescent Antisocial Behavior Check List has fair reliability and validity, as well as evidence of sensitivity to change (for the total score, not for scores on direction of violence— property, others, self). Kazdin et al. (1983) indicate that while children are able to self-rate their dysfunctional behaviors in these settings, they tend to provide lower estimates of the severity of their problems than their parents.

Spielberger et al. (1983) have developed the State–Trait Anger Scale (STAS) for adults. State anger refers to an emotional state consisting of subjective feelings of tension, annoyance, irritation, fury, and rage, along with concomitant activation or arousal of the autonomic nervous system. State anger varies with temporal and situational context. Trait anger refers to individual differences in the frequency that state anger was experienced over time. The STAS has excellent psychometric characteristics. However, there are only 10 items for each scale (state and trait), thus reducing its usefulness for the assessment task of concern here. There is not much evidence concerning the STAS' sensitivity to change. At the present time, the STAS appears to be most useful as an efficient research measure, and, with additional data, might serve as a brief measure that can be administered repeatedly and provide an index of change.

The Buss–Durkee Hostility Index (Buss & Durkee, 1957) and the Anger Self Report (Zelin, Alder & Myerson, 1972) both have an adequate sampling of items (66 and 64, respectively) for assessing anger-arousing situations for adults. Both measures have adequate reliability, concurrent and predictive validity data. The two measures correlate highly with one another (Biaggio, 1980), so there is little need to use both. Both measures are subject to social desirability ratings, and there is little evidence of sensitivity to change for either measure. Finally, Gottman and Levenson (1986) have reported that marital couple's self reports of affect under high conflict analogue discussions are very useful in assessing marital distress and change as a function of intervention. Filsinger (1983) presents many assessment measures helpful for assessing marital conflict.

All rating scales, including those previously mentioned, have the disadvantage of a likely mismatch between unique problems of a given client and his or her environment. That is, the particular situations included as items on a scale designed to present potentially anger arousing events may not be events confronted by a particular client or, if confronted, may not be of high salience for the individual. Given the desirability of individually tailoring the assessment of the aggressive behavior sequence, we will describe an approach for generating items and developing one's own measure to address this component of the sequence. This approach (used by Deluty, 1979, in the development of the CATS) is derived from the behavioral–analytic model of Goldfried and D'Zurilla (1969) as well as the more recent work of Dodge and Murphy (1984).

According to the behavioral–analytic model, items and response alternatives used in a self-report assessment measure are to be chosen on the basis of an empirical analysis of the relevant problem situations and of the likely courses of action undertaken by individuals representative of the population being studied or assessed. Items must be defined in specific situational terms. The situations described must be problematic in that they yield a variety of potential responses. The situations must be key, in that they represent the most pertinent and important environmental stimuli confronted by the individual or group.

The first stage in this approach is to conduct a situational analysis. For the change agent in the schools or agency, this analysis consists of a survey of relevant aggression-eliciting situations for the population of concern. The developmental level of the clients must be considered in this stage. For the change agent with an individual client, a detailed clinical interview with the client and significant others is necessary for this analysis. Interviewing significant others is important since often the client is unaware of problematic situations.

The second stage, or response enumeration stage, involves generating a list of possible discriminating responses to each of the pertinent situations selected in the first stage. Again, groups of individuals or a single client is surveyed concerning how they typically respond to each of the situations.

Response evaluation is the third stage in this approach. Here the client, groups of similar individuals, significant others and colleagues are asked to evaluate the most frequently cited discriminating responses in terms of anger arousal or aggressiveness. It is important that the clinician, or even the clinician's colleagues, not be the sole judge of the responses. The individual clients and significant others, in particular, are needed to make those evaluative judgments. The importance of the significant others in such evaluations cannot be emphasized enough since arousal and aggression typically occur in interpersonal situations. Such an emphasis is particularly important for child and adolescent clients since they are brought to professional attention primarily through the social judgments of others in the child's or adolescent's environment.

Malcommunication

Assessing this component of the aggressive behavior sequence involves the determination of communication skills and miscommunication patterns that are related to aggressive behavior, particularly within dyadic relationships. Relatively less research has been conducted in this area, and few formal measures are available for this assessment task.

At the indirect end of the continuum of methods are paper-and-pencil measures designed to assess family conflict and communication patterns. The Conflict Tactics (CT) Scale (Straus, 1979) was developed to assess three primary modes of dealing with conflict within families: reasoning, verbal aggression, and violence. The scale measures conflict resolution tactics among all possible family member dyads. For each item, the respondent is to indicate how often he or she engaged in the behavior over the past year, how often the other member of the designated dyad engaged in the behavior, and whether or not the behavior ever had occurred in the history of the dyadic relationship. Norms are available for a national sample of intact families. The verbal aggression (assessing the use of verbal and nonverbal acts that symbolically hurt another person) and violence subscales have high consistency, but the reasoning subscale (assessing an intellectual approach through the use of rational discussion, argument, and reasoning) has lower consistency. Substantial evidence for validity of the CT scale is available. Another paper-and-pencil measure with adequate reliability and validity data is the Parent–Adolescent Communication Scale (Barnes & Olson, 1982).

Gottman and Levenson (1986) emphasize the importance of more direct measures of communication patterns in marital as well as other family interactions. Robinson and Eyberg (1981) described the Dyadic Parent–Child Interaction Coding System (DPICS) for use in both direct naturalistic observation and analogue observation. There are 29 behaviors observed during event recording within 5-minute segments. Maternal behavior categories include total praise, critical statements, total commands (direct and indirect), no opportunity commands (where the child has no opportunity to comply) and direct commands. The child categories include total child deviance, and noncompliance. Webster-Stratton (1985) found the DPICS to be highly useful within a structured clinical observation setting (analogue observation). In her situation, the interaction was parent-directed where the parent was to choose something to play and get the child to play as well. Comparing observations under an unstructured clinical observation ("do what you normally do," or "follow your child's lead") to the structured analogue observation, she found higher rates of parental commands which resulted in greater child deviance and noncompliance under the analogue observation conditions. Behavior in this structured context correlated most highly with parent ratings of aggression and conduct problems. Webster-Stratton suggested the structured clinical observation was highly efficient and analogous to a challenge test in medicine where, for example, someone suspected of having an allergy is presented with a symptom-producing substance. Similarly, when an unstructured baseline observation is followed by the analogue observation, if there is a significant change in parental behavior and a significant increase in child deviance and noncompliance, then this suggests a more seriously disturbed parent–child dyad. The observational results provide specific intervention suggestions for improving the communication and interactional patterns.

Prinz et al. (1979) provide a description of a comprehensive assessment battery for use in evaluating parent–adolescent conflict. The Conflict Behavior Questionnaire (CBQ) consists of 73 (adolescent version) or 75 (maternal version) items that describe conflict-related behaviors. Four scores are derived from the CBQ, including the adolescent's appraisal of the mother, maternal appraisal of the adolescent, the adolescent's appraisal of the dyad, and maternal appraisal of the dyad. The Issues Checklist (IC) assesses the frequency and intensity of discussions associated with specific issues that might arise at home, and the frequency and intensity of disagreements about specific issues. Six derived scores are obtained, including maternal/adolescent quantity of issues, maternal/adolescent intensity of issues, and maternal/adolescent intensity-by-frequency of issues. A parental control measure along with a measure of the adolescent's dissatisfaction of parental control are also obtained. The Decision-Making Questionnaire measures the relative balance of power between members of the dyad, an appraisal of decision making, and adolescent dissatisfaction with decision making. Daily home reports were obtained for one week, consisting of positive and negative (yes/no) descriptions of parent and adolescent behavior. The reports included an estimate of the ratio of the arguments to pleasant or neutral interactions for each day. Finally, 10-minute tape recorded discussions were submitted. The discussions concerned something the adolescent wanted to change and that would involve implementing a course of action in the home. Ratings from the recordings were made of negative behavior (adolescent/mother), positive behavior (adolescent/mother), insults (dyad), friendliness (dyad), resolution of problem (dyad), and problem-solving effectiveness (dyad).

Interobserver reliabilities were very high. All measures had solid psychometric characteristics. The most effective discriminators between conflicted and non-conflicted dyads were the CBQ (especially the mother's scores) and the ratings of the taped discussion. Similarly effective discriminators were the ratings (from both mother and adolescent) of the intensity of issues on the IC, not frequency, and adolescent dissatisfaction with parental control. While parents and adolescents differ on many issues, their data indicated that the most critical factor was the way the differences were handled (not the frequency of differences), and most particularly how the dyad talked to one another. Therefore, an important assessment strategy for this component is to obtain samples of how issues were discussed and handled. Reports of positive and negative communication behaviors related to conflict situations are also important. For greatest reliability and validity, reports must concern recent specific quantifiable events, not reports of general past child rearing practices which tend to be unstable and distorted. These samples and reports lead directly to specific targets for intervention within this component of the aggressive behavior sequence.

Mismanagement of Contingencies

The basic assessment task for this component of the aggressive behavior sequence is the examination of those environmental events that serve to maintain aggressive behavior and its concomitants, as well as those environmental events that reduce the likelihood of the individual engaging in prosocial alternatives to aggressive behavior. This is typically done through the functional analysis of behavioral interactions among the individual client and significant others. There is extensive literature on the use of clinical interviews and direct observation as part of this functional analysis (e.g., Kazdin & Frame, 1983; Keller, 1986). Our focus will be upon issues pertinent to this assessment task and some of the molar variables derived from detailed systematic observations that have been shown to be related to aggressive behavior. Much of this work revolves around observations of parent–child interactions.

It is always desirable to observe not only the aggressive behaviors that we want to reduce, but also those prosocial alternatives we wish to enhance. While direct observation is the most thorough means of conducting this assessment task, more indirect approaches such as clinical interviews and rating scales can be helpful both in and of themselves and as aids to focusing the observational assessment. The interviewer must take care to elicit information as descriptive as possible from the client and significant others. General questions concerning how the parent relates to or disciplines the child client should be avoided. Rather, interviewees might be asked to describe in detail a recent day, a recent positive experience with the client, a recent instance where the client controlled his or her anger, a recent conflict that resulted in aggressive behavior, or a recent disciplinary action. Often, getting the interviewee to image the day or conflict and to describe the scene and event in great detail is a helpful means of getting the person into a descriptive mode and away from dealing with generalities.

Behavior ratings scales (Martin, Hooper & Snow, 1986), while being static measures of behavior, can be helpful in directing the focus of interviews and observations. The previously cited CT scale (Straus, 1979) could provide information concerning intrafamily interactional patterns surrounding conflict. Achenbach and Edelbrock's (1983) Child Behavior Checklist (CBCL) is a thoroughly normed and standardized broad-band parental checklist that includes aggressive behavior and other undercontrolled behaviors as well as overcontrolled behaviors such as withdrawal and anxiety. As indicated earlier, the combination of aggression and withdrawal has been shown to be particularly resistant to therapeutic efforts so such a combination of behavioral characteristics would require careful planning of a comprehensive treatment program. An additional advantage of the CBCL is that it has been shown to be sensitive to therapeutic change and therefore could be used as a general measure of treatment outcome. Further, Achenbach and Edelbrock have developed a teacher report form (CBCL-TRF), a youth self report form (CBCL-YSR), and a direct observation form (CBCL-DOF) to accompany the CBCL.

In addition to the previously described DPICS analogue observation approach of Robinson and Eyberg (1981), which was demonstrated to be effective in identifying targets for treatment and for measuring treatment efficacy (Webster-Stratton, 1985), Abramovitch, Konstantareas, and Sloman (1980) described a free-play analogue observational procedure for children 5–7 years of age. Their behavioral categories included aggressive, prosocial and imitative acts, plus a derived prosocial/aggression ratio. The measures were found to be highly sensitive to change for a treatment program focusing upon increasing prosocial behavior and decreasing aggressive behavior.

Patterson and his colleagues (Loeber & Schmaling, 1985b; Patterson & Bank, 1986; Patterson & Stouthamer-Loeber, 1984) describe both direct and analogue observational procedures for assessing mismanaged contingencies related to aggressive behavior. Two derived measures that have been found to account for most of the variance in official data as well as self-reported delinquency and aggression include parental monitoring and discipline. These two variables were found to be significantly more important than specific parental reinforcement contingencies. Monitoring refers to parents' failure to note or to believe reports of major antisocial episodes outside the home, parental perception of supervision of children as unimportant, amount of sharing by child about his/her activities, and discrepancy between child's report of activities in the past week and parent's report of child's activities over the same interval. Monitoring was measured through direct observation, taped discussions in the home, and phone interviews concerning activities. The most important aspects of the discipline variable were the degrees of consistency both within a parent and between parents, and maternal followup to commands. For more severely antisocial children (Patterson & Bank, 1986), inept discipline included parental tendency to scold, threaten and nag as reactions to both trivial and significant antisocial behaviors, a tendency to use significantly more extreme forms of physical punishment (i.e., hitting, grabbing, or beating with an object), and the occurrence of explosive, unpredictable discipline. The potential breadth of impact of the monitoring variable is illustrated further by Boike, Gesten, Cowen, Felner and Francis (1978). They found that minimal parental interest in a child's educational situation, little monitoring of study habits and homework completion, and little reinforcement for academic involvement or achievement were related to both greater learning problems and aggressive acting out problems.

Again, a multi-method approach to assessing whether or not mismanagement of contingencies is a significant component in a given individual's aggressive behavior is important. Particular emphasis should be placed upon the explicit delineation of parental monitoring and parental disciplinary strategies in assessing children's aggressive behavior. Successful contingency management intervention also is dependent upon a thorough job of doing those assessment activities in preparation for such treatment stategies (cited in chapter 7). At the same time, concern should be addressed to the contingencies maintaining, or reducing the likelihood of, the use of prosocial skill alternatives over aggressive behaviors.

Prosocial Skill Deficiencies

Prosocial skills are highly situationally and task specific (Dodge, McClaskey & Feldman, 1985; Freedman, Rosenthal, Donahoe, Schlundt & McFall, 1978; Gaffney & McFall, 1981; Hartwig, Dickson & Anderson, 1980). Therefore, the basic assessment task for this component of the aggressive behavior sequence is to identify an individual profile of situationally task-specific prosocial skill strengths and weaknesses. Our suggested assessment strategies for this component follow the social information processing model of social competence proposed by Dodge and Murphy (1984). Selection of situations and tasks for prosocial skill assessment should follow the behavioral–analytic model (Goldfried & D'Zurilla, 1969) described earlier for situations eliciting heightened anger arousal (i.e., situational analysis, response enumeration, and response evaluation).

Within this model, social tasks must be defined in specific situational terms. Tasks must be problematic in that they yield a variety of responses. Tasks must be key in that they represent the most pertinent and important environmental situtations confronted by the individual or group. Social competence, because it is interpersonal in nature, involves a judgmental process. An individual is socially skilled to the degree to which he or she is judged to be successful at solving or completing social tasks. Competence, therefore, is determined by the criteria of judges, or significant others, so it must be recognized that judgments may vary with characteristics of the significant others.

Social competence involves what Dodge and Murphy (1984) refer to as social information processing skills. These component skills include the ability to decode and interpret social cues in the environment, response decision (involving memory search for possible responses, evaluation of the adequacy of each response, and response selection), and enactment (task-specific verbal and motor skills). Overriding skills include the ability to integrate subcomponent skills, and, most importantly, self-monitoring skills and resulting modulation of behavior.

The specific assessment framework derived from this model includes the following steps:

1. Identification of the client, identification of who judged the client as incompetent, and the bases of that judgment.
2. Survey of pertinent social tasks. A detailed clinical interview is conducted with the client and significant others, perhaps starting with one of the general rating scales of situationally derived social tasks (discussed on pp. 16–17).
3. Identification of the situational sources of incompetence. This involves the determination of which subset of tasks provides the most problems for the individual. That is, which tasks result in behaviors that are judged incompetent? This can be done by asking the client directly, though often the client is unaware of those tasks that provide the most difficulty. It is therefore important to get this information from significant others. Alternatively or additionally, the client can be asked how he or she typically responds to each of the social tasks, then the responses can be judged for competence by

significant others (or, less preferably, by the clinician). It is important that clients be asked "What do you do?" in response to a particular situational task, rather than "What is the best thing to do?". The
latter type of question might be helpful in determining whether
there is a knowledge deficit or a skill deficit.

4. Assessment of subcomponent skills and deficits. Determine the
   specific locus of the client's incompetence in each identified task.
   Which subcomponent process is the source of incompetent performance in specific tasks?
5. Construct a profile of specific skills and deficits.
6. Design an individually specific and appropriate prosocial skills
   intervention.
7. Evaluate the efficacy of the intervention.

Self and other ratings of prosocial skills, along with detailed clinical
interviews, comprise the primary method of assessment for this component of the aggressive behavior sequence. While role play analogue
observations have been the mainstay of much of the social skills assessment literature, research has not found role-plays to be valid indices of
directly observed prosocial skills or of self or other ratings of social skills
(Farrell, Curran, Zwick & Monti, 1983; Kazdin, Matson & Esveldt-
Dawson, 1984; Monti, 1983; Monti, Wallander, Ahern, Abrams & Munroe, 1983). Time constraints are such that role-plays do not include a
broad enough range of situations and social tasks. Role-play analogue
measures of social skills can be effective proximal pre- and post-
measures of treatment efficacy. That is, they can be designed as
measures of training specific skills to make certain that the trained skills
were acquired as a result of the intervention. Such training-specific
acquisition is necessary before examining more important generalization and transfer effects of intervention.

There are a variety of prosocial skills rating scales for children. Three
quick screening measures might be useful in a school setting to help
identify children at-risk for prosocial skill deficits and in need of more
comprehensive assessment. These measures are the social competence
subscale of the CBCL (Achenbach & Edelbrock, 1983), the Classroom
Adjustment Rating Scale (CARS) (Lorion, Cowen & Caldwell, 1975), and
the Children's Assertiveness Behavior Scale-Teacher (CABS-T) (Shapiro, Lentz & Sofman, 1985). None of these measures are sufficiently
broad-based to serve the function of surveying pertinent social tasks.
The CBCL does have the advantage of including both the general social
competence rating and broad-based ratings of problem behaviors
(many of which might be concomitants of social skill deficits and targets
of intervention in their own right).

AB-C

The Student Skill Checklists and Teacher Skills Checklists for children (McGinnis & Goldstein, 1984) and for adolescents (Goldstein, Sprafkin, Gershaw & Klein, 1980) have excellent treatment validity because they identify specific skill areas (classroom survival skills, friendship-making skills, skills for dealing with feelings, skill alternatives to aggression and skills for dealing with stress) in need of intervention. The skill areas and checklists have been used in an extensive set of intervention studies. Concurrent validity between the student and teacher checklists is good, but there is no evidence on predictive or concurrent validity to independent measures of social skills.

Deluty's (1979) CATS provides a situational survey of assertiveness skills for children. Another useful specific domain for skills assessment that has been demonstrated to be relevant to aggression is the assessment of academic skills (Boike et al., 1978; Dishion, Loeber, Stouthamer-Loeber & Patterson, 1984).

Two broad-based measures of social skills in children include the Taxonomy of Problematic Social Situations for Children (TOPS) (Dodge et al., 1985) and the Matson Evaluation of Social Skills with Youngsters (MESSY) (Matson, Rotatori & Helsel, 1983). The TOPS is a teacher rating scale with 44 items. It addresses six factors, including peer group entry, response to peer provocations (found to be most problematic for rejected and aggressive children), response to failure, response to success, social expectations, and teacher expectations. This measure has been demonstrated to successfully identify situational contexts of children's social incompetence, as well as subcomponent skill deficits. The MESSY consists of a 62-item self report and a 64-item teacher report. The self-report scale yields five factors, including appropriate social skills, inappropriate assertiveness, impulsiveness/recalcitrance, overconfidence, and jealousy/withdrawal. The teacher report yields two factors, inappropriate assertiveness/impulsivity and appropriate social skills. The MESSY has been shown to correlate highly with independent teacher and parent ratings of social skills in children (Kazdin et al., 1984).

For adolescents, two broad-based measures of social skills have been developed separately for males and females—the Adolescent Problems Inventory (API) (Freedman et al., 1978) and the Problem Inventory for Adolescent Girls (PIAG) (Gaffney & McFall, 1981). Both measures have been shown to be reliable, stable, and valid scales. The API has 44 items and the PIAG has 52 items.

The Social Performance Survey Schedule (SPSS) (Lowe & Cautela, 1978) is the only broad-based measure of social skills for adults. However, while it has been found to correlate well with role-play analogue measures of social skills (Miller & Funabiki, 1983; Monti, 1983), it has not been shown to relate to in vivo staff evaluations of hospitalized psychiatric patients (Monti, 1983). Hardly any other psychometric data are available on the measure. It might serve as a useful beginning point for a thorough clinical interview. More specific rating scales of adult assertiveness skills include the Conflict Resolution Inventory (Hartwig et al., 1980) and the Personal Assertion Analysis (Hedlund & Lindquist, 1984). Both assertiveness scales have adequate reliability, stability, and convergent and discriminant validity.

Prosocial Value Deficiencies

This component of the aggressive behavior sequence is viewed from a developmental perspective (see chapter 9 for detailed discussion of the theoretical foundations for the associated intervention), with focus upon those values that concern regard for the needs and perspectives of others. Kohlberg's (1969) theory of the development of moral reasoning is the specific conceptual basis for this area. The assessment task therefore is to determine the moral reasoning stage of the individual. Assessment tools in this area have been developed and used primarily as research tools. We have found the Sociomoral Reflections Measure (Gibbs & Widaman, 1982) helpful in this task. It consists of two moral dilemmas and a series of probe questions for each. An estimate of the individual's level of moral reasoning is obtained. The measure has very good reliability, stability, and convergent and discriminant validity. Performance on the measure has been shown to relate to antisocial and aggressive behavior in adolescents. A disadvantage of the measure is that it takes extensive training in the administration and scoring procedures in order to attain high levels of interscorer reliabilities.

A simpler measure of moral judgments, also yielding an estimate of the individual's stage of moral development, was developed by Carroll and Rest (1981). The measure consists of 40 statements written to give moral advice representing the first four of Kohlberg's stages and a composite of the principled stages (5 and 6). Items were written in the context of four moral dilemmas. Each of the five stages was represented by eight moral advice statements. There were two statements representing each stage for each of the four stories. Items were rated on a four-point scale (reject to accept). This measure was found to have adequate reliability and showed consistent developmental differences. While the authors suggest its use in intervention studies, insufficient research has been conducted with this measure.

As will be indicated in chapter 9, the moral reasoning trainer must continually assess the moral reasoning stage of group participants during the intervention. This ongoing assessment task requires a thorough grounding in Kohlberg's (1969) conceptual framework. Chapter 9 and the description of the moral reasoning component of our aggression replacement training (Goldstein & Glick, 1986) should be helpful in the application of this task as well.

To summarize, assessment of the aggressive behavior sequence requires a multi-method, multi-level approach that is developmentally based and individually tailored. A variety of available measures and strategies have been discussed and are listed in Table 2.1. It is critical that assessment be conducted in a manner that leads directly to interventions and to the evaluation of the effectiveness of those interventions. Continuity of assessment and evaluation is important. We will now consider measurement of intervention efficacy, a necessary component of treatment implementation.

Table 2.1. Assessment of the Aggressive Behavior Sequence

Arousal-Heightening Interpretation of External Stimuli
  Interview
  In Vivo Thought Sampling (Kendall & Korgeski, 1979)
  Rating Scales
    Children's Action Tendency Scale (Deluty, 1979)—Children
    Affect Questionnaire (Garrison & Stolberg, 1983)—Children
    Reaction Inventory (Evans & Strangeland, 1971)—Adults
    or
    Anger Inventory (Novaco, 1975)—Adults

Heightened Affective Arousal
  Individually Tailored via Behavioral-Analytic Model
    Situational Analysis
    Response Enumeration
    Response Evaluation
  Rating Scales
    Children's Action Tendency Scale (Deluty, 1979)—Children
    Affect Questionnaire (Garrison & Stolberg, 1983)—Children
    State–Trait Anger Scale (Spielberger et al., 1983)—Adults
    Buss–Durkee Hostility Index (Buss & Durkee, 1957)—Adults
    or
    Anger Self Report (Zelin et al., 1972)—Adults

Malcommunication
  Rating Scales
    Conflict Tactics scale (Straus, 1979)
    Parent–Adolescent Communication Scale (Barnes & Olson, 1982)
  Analogue Observation
    Dyadic Parent–Child Interaction Coding System (Robinson & Eyberg, 1981)
  Comprehensive Battery (Prinz et al., 1979)
    Conflict Behavior Questionnaire
    Issues Checklist
    Decision-Making Questionnaire
    Daily Home Report
    Taped Discussions

Mismanagement of Contingencies
Rating Scales
    CBCL (-TRF, -YSR, -DOF) (Achenbach & Edelbrock, 1983)
Analogue Observation
    Dyadic Parent–Child Interaction Coding System (Robinson & Eyberg, 1981)
Derived Measures from Observation and Other Methods (Loeber & Schmaling, 1985b;
        Patterson & Bank, 1986; Patterson & Stouthamer–Loeber, 1984)
Parental Monitoring
Parental Discipline

Prosocial Skill Deficiencies
Behavioral–Analytic Model
Social Information Processing Model of Social Competence (Dodge & Murphy, 1984)
    Identification of Client and Significant Others
    Survey of Social Tasks
    Identification of Situational Sources of Incompetence
    Subcomponent Skills and Deficits: Decoding, Interpretation, Response Decision,
        Enactment, Skill Integration, Self-Monitoring
    Profile of Skills and Deficits
    Intervention
    Evaluation
Rating Scales
    Screening—Children: CBCL (Achenbach & Edelbrock, 1983); Classroom Adjustment
        Rating Scale (Lorion et al., 1975); Children's Assertiveness Behavior Scale
        (Teacher) (Shapiro, Lentz & Sofman, 1985)
    Student Skills Checklist and Teacher Skills Checklist—Children: McGinnis &
        Goldstein, 1984; Adolescents: Goldstein et al., 1980
    Taxonomy of Problematic Social Situations for Children (Dodge et al., 1985)—
        Children
    Matson Evaluation of Social Skills with Youngsters (Matson et al., 1983)—Children
    Adolescent Problems Inventory (Freedman et al., 1978)—Adolescent Boys
    Problem Inventory for Adolescent Girls (Gaffney & McFall, 1981)—Adolescent Girls
    Social Performance Survey Schedule (Lowe & Cautela, 1978)—Adults

Prosocial Value Deficiencies
Sociomoral Reflections Measure (Gibbs & Widaman, 1982)
Carroll & Rest (1981)

Chapter 3
Evaluation of Intervention Efficacy

In this chapter, we will examine two assessment concerns. The first issue is the prediction of aggressive behavior. Can we identify individuals at-risk for becoming aggressive or at-risk for returning to aggressive behavior, for example, upon removal from incarceration or other restrictive settings (Goldstein & Keller, 1983; Webster, Ben-Aron & Hucker, 1985)? The second issue to be addressed is that of the evaluation of intervention efficacy. Evaluation of treatment is critical to efforts that successfully prevent and reduce the complex phenomenon of aggressive behavior.

PREDICTION OF AGGRESSIVE BEHAVIOR

Effective prediction could serve as a significant enhancer of prevention and control efforts. If the timing and target of aggression were adequately anticipated, steps could be developed and implemented to minimize or even eliminate the likelihood that overt aggression would actually take place. However, high levels of accurate prediction have proven to be difficult to obtain. On a broad macrolevel of inquiry, it has been sufficiently established that aggressive criminal behavior consistently correlates with demographic and related variables such as past criminal behavior, age, sex, race, socioeconomic status, and drug or alcohol abuse. But such group-focused, actuarial probabilities are of modest value at best in predicting the overt behavior of a given individual or individuals.

Some have posited that successful prediction might follow from accurate identification and use of childhood predictors of adult aggression. Many such possible predictors have been suggested; very few have been empirically examined to the point of successful cross-validation especially for purposes of predicting individual behavior. Hellman and Blackman (1966), as have many others, suggest enuresis, pyromania, and cruelty to animals be used for such predictive purposes. Based on surveys of mental health professionals, Goldstein (1974) concluded that a largely agreed upon constellation of childhood predictors of adult violence consisted of maternal deprivation, poor identification with father, enuresis, pyromania, cruelty to animals, and abuse by one or both parents. Empirical predictive studies are not totally lacking, however. Lefkowitz, Eron, Walder, and Huesman (1977) report such statistically significant childhood predictors of aggression at age 19 as (a) aggression at age 8 (single best predictor), (b) father's upward social mobility, (c) low identification of the child with his/her parents, and (d) a preference for watching violent television programs. McCord (1979) reported as statistically significant predictors: (a) lack of supervision during childhood, (b) mother lacking in self-confidence, and (c) chronic parental aggressiveness. Wolfgang, Figlio, and Sellin (1972) found number of residential moves, lower IQ, mental retardation, and fewer school grades completed to be reliable childhood predictors of adult aggression. It is apparent that the potential array of useful childhood predictors of aggression is modest and of limited utility when employed in attempts to predict overt aggression in the individual case. The findings reported are part untested speculation, part untested consensus, and part empirically identified postdictors of potential interest and usefulness, but largely awaiting predictive cross-validation.

Efforts to predict the overt aggression of any specific adult or groups of adults by means of other characteristics of such adults have generally yielded largely unsatisfactory outcomes. In his definitive work in this domain, *The Clinical Prediction of Violent Behavior*, Monahan (1981) critically reviewed the five major investigations that have sought to examine the utility of psychological test and interview data for predicting aggression. He demonstrated that clinical prediction of adult aggression yields a dismaying number of mispredictions. False positives, that is, prediction of aggression but no actual aggression ensuing, were very high across all studies reviewed. Monahan (1981) comments:

> [the] best clinical research currently in existence indicates the psychiatrists and psychologists are accurate in no more than one out of three predictions of violent behavior over a several-year period. . . . (p. 47)

Monahan correctly interprets the research as indicating our general inability to accurately predict individual aggression. Nevertheless, he urges further research on the demographic-aggression correlates and on certain postdictively identified childhood and adult behavioral predictors previously noted. The following paths are suggested by him.

1. Make base rates of violence a prime consideration. Monahan (1981) quite rightly notes that if the base rate of aggression in a given population is low, prediction of its occurrence is especially difficult. Perhaps, therefore, predictive efforts should focus mostly upon populations who have displayed such behavior earlier, for example, high base rate populations.

2. Obtain and use information of valid predictive utility. More information often does not mean better prediction, and may mean worse prediction. Crucial here is the demonstrated relationship between the predictor and criterion (aggressive behavior). As Monahan (1981) notes: "Focusing on a limited number of relevant and valid predictor items is more important than an exhaustive examination that yields much irrelevant and ultimately confusing information" (p. 88).

3. Make predictions based upon all relevant information. Attempt to include and properly weigh negative indices as well as potentially counterbalancing positive factors that would tend to decrease the individual's propensity to aggression.

4. If possible, combine the use of person and situation variables in attempting to predict aggressive behavior. Until very recent years, the effort to predict aggression was almost entirely based on the use of personality, psychometric, demographic, and related information about the potential perpetrator as the predictive base (the person-oriented model). In recent years, consistent with a parallel move toward person–situation interaction in personality theory in general, increasing efforts have taken place to consider situational and environmental information when attempting to predict aggressive behavior. Among the situational variables possibly predictive of the inhibition or facilitation of aggression are characteristics of one's family, peers, and job; the availability of intended victims; the availability of weapons; and the availability of alcohol, drugs or other possible disinhibitors.

Monahan (1981) presented a list of questions advantageously used by interviewers in trying to make accurate predictions. These questions appear in Table 3.1. While Monahan's insights and recommendations represent a major contribution in this area of predicting aggression, it is clear that our cumulative knowledge relative to predicting aggression currently remains inadequate, a conclusion further confirmed in yet another subsequent examination of the relevant theoretical and empirical literature (Webster et al., 1985). A great deal of predictor-identifying and prediction-testing research remains to be conducted. Perhaps such efforts will yield personality, demographic, situational, and other predictor information of use to this all-important task. Until such infor-

Table 3.1. Questions for the Clinician in Predicting Violent Behavior

1. Is it a prediction of violent behavior that is being requested?
2. Am I professionally competent to offer an estimate of the probability of future violence?
3. Are any issues of personal or professional ethics involved in this case?
4. Given my answers to the above questions, is this case an appropriate one in which to offer a prediction?
5. What events precipitated the question of the person's potential for violence being raised, and in what context did these events take place?
6. What are the person's relevant demographic characteristics?
7. What is the person's history of violent behavior?
8. What is the base rate of violent behavior among individuals of this person's background?
9. What are the sources of stress in the person's current environment?
10. What cognitive and affective factors indicate that the person may be predisposed to cope with stress in a violent manner?
11. What cognitive and affective factors indicate that the person may be predisposed to cope with stress in a nonviolent manner?
12. How similar are the contexts in which the person has used violent coping mechanisms in the past to the contexts in which the person will likely function in the future?
13. In particular, who are the likely victims of the person's violent behavior, and how available are they?
14. What means does the person possess to commit violence?

mation is available, however, efforts to thwart or reduce aggression will of necessity occur primarily at a later point in the sequence of events that culminate in overt aggressive behavior, and closer in temporal proximity to the aggressive act itself.

EVALUATION OF TREATMENT EFFICACY

Assessment and intervention involve processes of systematically generating and testing hypotheses concerning an individual client. As such, they can be viewed collectively as a problem-solving process consisting of problem identification, problem analysis, plan implementation and plan evaluation. This process has many commonalities with the scientific method (Martens & Keller, in press). Chapter 2 addressed the first two stages of the problem-solving process. We will now discuss the fourth stage of this process, treatment evaluation.

Treatment integrity is a critical concern to determination of treatment efficacy. That is, we must make certain that the intervention was conducted in the manner in which it was designed. This is particularly critical when treatment is carried out by other staff through staff training or consultation (Keller, 1981). If the treatment was not implemented properly, then failure to bring about change cannot be attributed to the inefficacy of the intervention.

Consistent with our discussion of assessment issues, evaluation of treatment efficacy must also involve multiple measures at multiple levels. Such multi-method, multi-level evaluation allows the determination of generality of effects as well as the evaluation of unanticipated effects of interventions to prevent or control aggression. Chapter 10 discusses issues relevant to programming for generalization and transfer. It is important to evaluate treatment efficacy for generalization across time, settings, behaviors, clients, and response classes (Drabman, Hammer & Rosenbaum, 1979).

The question of *generalization and transfer* also relates to the use of proximal and distal measures. Proximal measures refer to those measures that assess direct and immediate effects of an intervention. For example, proximal effects of prosocial skill training with children (McGinnis & Goldstein, 1984) and adolescents (Goldstein et al., 1980) can be determined with role-play analogue measures of the specific social skills that were taught during the intervention. Such an evaluation indicates whether the skills were in fact acquired as a result of the intervention. Without such evaluation for acquisition, there is little point in examining more important generalization and transfer (distal) effects. That is, did the intervention have effects upon the daily life of the individual (contact with police, entry into or exit from the mental health system, school success, school truancy, etc.)? Did the specific skill enhancement lead to judgments of competence by significant others? Selection of measures for assessing proximal and distal effects requires consideration of psychometric issues and, in particular, measures demonstrated to be sensitive to change, many of which were identified in chapter 2.

Another concern of treatment evaluation is with *social validity* (Kazdin, 1977). Not only are we concerned with whether or not there was significant change in the target behaviors, but with whether the attained changes are meaningful and important to the client and to the client's significant others. This evaluation concern involves direct followup with those individuals via clinical interview.

The practitioner who must address problems of aggression rarely has the opportunity to conduct control group and comparison group designs with large sample sizes. Rather, individual clients or groups of clients are seen, and assessment and intervention require the repeated observation of a single individual or groups of individuals over time. Such constraints and demands upon the practitioner do not allow the use of large N inferential designs for *evaluating treatment efficacy*. Time series research methodology is more appropriately applied to the demands of the individual or agency practitioner. While time series methodology has been developed within the context of behavioral approaches, its application is not limited to such interventions (Barlow, Hayes & Nelson, 1984; Hersen & Barlow, 1976; Kazdin, 1980; Kratoch-will, 1978). Thorough consideration of the designs can be found in the above sources. Perhaps the most useful of these designs for evaluating the efficacy of interventions targeted to aggression are the multiple baseline (across individuals, across behaviors, across settings) and changing criterion designs.

A multiple baseline design can be illustrated through a description of the design applied across behaviors. This application allows the change agent to assess two or more behaviors in a single client or group. After a stable baseline is established on two or more behaviors, an intervention is introduced to only one behavior. It is expected that the intervention will change only the behavior to which it has been applied, with the other behavior(s) remaining stable. After stability is achieved in all behaviors, the intervention is applied to the second behavior with remaining responses continued on baseline. This sequential introduc-tion of interventions is continued until all behaviors have received the intervention. An intervention effect is said to occur when each behavior changes only when the intervention is introduced. The multiple base-line across settings or across individuals involves the sequential appli-cation of the intervention across settings or individuals, respectively. A major advantage of this design is that it promotes simultaneous measurement of several concurrent target measures. Examination of concurrent behaviors allows analysis of behavioral covariation. Relative to other designs, the multiple baseline design is perhaps most accepted by individuals in applied settings since there is no withdrawal of the intervention and no consequent return to a problematic baseline con-dition.

A changing criterion design requires initial baseline measurement of a single target behavior. Subsequent to baseline, an intervention pro-gram is implemented in each of a series of intervention phases. A step-wise change in criterion for a target behavior is applied during each intervention phase. Thus, each phase of the design can be conceptua-lized as a baseline for each subsequent phase. Treatment control is demonstrated through successive replication of change in the target behavior, which changes with each stepwise change in the interven-tion. This design seems especially advantageous in those situations where the change agent wishes to gradually change behavior over a period of time.

With thorough recordkeeping and documentation of treatment pro-cesses, data from individual clients can be aggregated over time for application of inferential statistics. Such aggregation of individual client data would allow consideration of the generality and specificity of treatment effects with respect to client and problem characteristics and would foster the development of prescriptive treatments (Goldstein, 1978; Goldstein & Stein, 1976). Such aggregation could occur not only across clients but also across change agents within an agency. Use of waiting lists would allow application of control group designs. Finally, collaboration with researchers at nearby colleges and universities might allow more elaborate control group and large N inferential designs within the context of service delivery to clients.

To summarize, the problem of aggression is so complex and our knowledge gaps are sufficiently large that we must be especially systematic, creative and energetic in our planning and gathering of relevant data. Such research will help identify predictors of aggressive behavior and the most effective means of preventing, controlling and reducing aggression. Research must address the prescriptive question of what treatments are most effective with what kinds of clients manifesting which component problems of the aggressive behavior sequence under what kinds of setting conditions. While these research questions require large-scale research endeavors, individual practitioners employing systematic time series research methodology with aggregation of systematically gathered data on individual clients can contribute substantially to this effort.

Part III
Intervention

Chapter 4

Anger Control Training

Although it is certainly not the case that all acts of aggression are preceded by anger on the part of the perpetrator, or that all instances of anger are necessarily followed by overt aggression, it is nonetheless true that very frequently anger leads to, instigates, and is the sufficient antecedent of overt aggressive behavior. Thus, it appears highly desirable to respond at this early step in the aggressive behavior sequence and attempt to intervene with an affect-oriented effort designed to substantially reduce anger arousal. Anger Control Training appears to be just such an intervention. To best understand Anger Control Training, and especially its core ingredient, self-instruction, we begin this chapter in what may seem to be a setting quite distant from the study of anger and its management, namely the experimental psychology laboratory of the Russian psychologist Luria. In an extended series of investigations, Luria (1961) explored the manner in which in the course of normal development, the child comes to regulate much of his or her external behavior by means of internal speech. Little and Kendall (1979) succinctly describe this unfolding pattern:

> The process of development of verbal control of behavior thus seems to follow a standard developmental sequence. First, the initiation of motor behavior comes under control of adult verbal cues, and then the inhibition of responses is controlled by the speech of adults. Self-control emerges as the child learns to respond to his own verbal cues, first to initiate responses and then to inhibit them.
>
> The 3- or 4-year-old child normally can follow rather complicated instructions given by an adult, and it is at this age that the child is said to begin to regulate his own behavior on the basis of verbal self-instruction . . . . Between the ages of $4\frac{1}{2}$ and $5\frac{1}{2}$, the child's self-verbalizations shift from overt to covert (primarily internal) speech. (p. 101)

In addition to Luria's seminal research, a number of other investigators have examined and confirmed this verbal mediation process

39

(Allport, 1924; Bem, 1967; Mussen, 1963; Vygotsky, 1962). But as with all normative development processes, there are children in whom the expected sequence fails to occur, or occurs only in part, or occurs in distorted or incomplete form. If the studies previously cited correctly lead to the conclusion, as we agree they do, that "There is considerable evidence to support the belief that self-control develops largely as a function of a child's development of internal language mechanisms . . . ", (Little & Kendall, 1979, p. 104), then what of the youngsters in whom this sequence fails to fully or correctly unfold? As we shall see, it is precisely such youngsters—deficient in the ability to regulate overt behavior by internal speech—who display the arrays of behavior associated with such terms as hyperactivity, impulsivity, poor self-control, acting-out, and the like. However, as we shall also see, such impulsive behavior in these very same, poorly self-controlled youngsters may be reduced by externally imposed interventions which very closely replicate the normal developmental sequence described by Luria.

Donald Meichenbaum and his research group have been especially active in this domain. Their initial investigations sought to further establish the relationship between impulsivity and poor verbal control of overt behavior. Meichenbaum and Goodman (1969), using what has become a standard measure for determining impulsivity/reflectivity, Kagan's (1966) Matching Familiar Figures Test, found that those youngsters who respond on the Kagan test quickly and make many errors (the impulsives) indeed exercise diminished verbal control over their overt behavior as compared to youngsters who take their time and make fewer errors (the reflectives). But just what do reflective and impulsive youngsters say to themselves, and how does their self-directed speech differ? To answer such questions, Meichenbaum and Goodman (1971) observed and recorded the play behavior and private speech of sixteen 4-year-olds, matched for age, intelligence and socioeconomic status, half of whom were reflective and half impulsive on the Kagan measure. Results indicated that

> The private speech of cognitively impulsive preschoolers was largely comprised of the most immature, self-stimulatory content. In comparison, reflective preschoolers manifested significantly more outer-directed and self-regulatory speech and significantly more inaudible mutterings . . . . The results of our observational studies suggested that cognitively reflective preschoolers use their private speech in a more mature, more instrumental, self-guiding fashion than impulsive preschoolers. (p. 28)

Other investigators concerned with self-directed speech in impulsive children reported concurring results (Dickie, 1973; Kleiman, 1974), and, of direct relevance to this book's concern, Camp (1975) extended the finding to a different category of youths often deficient in the developmental sequence described by Luria. She found that ". . . aggressive boys fail to employ verbal mediational activity in many situations where it would be appropriate, and when it does occur, covert mediational activity may fail to achieve functional control over behavior" (p. 151).

The nature of the normative developmental sequence described by Luria and found lacking in impulsive youngsters by Meichenbaum and others, led Meichenbaum (1977) to seek to duplicate the sequence as a remedial intervention for youngsters deficient in such self-regulatory skills. He comments:

> Could we systematically train hyperactive, impulsive youngsters to alter their problem-solving styles, to think before they act, in short, to talk to themselves differently? Could we, in light of the specific mediational deficits observed, teach the children how to (a) comprehend the task, (b) spontaneously produce mediators and strategies, and (c) use such mediators to guide, monitor, and control their performances? This was the challenge that sparked the development of self-instructional training. (p. 31)

SELF-INSTRUCTIONAL TRAINING
FOR THE IMPULSIVE YOUNGSTER

In research on self-instructional training, the typical sequence of instructional procedures is:

1. The therapist models task performance and self-instructs out loud while the child observes.
2. The child performs the task, instructing himself out loud as he does so.
3. The therapist models task performance and whispers self-instructions while the child observes.
4. The child performs the task, instructing himself in a whisper as he does so.
5. The therapist performs the task using covert self-instructions, with pauses and behavioral signs of thinking, for example, raising eyes toward the ceiling, stroking one's chin, and so forth.
6. The child performs the task using covert self-instructions.

Meichenbaum and Goodman's (1971) initial use of these procedures yielded decreased impulsivity and enhanced reflectiveness (i.e., increased response time and decreased error rate) in samples of hyperactive youngsters in comparison to appropriate control conditions. They indeed could learn, as the investigators put it, "to stop, look and listen." This early research also showed that observing a model utilize

covert self-instructions was not sufficient to obtain the desired outcome; the youngster had to covertly self-instruct also.

Other investigators reported essentially confirming results vis à vis
impulsiveness and hyperactivity (Bornstein & Quevillan, 1976; Camp,
Blom, Hebert & VanDoornivck, 1977; Douglas, Parry, Marton & Garson,
1976; Palkes, Stewart & Kahana, 1968) and began extending the apparent utility of self-instructional training to other, often related, types of
problem behaviors. These include problematic classroom behaviors
(Monahan & O'Leary, 1971; Robin, Armel & O'Leary, 1975), tolerance
for resisting temptation (Hartig & Kanfer, 1973), pain (Turk, 1976),
anxiety (Meichenbaum, Gilmore & Fedoravicius, 1971) and, as we shall
examine in detail shortly, anger and aggression.

Beyond confirmation of effectiveness, a number of these studies provide valuable information regarding conditions under which self-
instructional training effects may be maximized. Bender (1976), for
example, showed enhanced reduction in impulsivity when the child's
covert self-instructions included explicit strategies rather than just
general instructions. Kendall (1977), proceeding further in this direction, recommended that the content of self-instructions used by impulsive youngsters optimally should consist of:

1. Problem definition, for example, "Let's see, what am I supposed to
   do?"
2. Problem approach, for example, "Well, I should look this over and
   try to figure out how to get to the center of the maze."
3. Focusing of attention, for example, "I better look ahead so I don't get .
   trapped."
4. Coping statements, for example, "Oh, that path isn't right. If I go
   that way I'll get stuck. I'll just go back here and try another way."
5. Self-reinforcement, for example, "Hey, not bad. I really did a good
   job."

As is true for all psychological and educational interventions, not all
tests of the efficacy of self-instructional training have yielded results
confirming its value. Nonconfirming investigations include those of
Heath (1978), Higa (1973), Weinreich (1975) and Williams and Akamatsu
(1978). Self-instructional training appears to yield its hoped-for effects
with some youngsters, but not with others, and under some conditions,
but not under others. In a seminal discussion of this overall set of findings titled "Outcome Inconsistency and Moderator Variables", Kendall
and Braswell (1985) marshalled evidence from a large number of investigations to indicate that the effectiveness of self-instructional training
was influenced by the youngster's age, sex, socioeconomic status, cognitive level, attributional style, and apparent motivation. The import-

ance of these and other prescriptive moderator variables upon performance in the context of self-instructional training has also been emphasized by Copeland (1981, 1982), Pressley (1979), Braswell, Kendall and Urbain (1982), and Kopel and Arkowitz (1975).

SELF-INSTRUCTIONAL TRAINING FOR THE AGGRESSIVE YOUNGSTER

In 1975, Raymond Novaco sought to apply the self-instructional training approach to the management of anger. By way of definition, he comments:

> The arousal of anger is here viewed as an affective stress reaction. That is, anger arousal is a response to perceived environmental demands—most commonly, aversive psychosocial events. . . . Anger is thought to consist of a combination of physiological arousal and a cognitive labelling of that arousal as anger. . . . Anger arousal results from particular appraisals of aversive events. External circumstances provoke anger only as mediated by their meaning to the individual. (Novaco, 1975, pp. 252–253)

It is important to a full understanding of Anger Control Training to note in this definition the central role of affective arousal in forming the definition of anger. Novaco's attempt to apply self-instructional training to the management of anger was based not only upon the general success of such training in altering self-regulatory processes, but also upon a separate series of studies consistently showing the marked influence (increases and decreases) of covert self-verbalization upon a variety of arousal states. Rimm and Litvak (1969), for example, found that affectively loaded implicit self-statements increased both respiration rate and depth. Schwartz (1971), using similar procedures, found increased heart rate to result, and May and Johnson (1973) reported similar findings, plus an effect of inner speech on skin conductance. Russell and Brandsma (1974) also found such skin conductance changes.

These findings, viewed in the context of the work of Luria, Meichenbaum and others, led Novaco, (1975) to conclude that "a basic premise is that anger is fomented, maintained, and influenced by the self-statements that are made in provocation situations" (p. 17). The intervention he constructed and examined for its anger control value consisted of three stages. In the first stage, *cognitive preparation*, the client is taught about the cognitive, physiological and behavioral aspects of anger, its positive and negative functions, and especially its antecedents. During the second stage, *skill acquisition*, clients learn alternative coping skills to utilize in response to provocations. It is here that special emphasis is placed upon self-instruction. The third phase, *application training*, makes use of imaginary and role play inductions of anger, and homework assignments, to facilitate practice of the coping skills acquired—particularly skill in self-instruction. To operationalize this three stage intervention, Novaco (1975) construed the process of self-instructing to control anger as necessarily responsive to all phases of the provocation sequence: (a) preparation for provocation, (b) impact and confrontation, (c) coping with arousal, and (d) reflecting on the provocation. Table 4.1 provides examples of the self-statements relevant to each phase which were rehearsed by Novaco's subjects in his evaluation of self-instruction for anger management.

Novaco's (1975) initial research subjects were 34 persons who were both self-identified and externally assessed as having serious anger-control problems. Four treatment conditions were constituted, self-instructional training plus relaxation training, each of these separately, and an attention-control condition. The effect of these interventions was measured by self-report and physiological indices, subject response to role-played provocations, and by anger diary ratings. Results indicated that across these outcome criteria, the combined treatment, and to a lesser extent the self-instructional treatment alone, led to significant decreases in anger and significantly improved anger management. Novaco was able to later replicate this success both in a clinical case study (Novaco, 1978) and in a group comparison study involving probation officers (Novaco, 1978). Atrops (1978), Crain (1977) and Schrader, Long, Panzer, Gillet and Kornbath (1979) have each reported successful use of Novaco's self-instructional training with chronically angry adolescents or adult offenders. This result is buttressed substantially by numerous other investigations demonstrating a decrease in anger or aggression as a result of self-statements that contained more benign, cognitive reinterpretations of the provoking experiences (Green & Murray, 1973; Kaufman & Feshbach, 1963; Mallick & McCandless, 1966; McCullough, Huntsinger & Nay, 1977; Moon & Eisler, 1983; Schlichter & Horan, 1981; Stein & Davis, 1982). Though as we noted with the case of self-instructional training of impulsive youngsters, there are exceptions to its successful use with high-anger individuals (Coats, 1979; Urbain & Kendall, 1981).

Just as Meichenbaum needed to stand on the shoulders of Luria to view the remediation of impulsivity through Luria's insights about the normal development of self-regulation, just as Novaco needed Meichenbaum's impulsivity research results in order to extend self-instructional training to chronically angry individuals, the final psychologist in the lineage of Anger Control Training whose work we wish to consider, built upon the substantial foundation provided by Novaco. Eva Feindler and her research group have made important contributions to the development of Anger Control Training, both with important research findings and substantial refinements in technique

Table 4.1. Examples of Self-Statements Rehearsed in Self-Instructional Training for Anger Management

---

Preparing for Provocation

This is going to upset me, but I know how to deal with it.
What is that I have to do?
I can work out a plan to handle this.
I can manage the situation. I know how to regulate my anger.
If I find myself getting upset, I'll know what to do.
There won't be any need for an argument.
Try not to take this too seriously.
This could be a testy situation, but I believe in myself.
Time for a few deep breaths of relaxation. Feel comfortable, relaxed, and at ease.
Easy does it. Remember to keep your sense of humor.

Impact and Confrontation

Stay calm. Just continue to relax.
As long as I keep my cool, I'm in control.
Just roll with the punches; don't get "bent out of shape."
Think of what you want to get out of this.
You don't need to prove yourself.
There is no point in getting mad.
Don't make more out of this than you have to.
I'm not going to let him get to me.
Look for the positives. Don't assume the worst or jump to conclusions.
It's really a shame he has to act like this.
For someone to be that irritable, he must be awfully unhappy.
If I start to get mad. I'll just be banging my head against the wall. So I might as well just relax.
There is no need to doubt myself. What he says doesn't matter.
I'm on top of this situation and it's under control.

Coping with Arousal

My muscles are starting to feel tight. Time to relax and slow things down.
Getting upset won't help.
It's just not worth it to get so angry.
I'll let him make a fool of himself.
I have a right to be annoyed, but let's keep the lid on.
Time to take a deep breath.
Let's take the issue point by point.
My anger is a signal of what I need to do. Time to instruct myself.
I'm not going to get pushed around, but I'm not going haywire either.
Try to reason it out. Treat each other with respect.
Let's try a cooperative approach. Maybe we are both right.
Negatives lead to more negatives. Work constructively.
He'd probably like me to get really angry. Well I'm going to disappoint him.
I can't expect people to act the way I want them to.
Take it easy, don't get pushy.

Reflecting on the Provocation

    a. *When conflict is unresolved.*
      Forget about the aggravation. Thinking about it only makes you upset.
      These are difficult situations, and they take time to straighten out.
      Try to shake it off. Don't let it interfere with your job.
      I'll get better at this as I get more practice.
      Remember relaxation. It's a lot better than anger.
      Can you laugh about it? It's probably not as serious.
      Don't take it personally.
      Take a deep breath.

    b. *When conflict is resolved, or coping is successful.*
      I handled that one pretty well. It worked.
      That wasn't as hard as I thought.
      It could have been a lot worse.
      I could have gotten more upset than it was worth.
      I actually got through that without getting angry.
      My pride can sure get me into trouble, but when I don't take things too seriously. I'm
         better off.
      I guess I've been getting upset for too long when it wasn't even necessary.
      I'm doing better at this all the time.

(Feindler, 1979; Feindler & Fremouw, 1983; Feindler, Latini, Nape, Romano & Doyle, 1980; Feindler, Marriott & Iwata, 1984). This series of investigations provides consistent additional support for the anger control potency of the cognitive preparation, skill acquisition, application training sequence examined earlier by Novaco, and especially for its self-instructional components. In addition, these investigations provided valuable refinement of the Novaco three-stage sequence. In considering the Feindler program, it should be noted that while it derives empirically from work with aggressive adolescents, we have utilized it successfully with young children and we see no a priori reasons why its applicability ought not easily extend to adult populations. As constructed and implemented by Feindler and her group, Anger Control Training is a 10-week intervention sequence. Following introductory structuring material, participants are trained in the purpose and use of the hassle log (Figure 4.1). In essence, the hassle log is a diary-like means of recording and analyzing, as they occur, the provocative events experienced by the participant which, in his/her view, trigger increased levels of anger arousal. Participants are required to bring to each session one or more completed hassle log sheets. In the Anger Control Training meetings themselves, each participant in role play format is in turn required to enact the chain of arousal-reducing behaviors in response to re-enactments of *his* or *her own* hassles. That is, he/she is trained in alternatives to the anger non-control response that was utilized in reaction to the hassle as it actually occurred in real-life. The five links in the anger control chain, taught incrementally during the ten-session program, are (a) triggers, (b) cues, (c) reminders, (d) reducers, and (e) self-evaluation.

Triggers are the external events and internal appraisals or self-statements which functionally serve as provocations to anger arousal. While external events are initially often highlighted by participants when operationalizing this link (e.g., "He cut me off in traffic." "She said I could leave in a nasty way." "They left me out of the party."), training quickly focuses on the special provocative role very often played by interpretations made by the participant of such overt events. These instigating internal appraisals or self-statements, then, are a major focus of the initial Anger Control Training sessions.

Cues in the context of Anger Control Training refers to those kinesthetic, physiological experiences which, for the individual trainee, signal anger arousal. Attention to cues is important in three ways. First, chronically aggressive individuals are often stylistically impulsive, with very brief latencies intervening between perceived provocation and overtly aggressive response. It is functionally valuable to slow this process down, and to add a measure of reflectivity to it, in this case via directing attention to internal cues of anger arousal. Second, there exists some evidence that such individuals may be relatively deficient in the ability to discriminate among their affective states, at times confusing anxiety, fear, anger, and so forth. Enhanced ability to identify *anger* arousal, thus, is a prerequisite to decisions the individual must make regarding when it is and is not appropriate to use the Anger Control Training chain herein being examined. Finally, kinesthetic and physiological cues of anger arousal appear to be idiosyncratic in content, pattern, sequence and intensity. They include such experiences as accelerated heart beat, flushed cheeks, tightening biceps, "butterflies" in the stomach, hair on the neck standing up, and rapid shallow breathing.

Having learned what external and internal events trigger anger arousal, and how to identify when an increase in anger arousal is actually taking place, the Anger Control Training participant is ready to proceed to begin learning how anger arousal may be self-regulated. Consistent with the heavy emphasis we placed on self-instruction throughout this chapter, the first anger arousal reducing technique to be taught is self-instructional in nature.

Reminders, typically introduced by the fourth session, are self-instructional means for modifying one's level of anger arousal. Functionally, they may be viewed as the opposite of internal triggers. Reminders are of two broad types. What might be called "generic" reminders are self-statements designed to reduce anger arousal in any situation, and in response to any provocation, for example, "chill out," "calm down," or

FIGURE 4.1. Hassle Log

Date: _____	Morning _____	Afternoon _____	Evening _____

Where were you?

Classroom	_____	Bathroom	_____	Bedroom _____
Cafeteria	_____	Living Room	_____	Other _____
Gym	_____	Dining Room	_____	Outside/
Music/Art/Library	_____	Outside/home	_____	school _____

What happened?
_____ Somebody teased me.
_____ Somebody took something of mine.
_____ Somebody told me to do something.
_____ Somebody was doing something I didn't like.
_____ I did something wrong and was punished.
_____ Somebody started fighting with me.
_____ Other (describe): _____

Who was that somebody?

Another child	_____	Parent	_____	Teacher _____
Another adult	_____	Brother/sister	_____	

What did you do?

_____ Hit back	_____ Told parent/teacher
_____ Ran away	_____ Walked away calmly
_____ Yelled	_____ Talked it out
_____ Cried	_____ Told another child
_____ Broke something	_____ Ignored
_____ Was restrained (held)	_____ Anger Control (Describe) _____

What happened
   to you? _____
   to the other person? _____

How did you handle yourself?

1	2	3	4	5
Poorly	Not so well	Okay	Good	Great

How angry were you?

1	2	3	4	5
Burning	Really angry	Moderately angry	Mildly angry but still OK	Not angry at all

What can you do next time? _____

"cool it." Situation-specific reminders pertain to the substance of a particular provocation, for example, "I guess he's not picking on me, he's like that with everyone." "There are other meanings of what she said, and how she said it." The "Coping with Arousal" self-statements provided earlier (page 45) by Novaco (1975) are further examples of anger arousal-reducing reminders.

Reducers are the focus of the middle range of sessions, and represent a continuation of the effort begun by teaching reminders—to arm the participant with an array of means for reducing his or her level of anger arousal in real-life provocative situations. Some reducers are relatively simple, and are easily learned—counting backwards, deep breathing, imagining a peaceful scene. Others are less easily learned or utilized, for example, imagining the long-term consequences of one's behavior. In working with delinquent youth, for instance, it is useful (but difficult) for them to learn, "Yes, if I punch him in the face now, I'll get my cigarettes back, but I may also get time added to my sentence for starting a fight." Other reducers employed in Feindler's program include empathic assertion, escalating assertion, "broken record" and "fogging."

Self-evaluation is the final link taught in the anger control chain. Just as it is employed in many contingency management programs, self-evaluation skills are taught to enable the participant to appraise how well the preceding links were used and then either self-reinforce if used well or self-correct if used inadequately.

This chain of procedures represents the core of Anger Control Training. In Feidler's implementation of it, ancillary use is also made of contracting, assertion training, problem-solving training and, as our next chapter focuses upon, relaxation training.

Chapter 5
Relaxation Training

RELAXATION OF SELF

Relaxation training is the systematic application of tension-sensitizing and tension-release procedures in order to achieve a state of deep muscular relaxation. Rooted historically in techniques originated in Jacobson (1929–1964), popular in contemporary usage especially as a component of systematic desensitization procedures (Wolpe, 1969), and empirically demonstrated to be effective in an extended series of investigations (Grimm, 1980; King, 1980; Luiselli, Marholin, Steinman & Steinman, 1979; Rimm, DeGroot, Boord, Heiman & Dillow, 1971), relaxation training and its deep muscular relaxation consequence is an important technique for reducing the tension and arousal levels which so often function as immediate precursors to overt aggression.

Phase One: Tension-Relaxation Cycles

The first component of relaxation training is responsive to the just-noted observation regarding the heightened tension levels which frequently precede aggressive behavior. In order to both enable the individual to interrupt the tension build-up process as early as possible, as well as to maximize his or her awareness of the "feel" of relaxation by introducing procedures which actively contrast it with its opposite (tension), relaxation training begins with having the individual engage, in cyclical sequence, in tension-enhancing and relaxation-enhancing behaviors. To do so in the most effective manner, a series of steps are usually employed.

Step 1. The client is asked first to select an appropriate time and place where he or she will be undisturbed in a quiet atmosphere for approximately a half hour. Instructions to get comfortable then follow, that is, loosening clothing, dimming lights, finding a comfortable chair and position in it, and so forth.

Step 2. The essence of relaxation training, largely reflected in this step, is perhaps best communicated by quoting our exact instructions to clients when implementing this step (Goldstein & Rosenbaum, 1982):

> Let your eyes close gently, do not shut them tight. You are now ready to begin. Start with the hands. Tense them by making tight fists with both hands and hold the tensed position as you slowly recite T-E-N-S-E. Say one letter about every two seconds so that you are tensing the muscles for about ten seconds. After approximately ten seconds of tension, relax the hands quickly and let them continue to relax while you slowly recite R-E-L-A-X-R-E-L-A-X. Again, say one letter every two seconds so that you are relaxing for about twenty seconds. This is one tension–relaxation cycle. Repeat the cycle again, still with your hands. For each muscle group do two cycles (i.e., Tense–Relax, Tense–Relax) and then move on to the next muscle group. (p. 17)

Step 3. The client is then instructed in conducting two tension-relaxation cycles for the musculature in his or her arms, shoulders, neck, forehead, eyes and nose, mouth, chest and back, abdomen, and legs and feet. Phase one in its entirety, therefore, consists of twenty tension–relaxation cycles, that is, two each for ten muscle groups. Our further instructions to clients during this step are:

> As you do each of these exercises, let your mind relax as well as your body. Focus your attention within your body. As you tense and relax each muscle group, focus on the bad feelings of tension within that part of your body and then on the good feelings of relaxation in that part. Notice what it feels like when those muscles are tense, so that you will recognize tension when it occurs naturally. (p. 17)

Phase Two: Relaxation Only

The goal of phase two is to move the individual toward deeper levels of relaxation. The tension-sensitizing aspects of the training are deleted and the individual is instructed to concentrate on getting each muscle group more and more deeply relaxed. This phase seeks to establish a level of concentration on relaxation which will enable the final phase, deep relaxation, to occur.

> In Phase 1 you went through two tension–relaxation cycles for each muscle group and you should now be feeling very relaxed. Think of tense muscles as stretched rubber bands. You have now relaxed those rubber bands about halfway. There is still much more relaxation to be done. In Phase 2 there is no tension, only relaxation. Beginning with your hands, concentrate on each muscle group and focus on getting them more and more deeply relaxed. Remember, do not tense the muscles,

just think about letting them relax further and further. Spend about
thirty seconds thinking about relaxing on each group. (p. 18)

Phase Three: Deep Relaxation

As noted, an exact quotation here of our instructions to actual clients
provides the essence of this phase:

> Just let your entire body relax as you focus on a pleasant scene. It some-
> times helps to imagine yourself lying on a beach on a warm sunny day,
> or drifting peacefully on a raft in a pool, or lying under a shady tree in
> the cool grass on a warm day. Find and imagine a scene that makes you
> feel good and imagine it as you relax. Let the rubber bands unwind all
> the way. Sink deeply into your chair or bed. Breathe deeply, slowly,
> evenly. Tune out the outside world completely. Continue this final
> phase for about three minutes or so, then gradually open your eyes.
> You should feel refreshed and very relaxed. (p. 20)

Most clients, after approximately 2 weeks of daily practice of this
three-phase process, are able to drop the first phase and commence with
the "relaxation only" phase. In turn, a week or two of practice at this
level typically enables the individual to commence directly with phase
three, perhaps in response to the self-command, "Relax."

A great deal of research has sought to examine the effectiveness of
relaxation training. While conclusions safely drawn from this body of
literature must be tentative, cumulative findings are decidedly encouraging. Relaxation training has been studied as an intervention with
both adults and children experiencing a wide array of tension-
associated problems. Its effectiveness has been demonstrated in applications to insomnia (Borkovec, Grayson, O'Brien & Weerts, 1979; Pendleton & Tasto, 1976), essential hypertension (Taylor, Farquhar, Nelson
& Agras, 1977), tension headache and migraine (Luther, 1971; Warner &
Lance, 1975), test-taking anxiety (Delprato & Dekraker, 1976; Russell &
Sipich, 1974), public speaking anxiety (Goldfried & Trier, 1974; Weissberg, 1975), self-injurious behavior (Steen & Zuriff, 1977), and general
tension and anxiety (Borkovec, Grayson & Cooper, 1978; Sherman &
Plummer, 1973).

Mechanisms underlying such tension-reduction effects are not fully
clear. Some investigators have been able to demonstrate a relationship
of tension reduction to concurrent physiological changes (Jacobson,
1964; Paul, 1969). Others report the absence of such relationships
(Parker, Gilbert & Thoresen, 1978), and still others report mixed findings (Connor, 1974; Fee & Girdano, 1978). Yet an alternative view is that
a cognitive component rather than a physiological one is the determining basis for change in muscle relaxation (Rachman, 1968; Wolpin &
Raines, 1966). Thus, while the psychophysiological bases for the tension

reducing effects of relaxation training remain in need of further clarification, the effects themselves appear to be both substantial and relatively reliable across tension-associated disorders.

Rimm, DeGroot, Boord, Heiman and Dillow (1971) were able to demonstrate directly the value of relaxation training for persons who experience anger in automobile-driving situations. O'Donnell and Worell (1973) were able to provide similarly positive effects for relaxation in a study of anger in response to racial stimuli. Herrell (1971) reported similar success in a case study of a soldier who became excessively angry when given orders. Elitzur (1976), Evans (1971), McCullough, Huntsinger and Nay (1977) and Sanders (1978) have also presented case study descriptions of the successful application of relaxation procedures with aggressive individuals. Somewhat more ambiguous, but still encouraging outcomes have emerged in a further series of systematic applications of relaxation in yet other anger or aggression contexts (Evans, Hearn & Saklofake, 1973; Von Benken, 1977). Further evidence for the value of relaxation training for purposes of reducing anger arousal may be adduced from the demonstrated success of those multi-component treatment packages, of which relaxation training is a part, that have been employed for anger control purposes. We refer in particular to Novaco's (1975) stress inoculation approach, Feindler et al.'s (1980) Anger Control Training—both of which were examined in the previous chapter—as well as Schneider's (1974) and Robin, Schneider and Dolnick's (1976) turtle technique. Robin et al. (1976) describe this approach as involving physical withdrawal (figuratively, into the turtle shell), muscle relaxation, and social problem-solving. In their words:

> The goal of the first phase was to teach the children to emit the turtle response by pulling their arms and legs in close to their body, putting their heads down on the desks, and imagining that they were turtles withdrawing into their shells. They were taught to emit this response in four circumstances: (a) a child perceived that an aggressive interchange with a peer was about to occur; (b) a child became frustrated or angry at himself and was about to throw a tantrum; (c) the teacher called out "turtle;" (d) a classmate called out "turtle." The teacher introduced the turtle response through the use of the story [that follows]: "Little Turtle was a handsome young turtle very upset about going to school. He always got in trouble at school because he got into fights. Other kids would tease, bump, or hit him; he would get very angry and start big fights. The teacher would have to punish him. Then one day he met the big old tortoise, who told him that his shell was the secret answer to all his problems. The tortoise told Little Turtle to withdraw into his shell when he felt angry and rest until he was no longer angry. So he tried it the next day, and it worked. The teacher now smiled at him and he no longer got into big fights." After relating the story, the teacher demonstrated the turtle response and asked the class

to practice responding rapidly to the cue word "turtle" interspersed unexpectedly throughout her normal conversation. She then explained the four circumstances in which it was appropriate to emit the turtle responses and had students role-play instances of incipient aggressive interchanges followed by correct turtle responses. Throughout regular classroom periods the teacher cued children by calling out "turtle" whenever she saw an incipient fight. In addition, reinforcement for correct responses was provided in the form of praise and candy. Finally, peer support was encouraged by cueing and reinforcing children for telling each other to "do turtle" at appropriate times.

The second phase of the turtle technique, muscle relaxation, was introduced in order to help children defuse the strong negative emotions aroused by the original aggressive situation. During group practice sessions, children were taught to alternately tense and release the various muscle groups of their bodies according to the Jacobson (1939) relaxation induction. When the children had learned to release the tension in their muscles, they practiced relaxing while "doing turtle." In this manner the turtle response and relaxation were "chained" together.

The third phase, problem-solving, consisted of role-playing and discussion aimed at teaching the children alternative strategies for coping with the problematic situations which initially caused them to emit the turtle response. (pp. 450–451)

RELAXATION OF OTHERS

Intervention targets offered by the aggressive behavior sequence include not only the individual's anger arousal level, but also the anger experienced reciprocally by the other person involved in any given dyadic conflict. Our intermediate intervention goal is to create a low or zero level of anger arousal in the two (or more) combatants so that they might then more effectively proceed to efforts aimed at constructive conflict resolution. Having examined the use of relaxation training directed toward oneself in the previous section, we now turn to companion, relaxation-encouraging procedures that one party to a dyadic conflict might profitably direct toward the other. Before considering these specific, relaxation-of-others techniques, however, it should be noted that unlike the other aggression control procedures examined in this book, those designed to calm aggressive others do not for the most part rest on a strong empirical base. Modeling calmness, encouraging talking, listening openly, showing understanding, reassuring the other person, and helping them save face—the six procedures for calming others to be described—grow primarily from the clinical lore of the existential psychotherapies and the clinical experience of the crisis intervention movement. Our own two extended applications of these procedures are also more clinical–experiential than empirical in nature. The first application, *Police Crisis Intervention* (Goldstein, Monti, Sar-

dino & Green, 1978) sought to train on-line police officers in the effective use of these procedures when faced with highly aggressive individuals involved in marital or family disputes. The second, *Aggress-less*
(Goldstein & Rosenbaum, 1982), attempted to develop calming-others
expertise in lay individuals confronted with aggressive spouses, children and others. While both of these applications yielded effects which
appeared quite promising, the need for systematic and careful empirical
examination of these procedures remains clear.

Modeling Calmness

Modeling has an especially long and substantial history in psychology.
Vicarious or observational learning effects have been demonstrated in
connection with a particularly broad array of behaviors of diverse types,
including several demonstrations that aggression is often learned via
imitative or modeling processes. The opposite, modeling of aggression
control behaviors, is much less common, especially in research contexts.
Nevertheless, as noted previously, we feel there is a great deal of reason
(by extension of existing findings, and by clinical experience) to believe
that such modeling-instigated aggression control effects do obtain.

An individual, we suggest, can serve as a model of calmness—and
thus contribute to reducing the aggression of an observing other—by
means of facial expression, posture, gestures, what is said, and the tone,
speed, and loudness of how things are said. Specifically, the calm person's face shows an unwrinkled forehead, eyebrows not drawn down or
together, eyes open normally, with neither the staring or squinting of
anger or the wide openness of surprise, nose not wrinkled or nostrils
not flared, lips parted normally, not pressed together or pulled back as
in snarling. The calm person is more likely sitting than standing, with
arms at sides, that are not crossed, hands open, not in fists; movements
are slow and fluid, not fast or jerky; head, neck, and shoulders are
relaxed, not tense or rigid. The calm person's voice is even rather than
jumpy, soft or moderate rather than loud, slow or moderately paced
rather than rapid, the person avoids shouting, sharpness, or considerable unevenness and speech contains pauses. These are the several
overt signs of calmness which may be displayed by a model seeking to
calm an aggressive other.

Encouraging Talking

In the view of many clinicians, especially those subscribing to an
hydraulic model of aggression, the opportunity to talk it out, get it off
one's chest, or ventilate one's feelings is a primary approach to control-

ling aggressive behavior. While the authors of this book, holding a non-hydraulic, social learning perspective on aggression and its control, are less optimistic about the supposed potency for aggression-control purposes of ventilation; it is, we believe, appropriate to include this approach as but one of several contributing procedures to a multiple-determined calming-others effect. A useful and perhaps noninstigating strategy in doing so may be to help the aggressive person explain what he/she hopes might be constructively done about the aggression, rather than having the person explain why he/she became aggressive in the first place, which in fact is likely to reinstigate high levels of arousal and consequent aggressive behavior. Effective tactics for encouraging others to talk include asking open-ended questions (questions beginning with "what," "why," or "how"), responding to the person with encouragement to talk ("Tell me more." "Mm-hmm"), and other methods such as listening openly, showing understanding, or giving reassurance.

These steps all encourage the other person to talk more. Talking more will be especially useful as a calmative if, as the talk-elicitation procedures are used, other steps are taken to make sure that this increased talk is calm talk. This can be done in a number of ways. When asking open-ended or other questions, one should ask only one question at a time, and be as specific as possible. The aggressive person(s) should also be told that to make sure you understand them, you would like them to talk lower, slower, and more simply. One should also richly reward calmness as it is displayed, by telling the other person that their frankness, openness, and especially, their calmness is appreciated.

Listening Openly

As the aggressive individual begins to respond to the other person's modeled calmness and encouragement to talk, a further increment toward calming him or her which may be implemented is the other person's open listening. Open listening in this context means trying hard to pay attention to what the aggressive person is saying, and overtly showing this effort in one's behavior. Such attentional behaviors include looking squarely at the aggressive person when he/she speaks, nodding one's head when appropriate, leaning toward the other person, avoiding interrupting, and listening as carefully as one can to what is being said.

Showing Understanding

Calming of aggressive behavior is also a frequent consequence of believing that one's feelings and actions are understood. Sometimes, showing understanding is best operationalized very simply, for example, by saying "I see what you mean," "I can understand that," or by making similar statements. Other times, showing understanding is optimally implemented by use of restatement of content. This often-employed feature of nondirective psychotherapy involves, in our instance, the person seeking to calm the other by repeating, in different words than were used, the essence of what was said in the first place.

Often even more effective than such paraphrasing is to concentrate more on what the aggressive person is feeling than on the content of what is being said, and then letting the person know that those feelings are accurately understood. Such reflection of feeling can be a major aid toward calming aggressive individuals. Being skilled in the use of this procedure means first trying very hard to put oneself in the aggressive other's place. One should ask oneself what the other person is feeling and how strongly it is being felt. One must seek to go beyond the content of the aggressive person's words and focus more on how something is said—the tone, speed, and loudness of the words, the breathing rate, stammering, gestures, posture, facial expressions, and other clues to the nature and strength of the affect.

Here are a few examples of restatement of content that seek to paraphrase content and reflection of feeling, and that seek to communicate an understanding of affect:

> Aggressive person to you: "You shouldn't have left!"
> Restatement: "You think I was wrong to have left."
> Reflection: "You're really upset that I left."
> Aggressive person to you: "Why the hell did they stop before the end!"
> Restatement: "You believe they gave up too easily."
> Reflection: "You feel let down that they didn't try hard enough."
> Aggressive person to you: "Damn it, they took it and it was mine!"
> Restatement: "You think you've been cheated."
> Reflection: "You're really steamed, and feel cheated."

Reassuring the Other Person

People who are behaving aggressively often either have not attempted less forceful solutions to the problems upsetting them or, if they have, such attempts haven't succeeded. It will frequently be helpful in calming such persons to reassure them that nonaggressive alternatives do exist, and further, that one is willing to help the other individual attempt such alternative problem solutions.

Reassurance may be expressed in a number of ways. Statements can be offered such as, "It will be OK, we've worked this out before." "I think we'll be able to handle this a step at a time." "I'm really interested in solving this with you." In addition, the aggressive person can be reminded of times in the past when he/she or others in fact successfully found and used nonaggressive solutions to this or similar problems. The reassurance offered should be aimed at reducing threat, arousing optimism for problem resolution, clarifying ambiguities, and express- ing a willingness to help solve the given problem. Reassurance is best offered warmly and sincerely and, when appropriate, with a physical gesture of support, such as a hand on the other's shoulder. If not over- used, and if one avoids minimizing the seriousness of real problems, reassurance can clearly be an effective component of efforts to calm aggressive others.

Helping Save Face

At times, calming others is especially problematic because the source of the other individual's aggression and the person seeking to calm the other are one in the same. If person A is, therefore, trying to calm person B—whose aggression is being directed toward A—A will be more suc- cessful to the degree he can aid B in listening openly, thinking objec- tively, and become more willing to consider compromise or other nonaggressive problem solutions. One means for meeting these ends involves helping person B save face, that is, making it easier for him/her to retreat, back off, or back down gracefully. One can do so in several ways. A should avoid audiences in talking with B and, if necessary, pro- vide face-saving rationalizations. A should also control the pace of his/ her own concession-seeking and B's concession-giving by not asking for too much too soon. Perhaps most important to this face-saving, per- son A should also contribute to a compromise, and offer B at least some substantial part of what B is aggressively demanding.

These several calming-others procedures appear from the perspective of clinical application to be useful and effective means for reducing anger arousal in others. Their apparent utility is sufficient to warrant our strong encouragement of their rigorous and systematic investi- gation.

Chapter 6

Communication, Negotiation and Contracting Training

It often will be appropriate that the major procedures described in this book be viewed as optimally utilized in combination and in essentially the sequence in which we have presented them. Thus, anger control training and self- and other-directed relaxation procedures are logically followed in dyadic conflict situations by efforts which permit the parties in conflict to engage in conflict-reducing, constructive problem-solving attempts. Constructive problem solving has typically been operationalized in practice by training disputants in open communication procedures which, in turn, have the positive potential for leading to negotiated conflict resolutions, where terms are contractually secured. In keeping with our goal of sequencing chapter topics to parallel the likely flow of an entire aggression control event, communication, negotiation and contracting are the respective topics of the present chapter.

COMMUNICATION TRAINING

Interest in conflict-laden communication, and a companion focus upon training in problem-solving, constructive communication has been a central concern in recent years among professionals interested in marriage and marital therapy. The systems theory views of Lederer and Jackson (1968) and Watzlawick, Beavin and Jackson (1967) placed early emphasis in their descriptions of marital disharmony on the high levels of ambiguous and vague communication between spouses in such marriages. Friedman (1972) similarly highlighted the role of inconsistent and often contradictory verbal and nonverbal communications as sign-

59

posts of disordered marriages. Knox (1971) has described marital disharmony largely in terms of the lack of honest and direct communication, and both Eisler and Hersen (1973) and Fensterheim (1972) have
stressed the couple's inability to express either positive or negative feelings. Related communication skills deficits have been central to the
marital therapy and communications training work of most other investigators concerned with discord, conflict, and aggression in marital contexts (Bornstein, Anton, Harowski, Weltzein, McIntyre & Hocker-
Wilmot, 1981; Carkhuff, 1971; Gottman, Notarius, Markman, Bank,
Yoppi & Rubin, 1976; Guerney, 1964; Jacobson & Martin, 1976; O'Leary
& Turkewitz, 1978; Rose, 1977; Stuart, 1971; Weiss, Hops & Patterson,
1973). Improved communication patterns and reduced dyadic conflict
have also recently been the shared goals of considerable communication
training research involving parents and their children (Bright & Robin,
1981; Kifer, Lewis, Green & Phillips, 1974; Parsons & Alexander, 1973).
The communication training contents and constructive communication
rules to which we now turn are a distillation from these several investigators of their major recommendations or curricula for discordant and
conflicted marital and parent–child communicators. As is true for most
other types of skills training efforts, the communications skills which
follow have typically been taught by means of such procedures as
instructions, modeling, behavioral rehearsal, and performance feedback. These procedures are described in greater detail in chapter 8.

Retargeting Communication Goals

An important first step in communication training is to aid the disputants in refocusing their efforts away from "winning" and toward more
collaborative problem solution seeking behavior. As we state when
instructing conflicted couples toward this end (Goldstein & Rosenbaum, 1982):

> Assume for a moment that you are about to have a serious argument with
> your spouse, your child or a co-worker. One of the most important fac-
> tors determining the outcome of the argument is how you want it to
> come out. Is your goal to win, to beat the other person, to cut him
> down, to humiliate her? Remember, your intentions are crucial. If they
> are to defeat the other person, if it is you versus them, it is going to be
> quite difficult to either reduce the level of anger and aggression, or
> solve the aggression-causing problem constructively. If, however, your
> goal is to join with (not against) the other person to defeat the problem,
> and not the other person, your argument is off to a very positive start.
> (p. 42)

The win–win constructive communication strategy (Filley, 1975) to
which these instructions point, urges the disputants to consider both

their own needs and the other person's, and to try to join with the other person to find a shared problem solution that is satisfying to both of them. This strategy contrasts sharply with the win–lose stance characteristically adopted by most dyadic disputants, a stance in which one (and usually both) party seeks to defeat the other.

Preparing for Communication

In addition to self-instruction, relaxation, calming others, and retargeting goals, there are other preparatory steps which disputants profitably may take for purposes of readying themselves for constructive communication.

1. *Plan on dealing with one problem at a time.* Constructive communication in the context of aggression is complex and difficult enough to achieve when a single issue or problem is at focus. To attempt simultaneous solution of two or more such matters seriously increases the chances of failure. Thus, the rule we recommend is one problem at a time, sequencing them in order of significance if more than one exists.

2. *Choose the right time and place.* Disputants should be encouraged to take setting and time influences into consideration when planning communication attempts. Privacy is usually vital, as audiences typically hinder much more than assist. Potential interruptions should be minimized and, in general, a facilitative location and time should be selected.

3. *Consider one's plan.* A final preparatory step involves reviewing one's own views and feelings, as well as one's expectations about the other disputant's position. The communications trainee is thus urged to consider why he or she thinks and feels a particular way, why particular outcomes are desired, and how he or she can contribute concretely to a win–win solution—and also the likely thoughts, feelings, hoped-for outcomes, and possible constructive contributions of the other disputant.

Constructive Communication Rules

Once preparatory efforts are completed, constructive communication can commence. In communication training, specific rules for aggression-reducing problem solving frequently include the following:

1. *Acknowledge subjectivity.* To help establish a facilitative climate for nondefensive communication, communication training often seeks to increase disputants' awareness of their own subjectivity. While disputants are often quick to perceive each other's beliefs and behavior as

biased and highly subjective, they clearly tend to be disinclined to acknowledge reciprocal subjectivity in their own conflict-relevant behavior. In our approach to this step, we train disputants to be more aware of such lack of objectivity, but also to be explicitly open about it especially in the beginning stages of potentially conflict-reducing confrontation. Phrases such as "I believe that . . ." or "It seems to me that . . . " are examples of such openness to possible subjectivity.

2. *Be rational.* Disputants are trained to present their position in a logical, step-wise, systematic manner. To maximize the clarity of their communications, they are urged to carefully explain the reasoning behind their views and the bases for their interpretation of events, as well as to define terms and ideas whenever there appears to be a possibility of misinterpretation.

3. *Be direct.* Communications training urges disputants to present what they have to say to the other person in a direct, straightforward, nonhostile manner. When offering what one believes, feels, and prefers, the effort must be made to avoid or minimize censoring or half-truths. One's needs, feelings, intentions, and expectations should be presented as clearly as possible.

4. *Make ongoing communication checks.* Rather than assume one is being understood, disputants are taught to take overt steps in order to encourage the other person to ask questions, to be repetitious on possibly hard-to-understand content, to explain their own ideas using the other person's language and concepts as much as possible, and to check out how successfully they are communicating in other ways.

5. *Focus on behavior.* Most approaches to communications training are decidedly behavioral in orientation, not only in how communication rules are taught, but also with regard to the rules themselves. In our procedures, for example, when describing to the other person one's own view of what happened and what one would like to have happen, disputants are instructed to concentrate on actual actions the person has taken or might take—what was done, where, when, how often, how much. If the communication focus is on the other disputant's values, beliefs, personality, intentions, motivations, or other inner, unobservable qualities, we believe the likelihood of aggression-reducing constructive communication is substantially reduced. Simply stated, we hold this view because character, personality, intentions, and other targets for potential change that cannot be seen are considerably harder to alter and considerably more threatening as targets of change than are communication goals which are behavioral and observable—coming in on time, spending less money, picking up one's bicycle.

6. *Reciprocate.* Consistent with the spirit of preparing for problem-solving encounters whose goal is both aggression-reduction and the

search for win–win problem solutions, we have found that willingness to reciprocate is an important lesson to learn in communication training. Disputants are taught to focus not only upon what they'd like the other person to do, but also their willingness to change their own behavior in specific and concrete ways. In addition to willingness to contribute to problem solutions, constructive communicators also acknowledge their contribution to problem causation, and thus disputants should be encouraged to do so.

7. *Disclose yourself.* Closely related to the theme of reciprocity is that of self-disclosure. Constructive communicators should be taught that they can encourage openness in others by being open about themselves. Such self-disclosure, when done gradually and offered appropriately in terms of its timing, depth, intimacy, and length, can contribute importantly toward fuller mutual understanding between communicating disputants.

8. *Be empathic.* In our earlier discussion of useful means for calming aggressive persons, we described the value for this purpose of showing understanding of the other person's feelings. Such empathic responding is also an especially valuable component of the type of constructive communication we are aiming for in this chapter between disputants, one or more of whom are overtly aggressive. As we have commented elsewhere in connection with this communication rule (Goldstein & Rosenbaum, 1982):

> Your first step is to try to put yourself in the other person's place. Ask yourself what he or she is feeling, and how strongly. Communicating to the other person your understanding of his or her feelings is a crucial step in the problem-solving process. Your communication of empathy might be at the reflection level, in which you let the other person know your understanding of his or her feelings at the same level as they were shared with you. Or it might be at the implicit level, in which you go beyond what the person actually said to you, and beyond the person's own perception of his or her feelings, to share what you think may be the deeper, underlying feelings. . . . Your effort at being empathic . . . will help make the other person feel better understood. They . . . often will respond by becoming calmer, feeling closer, and trying to be empathic in return. (p. 46)

9. *Check it out.* Disputants should be trained to regularly take steps to make sure the message one thinks one is communicating is in fact the message heard by the other individual. By either directly asking the other person, or by judging from their overt responses, one should periodically check to be sure accurate communication is occurring.

10. *Pay attention to nonverbal behavior.* For purposes just described, that is, checking out messages received, as well as an aid to several of the other communication rules presented above, a skilled communi-

cator regularly attends to the other person's nonverbal behavior. Gestures, posture, facial expression, skin color, breathing rate, and many other nonverbal behaviors signify to the attentive observer a great deal about the other person's feelings, acceptance of one's views, willingness to continue talking and listening, and overall progress toward problem solution.

11. *Avoid communication blocks.* In addition to the several "do's" represented by the ten communication rules just described, aggression-reducing and problem-solving discourse is optimized when disputants avoid a number of aggression-enhancing, solution-avoiding communication errors. These include threats, commands, interruptions, sarcasm, put-downs, counterattacks, insults, teasing, and yelling. In addition, constructive communication will often be blocked by overgeneralizations ("You never . . . ," "You always . . ."), not responding (silence, sulking, ignoring), exaggeration (of the other's wrongness or one's own rightness), speaking for the other person, offering advice prematurely, lecturing, or shifting the topic inappropriately. Finally, and particularly to be avoided, as they are especially potent instigators to renewed aggression, are "kitchen-sinking," "building straw men," and the use of guilt arousal.

In addition to our own utilization of this communications training curriculum (Goldstein & Rosenbaum, 1982; Goldstein, Sprafkin & Gershaw, 1976), a number of other approaches to reducing aggression and enhancing communication in discordant and conflicted dyads using largely the same or analogous communications training contents have been both reported and systematically examined. Carkhuff's (1971) Systematic Facilitative Training is one such communications training approach, where special emphasis is placed on teaching empathy, warmth, and genuineness as a communicative base. Wells, Figurel and McNamee (1975) successfully demonstrated the utility of Systematic Facilitative Training in enhancing marital adjustment among high conflict married couples. Pierce (1973) worked with couples who acknowledged serious communication skills deficits, and showed the Carkhuff approach to be more useful vis à vis communication-enhancement than was the more traditional insight therapy. Hickman and Baldwin (1971) reported an analogous positive demonstration of the effectiveness of this approach, in this instance as compared to both programmed text and no treatment conditions.

Guerney's (1964) Dyadic Relationship Enhancement method for communications training also rests on a reasonable foundation of empirical support. Ely and Guerney (1973) describe the impact of this approach as including diminishing hostile attitudes, increasing mutual understanding, and more effective communication patterns. Miller (1971), Nunally

(1971), and Rappaport (1971) have each provided additional confirming evidence in support of the communication skill enhancement value of the Dyadic Relationship Enhancement method. Rose's (1971) Communications Skills Workshops, the Couples Communication Program (Miller, Nunally & Wackman, 1975), the Association of Couples for Marriage Enrichment (Mace & Mace, 1976), Marriage Encounter (Bosco, 1973), Structured Marriage Enrichment Programs (L'Abate, 1975), Jacobson and Margolin's (1979), Problem-Solving Training, the Pairing Enrichment Program (Travis & Travis, 1975), and Gottman, Markman, Notarius and Gonso's (1976) Communication Training are other formal programs which purport to effectively teach an array of communication skills similar to those we have described. In addition, systematic communications training of the types previously mentioned have been reported and empirically investigated with favorable results by Allred (1977); Argyle, Trower and Bryant (1974); Brock (1978); Burka, Hubbell, Preble, Spinelli and Winter (1971); Curran (1977); Ewart, Taylor, Kraemer and Agras (1984); Foster, Prinz and O'Leary (1983); Gottman, Notarius, Gonso and Markham (1976); Hanson (1971); Heiman (1973); Lieberman, King, DeRisi and McCann (1975); McFall and Twentyman (1973); Rhode, Rasmussen and Heaps (1971); Robin, Kent, O'Leary, Foster and Prinz (1977); Terkelson (1976); Wyckoff (1978); and Zimmerman (1978).

NEGOTIATION TRAINING

This section focuses on the training of one other type of communication skill, singled out here for separate consideration to reflect its singular importance in the aggression-reduction and problem-solving arenas. We refer to negotiation skill. It will be recalled that in our consideration of communication goals, the win–win outcome was described as the optimal communication target. In such conflict solutions, both parties get all or most of whatever they are seeking. While win––win goals should indeed remain first in one's communication strategy, it must be recognized that such outcomes are often hard to plan for or reach. It will very often be true, in interpersonal conflict situations, that one and usually both of the people involved will have to surrender at least part of their ideal outcome. By a process of bargaining, give and take, trading off, or negotiation, compromise can be mutually sought and successfully reached. Thus, while win–win solutions may be ideal, compromise outcomes—in which each party gains part of what he or she is seeking, and each also loses a part—may be the optimal solution that can realistically be expected in many instances. Clearly, such compromises in the face of conflict are preferable to a third and rather frequent type of interpersonal conflict outcome, the win–lose situation—

in which one party obtains all that he or she sought and the other obtains nothing.

Preparation for Negotiation

A few preparatory steps exist that will aid potential negotiators in maximizing the chances that their subsequent negotiations will be effective and result in a mutually satisfactory compromise.

1. *Remain calm.* Perhaps this first step need not be reiterated, but it is indeed a crucial determinant of the negotiations climate, and hence its eventual outcome. This step urges that the negotiators remain sensitive to their own and the other's anger-arousal level, and reuse techniques for the relaxation of self and others whenever their respective anger levels warrant.

2. *Choose negotiation goals.* A second useful preparatory step involves negotiators getting their priorities and hoped-for conflict solutions clear in their own minds. Obviously, if compromise is their intent, the greater the range and number of goals which are acceptable, the greater the likelihood of a successful negotiated outcome. In our negotiation training (Goldstein et al., 1976; Goldstein & Rosenbaum, 1982), we urge negotiators to select goals based upon (a) what is fair; (b) what is manageable in terms of size or scope of the goals selected (when anger is high and trust low, smaller goals should be dealt with before larger ones); (c) their relationship with the other person, and what they would like it to be after the negotiation is completed; (d) the importance to the parties of whatever is being negotiated; (e) the level or risk each party is willing to run; and (f) each person's history as a negotiator, both in general and with the particular person involved in the present conflict.

3. *Where and when to negotiate.* As we suggested in connection with constructive communication, negotiation proceeds best when there is privacy and little chance of being interrupted. The presence of others during conflict negotiations has been shown to increase face-saving attempts, lengthen the negotiations, add outside pressures, and decrease openness and objectivity. Privacy, therefore, seems to be an especially desirable characteristic of effective negotiations. There are additional time and place considerations. Negotiations ideally should be conducted at a neutral location—not her office, his den, or their apartment. Bargainers have been shown to be more assertive and less inclined to compromise when they are in their own surroundings, thus our recommendation of a neutral location.

4. *When to negotiate.* If possible, time limits should be avoided. Though time pressures can sometimes increase the likelihood of compromise, they more often lead to counterproductive consequences—a

lowering of goals, an increase in demands, an increase in bluffing, and other nonconstructive communication. Finally, conflict negotiations ideally occur in person, on a face-to-face basis, and not by telephone. In negotiations conducted by phone, important matters are more likely to be omitted, time pressures become greater, the person called is often less prepared than the caller to negotiate, interruptions are more likely, facial expressions and gestures are not visible, misunderstandings may be more frequent, and it is easier for one of the parties to say "no" and thus end the negotiations in a noncompromising failure. These several reasons underscore the value of direct, in-person negotiations.

Negotiating Procedures

In our version of negotiation training (Goldstein & Rosenbaum, 1982), after appropriate attention to preparatory rules, trainees are instructed in the following, five-step negotiating sequence:

1. *State your position.* This is your opening statement. It is determined by the goals you are aiming for, the negotiating tactics you have decided to use, and how well you have prepared yourself to negotiate. Your opening position has a significant effect on how the negotiation eventually works out. It can help create a facilitative psychological climate between you and the other person—trust, level of toughness, cooperativeness, and so forth. We therefore urge a moderate opening position in which you demand neither too much nor too little.

2. *State your understanding of the other person's position.* After presenting your viewpoint, this second negotiating step lets the other person know you are trying to understand his/her viewpoint. In a conflict situation, especially when anger levels are high, it is often difficult to be accurate about what the other person believes, wants, or is demanding. Yet, for a compromise to be reached, truly understanding the other person's position is vital. So, when the other person is having trouble understanding your position, we recommend you make use of a technique called *role reversal*. You take the other person's part and try to explain, argue for, and defend that position; and the other person should do the same for your position. Try to really be the other person. Go over and sit where he/she was sitting, and have him/her take your chair. Use the other person's name as your own. Try to "get into his/her skin," and have the other person reciprocate. If you both do this energetically, your empathy for and understanding of each other's position will increase substantially.

3. *Ask if the other person agrees with your statement of his/her position.* This step is the "checking it out" we urged you to do in other attempts at constructive communication. This sequence of steps is building to

the final one, in which you actually propose a specific compromise. Before doing so, you must be sure you accurately understand the other person's position, and this step is your way of doing it. So, be sure to "check it out."

4. *Listen openly to his or her response.* The emphasis in this step is on the word "openly." One or both of you is angry. One or both of you is behaving aggressively. It may be easy to hear (especially if you both are shouting!), but hard to really listen. So, as you listen openly to the other person's response to your statement of his/her position, you should follow all the good listening rules we described in our discussion of calming others, and also (a) don't interrupt, (b) don't "tune out" information you don't like, (c) don't speak before thinking, (d) discourage distractions, do nothing but negotiate, and (e) try to listen as though you have to summarize to someone else what the other person is saying.

5. *Propose a compromise.* When you and the other person have gone through the first four negotiating steps enough times so that you feel there has been a sufficient exchange of information and a sufficient increase in understanding each other's positions, it is time for compromise solution to be proposed. Whether the compromise is some sort of 50–50, split-the-difference proposal, or some other arrangement, it is important that it meets some of the important needs and demands of each of you. Remember in compromise solutions both of you win some of what you want, and both of you must lose at least a little also. It is often helpful if the compromise you propose is one that you would find acceptable if it were offered to you.

In proposing a compromise, you both demand and concede. You earlier chose your negotiating goals and set your priorities; and now, through negotiation, you've gotten added information to help you adjust your goals or demands. When proposing to the other person what you want to get out of a compromise solution (these are your demands), and before you state what you are willing to give up or yield on (these are your concessions), try to (a) be direct, (b) be specific and behavioral (state exactly who you want to do what, where, when, and with whom), (c) explain the reasons for your demands, and (d) be sure you are reflecting your own priorities.

Tell the other person that if he or she will meet your demands, you will reciprocate with certain concessions. As with your demands, rank your possible concessions before proposing the compromise, and offer at first, concessions which are of somewhat lesser importance to you; those that rank low. Your goal should be to give away enough to satisfy the other person, but not so much that the compromise is a bad deal for you. When trust is low, you may have to make somewhat larger concessions or more frequent concessions in order to stimulate the other person to do likewise. But when you do so, do not "burn your bridges behind you." Make sure your concessions are tentative and reversible so that you can pull back if, after you have done a good bit of conceding, the other person does not reciprocate.

You have negotiated toward a compromise, made your demands, offered concessions. When the two of you agree, the conflict can, at least temporarily, be considered over. But what about those times when you have proposed what you feel is your best compromise offer, and it is not accepted, and you feel there are no more concessions you can make? To prepare for this eventuality, disputants must also be trained in techniques for breaking deadlocks.

Breaking Deadlocks

There are a number of things that can be done that have a reasonable chance of breaking even "dug in" negotiating deadlocks.

1. *Increase bargaining room.* This attempt to get things rolling again toward an acceptable compromise may mean lowering your goals a bit. The deadlock may end if you can add options or alternatives, change your terms or demands, concede a bit more, and increase your willingness to take risks.

2. *Help the other person save face.* The other person may be avoiding acceptance of your proposed compromise not because he or she actually needs further concessions from you, but because of fear that giving in or yielding means defeat or weakness. Often you can bring the negotiation to a successful conclusion if you can help the other person save face. This can be done by reminding the person about what you are conceding, by acknowledging the parts of his or her position you do agree with, and by showing that you respect his/her right to those parts of the views you disagree with.

3. *Take a break.* Good negotiated solutions come from rested negotiators. Tired negotiators are usually less rational, more likely to make mistakes, and more likely to settle on outcomes they may later regret. So, if one or both of you is fatigued and negotiating poorly, call for time out and take a break from the negotiation and from each other. Use the time to relax, to review your position and the other person's, to consult other people who may be helpful, to analyze the implications of both of your positions and the deadlock, or to simply distract yourself with another activity for a while.

4. *Bring in a mediator.* We all need help sometimes, and you should not be reluctant to seek it. If you and the other person seem firmly deadlocked, and can't break free on your own, the two of you may have to find a third person to mediate your conflict. It must be someone you

both agree on, and someone who, hopefully, can help you both with at least some of the following deadlock breakers: reduce irrationality and think more objectively; clarify intentions, expected gains, and likely costs; explore the implications of your proposed compromise, the reasons for your deadlock, and possible new solutions; help in graceful retreats; referee; protect; encourage openness; help you both stay cool; and help you both continue engaging in constructive communication. The person can be a friend, relative, a counselor, or someone else. Many such people exist, so do not hesitate to seek one out.

Obstacles to Negotiation

Beyond potential negotiating deadlocks, a number of additional obstacles to successful negotiation outcomes may arise, and disputants optimally should be trained to both anticipate and overcome them. Some may be the communication blocks we examined earlier. Others are especially likely to arise in and sabotage negotiations when the conflict is a heated one. One such obstacle is known as a self-fulfilling prophecy. This is an instance when your expectation that the other person is likely to do something causes you to behave in ways that increase the chances that the person actually does behave that way. So, check yourself. If you anticipate that the other person is going to demand more, or cheat, or become physically abusive, or whatever, try to figure out how realistic your expectation is and whether you are communicating it to the other person. If you are, you may be bringing on yourself the very things that you do not want to occur.

Also, you may be provoking the other person in other ways. Are you challenging him or her unnecessarily, cornering and leaving little room for the other person to maneuver? Do you have a "chip on your shoulder," is the other's aggression due mostly to your provocation? Are you making extreme or nonnegotiable demands? Are you sending contradictory or conflicting messages that say "come close but stay away," or "that's a sufficient concession but I need still more," or "this is my final offer but I might have another one?" Are you both having trouble reaching a compromise because power, honor, self-esteem, reputation, saving face, or status have become more important than the issues you have been negotiating? Especially crucial here is when giving in or conceding becomes equal to weakness. Are you laying down other smokescreens which are negotiation obstacles, such as focusing at length on minor details, stalling, coming up with new issues as the first one gets "close to home," getting something to eat, or making a phone call, or going to the bathroom, or avoiding confrontation in other ways?

These several obstacles, smokescreens, avoiders, or end runs all serve as blocks to successful, compromise-reaching negotiation. When your negotiations are stalled or seem to be failing, these are the issues to explore. Have the other person do the same. If you both can honestly deal with self-fulfilling prophecies, unnecessary challenging, extreme demands, contradictory messages, symbolic issues, and the various smokescreens we have described, you are well on your way back to concluding a successful negotiation.

CONTRACTING

Solutions to volatile interpersonal conflicts, whether achieved through negotiation or by other means, are often fragile. They frequently are solutions which may be not only hard to reach, but also quick to crumble. The original conflict and its accompanying anger and aggression may re-escalate; one of the parties may have second thoughts; the agreement may not work the first time it is tried, and one of those involved may not wish to risk a second try; someone may need to save face; or brand new conflicts or complications may enter the situation. For these several reasons, new compromise or win–win solutions often may not be lasting solutions. Whatever can be done to make them more enduring, more binding, more likely to really be tried-at some length before those involved decide to keep, change, or drop them, the better the outcomes are likely to be. One such "binder," designed to increase the chances that those making an agreement will actually try to carry it out, is the use of contracts. We recommend that disputants be thoroughly trained in their design and use.

A contract is basically an exchange agreement which spells out who is to do what, for whom, and under what circumstances. It makes expectations explicit, and enables the people involved to know the relative costs and benefits of doing something. A good, behavior-change contract consists of the following components:

1. *Relevant Dates.* Every contract should specify the dates it begins, ends, or is to be renegotiated.

2. *Behaviors Targeted for Change.* This is the contract's goal, what the parties to the contract will do to meet the agreement. As much as possible, the goals or targets of a contract should be determined by the people who will have to meet the contract. When the parties involved actively participate in setting goals and related contract-building procedures, they are much more likely to have the commitment and motivation to see them through. It is for such reasons that negotiation and contracting have so frequently been utilized together in behavior modification interventions.

In our view, goals set should ideally be behavioral goals, avoiding general targets or ambiguous planned changes. The specification of goals should make explicit what behaviors will be changed, by whom, where, when, how much, how often, and any other considerations which lead to concrete and clear behavioral targets. General goals such as "behave better," "control myself," or "stay out of trouble" are harder to both define or keep track of than such concrete goals as "avoid yelling for 3 days", "talk quietly and slowly to my spouse," or "respond by telling my boss what I honestly believe or disagree about when he tries to bulldoze me." In setting such goals, one should remember to aim low at first by contracting for easier-to-change behaviors initially, and gradually work up to goals which are harder to reach.

The behavior targeted for change can be aggression itself, with the goal of the contract being aggression reduction, control, or management. However, it is recommended strongly that, whenever possible, goals be stated in terms of what the parties of the contract will do, not what they will seek to avoid doing. Better to make one's goal "speak at a normal level" than "avoid yelling." "Dealing with others in a friendly manner" is a better way of stating one's goal than is "staying out of fights." "Listening openly to my wife" is preferable to "not tuning her out." So, we urge that contractual goals not only be concrete, but also stated in terms of acts which will actually be performed, not whose performance will be avoided.

3. *Rewards.* A crucial part of every contract are the rewards that are promised if the individual changes the behavior targeted as goals. This is the person's incentive or motivation for agreeing to the contract. Several aspects of the reward influence its behavior-change potency.

Types of Reward: Rewards can be objects, events, or other behaviors performed by the parties to the contract. In setting up a contract, it is highly desirable to make sure that each person involved has a major say in choosing his or her own potential rewards. In this way, one increases his/her motivation to succeed in reaching the contract's goals. Sometimes reward selection can be done best by presenting the person with a list of rewards or a "reward menu" from which to choose. In contracts between spouses, some of the rewards that have been used are gifts, displays of affection, quiet conversation time, going to a movie and a special dinner, or a way of dressing. Teenagers have been parties to contracts specifying such rewards as increased allowance, time watching TV, staying out longer, having a party, and being allowed increased number or length of phone calls. And reciprocally, their parents' contracts have called for such payoffs as the teenager doing certain chores, homework, introducing friends, or getting up each morning with no hassle. Almost any event or object can serve as a reward if desired by the individual.

Amount of Reward: The amount of reward to be specified in the contract should fit the difficulty of the contract's behavior-change goal. Easier goals should mean smaller rewards; difficult goals should result in promise of greater rewards. Ideally, the first time or two one uses contracting to help change one's own or someone else's behavior, modest goals should be set and small rewards for reaching them promised.

When to Reward: It should be made clear in formulating every contract that the reward is to be delivered after the person enacts the behavior contracted for, never before. Thus, it would be appropriate contractually to state: "If you do your English and chemistry homework now (behavior change goal), you may go out for 2 hours later (reward)." The other way around, that is, reward before behavior change, will almost always prove to be an ineffective contract (i.e., "You can go out for 2 hours now, if you promise to do your English and chemistry homework later").

Other Reward Rules: Reward should be given as soon as possible after the behavior change occurs. If the behavior change called for in the contract is difficult, reward should be contracted for and given for clear progress toward the overall goal. And, finally, contracts should be drawn up to reward accomplishment, not obedience. The contract should state, "If you do X, you'll be rewarded with Y," not "If you do what I tell you to do, I will reward you with Y." The first approach, rewarding accomplishment, leads to independence. The second, rewarding obedience, encourages dependence.

4. *Penalties.* Just as progress toward and accomplishment of a contract's goals should be rewarded, lack of progress or failure should be penalized. The penalty included in the contract, just like its rewards and goals, should be specific, concrete, behavioral, and, if possible, determined by the people involved in the contract. Penalties may take many forms. Losing routine pleasures (TV, dessert), doing unpleasant household chores, contributing money to political or other causes opposite to those one actually believes in, postponing or canceling special events (trips, visits). Whatever the penalty chosen, the parties involved need to be sure it hurts enough that there will be motivation to avoid it. Some penalties are what psychologists call "linear," that is, they even up the failure. For example, a contract may be written so that a child loses a minute of play time for every minute he fights with his brother. Being 10 minutes late yields a penalty of 10 minutes less play time. In other contracts, a geometric penalty is used—there is a doubling or tripling in the penalty of the nature of the failure. Coming to dinner 10 minutes late brings a penalty of 20 or 30 minutes lost play time. Yet another type of penalty involves what has been called a performance deposit. At the

beginning of the contract, the person puts up an amount of money or valuables and gets them back or gives them up permanently as he or she meets or fails to meet the behavior change goals of the contract. Regardless of the type of penalty used, the important thing is that, just as the reward given should fit the difficulty of the behavior changed, the penalty imposed should correspond to the nature of the failure which occurs.

5. *Bonuses.* It is often wise to include a bonus clause in behavior change contracts. These are special rewards to be given if the person exceeds the behavior change goal he agreed to try for, or reaches the agreed-upon goal much more quickly than contracted for. Bonuses can be the same rewards contracted for already, but in greater quantity; or bonus rewards can be different and even more special things one does or gets following exceptional change.

6. *Recordkeeping.* It will often be difficult to know whether or not the people involved in the contract have reached their behavior-change goal, and thus should be given a reward, penalty, or bonus, unless a clear record of their behavior is kept. One or both parties to the contract may have a general feeling of progress, but may not be sure. Keeping record avoids this uncertainty. When a compromise or other conflict solution has been negotiated, and a contract drawn up to help make it work, it usually is a good idea to start keeping a record of the behavior involved a week or two before the contract starts. This baseline information can then be used as the standard or reference point to judge progress after the contract has gone into effect. Different ways, all of them simple, have been used to keep such records—a tally sheet put up on a closet door, an index card carried in one's purse or pocket, marks made on a calendar, a golf wrist counter, and so forth. Such baseline recording also provides an index of client compliance and motivation for change.

We have now described the clauses or components that make up a typical behavior-change contract—relevant dates, behavior change goals, rewards, penalties, bonuses, and recordkeeping. In addition to these components, there are a number of steps one can take to strengthen contracts still further.

Contracts Should be Written. Contracts should always be in writing. It makes them seem like legal documents, and increases the sense of commitment and involvement of the people whose contract it is. Putting things in writing also decreases the chances that there will be a misunderstanding later on.

Contracts Should be Signed. The parties involved in the contract should sign it, as should one or two witnesses, if they are available. If appropriate, the signing should be a bit of a ceremony with some fanfare.

Getting signatures in this manner will also help increase commitment to the fulfillment of the contract.

Contracts Should be Fair. Rewards, penalties, and goals should be consistent. As in business contracts, one must be careful to avoid ambiguous words or ideas, hidden clauses, double meanings, and "fine print." All of the people who are involved in the contract should have an equal part in writing it. Force or coercion must be avoided, either in setting the terms of the contract or as the person tries to carry them out. Above all, one should not enter into a contract unless one fully intends to try to meet its terms.

Contracts Should be Public. Behavior-change contracts exist to help people in conflict situations change their behavior. Unlike business and other legal contracts, behavior-change contracts work best when they are not kept in a desk drawer, strong box, or bank vault. The more public they are, the more they can serve as a spur or reminder to the parties involved to meet their terms. Therefore, we recommend that contracts be posted where they can be regularly and easily seen—a door, a bedpost, a refrigerator, and so forth.

Contracts Should be Reviewed Regularly. Human behavior is never static. Especially in the volatile situation of conflict and the fragile circumstances of compromise, what was true yesterday may change by tomorrow. Those involved in the contract should use their recordkeeping to judge whether progress is being made. If the answer is no after a reasonable amount of time, adjustment in the terms of the contract may be necessary, or an entirely new contract may be appropriate. The behavioral goals may be too difficult, the rewards may be too miserly, the penalties may be too great. Thus, it is clearly important that contracts be reviewed regularly.

We have so far in this section explained what a contract consists of, and steps that can be taken to strengthen its effectiveness. Before presenting some examples of actual contracts, there remains one more topic to examine. The contractual terms we have described can be used in two different ways. Especially for people in conflict situations, the contractual arrangement that is chosen may make a great deal of difference in whether or not the behavior-change goal is reached.

Good Faith Contracts

If a husband and wife, parent and child, or two office mates are in conflict, each member of the given pair may agree to a contract in which "If I do X, I'll get Y," whatever the other person in conflict does. Both people in conflict agree to their own contractual stipulations. The two contracts are not tied to each other. They are parallel, independent contracts. For each person, the possible reward is an outside event or object, not a change in the other person's behavior. The important point here is that if the two contracts are tied together (as is the case we discuss below), and one fails, they consequently both fail. For example, if they both sign a contract which states "If I do X, the other will do Y" and one fails to meet the responsibility involved, then there is no contractual reward motivating the other person to change. It makes considerable sense to us to recommend that the use of contracts, in most conflict relationships, start with these good faith or parallel contracts. When trust may be low, and common fate a risky strategy, good faith contracts are the wisest choice.

Quid Pro Quo Contracts

A quid pro quo contract is a linked-together exchange, give-and-get contract in which both parties agree to a "You do X, I'll do Y" arrangement. Unlike the good faith contract, where the rewards indicated were outside events or objects, the reward in a quid pro quo contract is always a reduction or change in someone else's problem behavior. A quid pro quo (something for something) contract is a common fate contract. If one party decides not to deliver, the contract is in trouble. All things considered, the risk of failure is greater for a quid pro quo contract than a good faith contract. But a quid pro quo contract, when it works, results in the two people involved providing each other with reciprocal rewards. This is the opposite of what happens in an aggressive, interpersonal conflict situation, where the parties engage in reciprocal punishment behavior. Thus, the quid pro quo arrangement is indeed one to aim for. It provides the exact relationship one should ultimately seek when trying to build nonaggressive, mutually rewarding dyads.

It seems that the wisest overall strategy in the use of contracts, therefore, is to begin with good faith contracts. This is consistent with the plan we have recommended a number of times elsewhere in this chapter of aiming relatively low at first, and then graduating to larger possible risks and rewards. When one sees that this first type of contract is succeeding, moving on to the use of quid pro quo arrangements then becomes appropriate. Sample contracts are depicted in Figures 6.1 and 6.2.

A sample case is as follows: Jane Smith was pleased that she and her husband reached a compromise regarding her parents' visit, but was concerned that John had carried on so—yelling, shouting, threatening—on the way to reaching the compromise. They decided to draw up a good faith contract for John (Figure 6.1).

FIGURE 6.1. A Sample Good Faith Contact

Behavior-Change Contract

Behavior-Change Goal: To speak to Jane at a normal, conversational level whenever I speak to her at home or outside.
Reward: Buy myself the tie I've been admiring in the window of the Men's Shop.
Penalty: Not watch the bowl game next Saturday.
Bonus: Get the tie and take in the movie I've been wanting to see if our conversations go especially well.
Recordkeeping: Mark tallies on the wall calendar every time I speak to her the right way.
Beginning Date: 7/19 Ending Date: 7/26

Signature: ....

Another sample case follows: Two assistant managers in an office, Fred White and Ron Jones, frequently and forcefully argued over who had access at given times to the services of their shared secretary. Their negotiations which they held led to a quid pro quo contract (Figure 6.2).

FIGURE 6.2. A Sample Quid Pro Quo Contract

Behavior-Change Contract

It is hereby agreed that:
(A) Fred White will make use of his shared secretary's services only until 3.30 pm Mondays and Thursdays and all morning on Wednesday if, in return, Ron Jones avoids seeking her services during these time periods.
(B) Ron Jones will make use of his shared secretary's services only until 3.30 pm on Tuesdays and Fridays and Wednesday afternoons until 3.30 pm if, in return, Fred White avoids seeking her services during these time periods.
(C) Every day at 3.30, the shared secretary will stop whatever task she is working on, check with Fred White and Ron Jones about rush work and, if any exists from either party, she will give that work priority.

Date: 7/9/82

Signatures: ....(Fred White)
              ....(Ron Jones)
              ....(Al Harrison, witness)

Research on Contracting

A number of investigations have been conducted in an effort to evaluate the behavior change potency of contracting procedures. In some of these studies, contracting was examined as it operated alone; in others, a treatment package was constituted and studied. While these studies are modest in number, their combined thrust is clearly in support of the efficacy of contracting for behavior change purposes.

The first such investigation was conducted by Stuart (1969), who utilized quid pro quo contracts with four husbands who receive tokens under their contracts for accelerating their time spent engaged in conversation with their wives. The tokens were exchangeable for increased physical contact with their wives. Study results in all four cases were substantial increases in both conversational and physical contact behaviors, behavior changes maintained on follow-up measurement also. Rappaport and Harrell (1972) also report an early case study of successful use of contracting. Stuart (1971) conducted a successful extension of contracting in a case study involving a delinquent girl and her family. Stuart's early work stimulated a series of subsequent investigations involving use of contracting which were conducted by Weiss, Patterson, and their associates at the Oregon Research Institute (Weiss, Hops & Patterson (1973). In these studies, contracting was a component of a treatment package containing communications training, negotiation training, and contracting. These studies, essentially replicated case studies, did not seek to partial out the behavior change impact of the three separate components, but did indeed suggest the potency of the package as a whole. In terms of both effectiveness of communication for problem-solving purposes, and reward, that is, the extent to which spouses reward rather than punish one another, conflicted couples undergoing the treatment package reported substantial gains, most of which sustained on 3–6 month follow-up (Patterson & Hops, 1972; Weiss, Birchler & Vincent, 1974; Weiss, Hops & Patterson, 1973). The problem-solving and reward findings previously noted as well as enhanced marital satisfaction, were also reported by Jacobson (1977) in a study evaluating the same treatment package, but this time against the concurrent behavior and satisfaction change reported by a minimal treatment control group not receiving the treatment package.

Azrin, Naster and Jones (1973) evaluated a similar treatment package, one they termed *reciprocity counseling*. Here, negotiation and contracting were utilized to teach couples to behave in more reciprocally rewarding ways to one another. All but one of the 12 participating couples reported significantly greater marital happiness after the reciprocity counseling as compared to behavior change as a result of their earlier participation in a placebo therapy procedure. A further, more recent empirical demonstration of the effectiveness of contracting in conflicted marital dyads is provided by Baucom (1982).

We concur with Jacobson and Martin (1976) and Liberman, Levine, Wheeler, Sanders and Wallace (1976) who view the studies briefly described therein as providing suggestive positive evidence for the utility of contracting, and treatment packages of which it is a part. As they each remind us, definitive studies of contracting's impact are yet to be conducted, and clearly well-deserve to be, in response to the encouraging beginnings we have described.

Chapter 7

Contingency Management Training

Contingency management is a set of behavior modification techniques that by one means or another, contingently present or withdraw rewards or punishments (e.g., environmental consequences) to alter the behavior which precedes these consequences. Specifically, if one's goal is to increase the likelihood that a given (e.g., prosocial) behavior will occur, one follows instances of its occurrence with positive consequences, that is, by means of one or another technique for presenting reward or removing an aversive event. In a directly analogous management of contingencies, if one's goal is to decrease the likelihood that given (e.g., antisocial) behavior will occur, one follows instances of its occurrence with negative consequences, that is, by means of one or another behavior modification technique for presenting an aversive event or removing a rewarding event. To decrease the disruptiveness, aggression, or acting-out behavior of a given youngster, for example, and to simultaneously increase the chances that he or she will behave in a constructive manner, the skilled contingency manager will often use a combination of aversive or reward-withdrawing (for the aggression) and aversiveness-reducing or reward-providing (for the constructive behaviors) techniques.

Thus, contingency management consists basically of two core sets of procedures. The first is designed to increase or accelerate the frequency of desirable, appropriate behaviors, and is operationalized by one or another means of delivering positive reinforcement contingent upon the performance of such behaviors. The second, designed to decrease or decelerate the frequency of undesirable, inappropriate behaviors is punishment, either in the form of removal of positive reinforcers (extinction, time out, response cost) or the provision of aversive stimuli (reprimands; overcorrection; unpleasant tastes, sounds or odors). We will examine each of these several contingency management procedures.

Though much of the basic thinking relevant to the contingency management approach to human behavior has been available for a number of years (Mowrer & Mowrer, 1938; Skinner, 1938; Watson & Rayner, 1920), it wasn't until the 1950s that it began to find substantial, overt implementation in hospitals, clinics, schools, and other institutions where one found disturbed or disturbing adults and youngsters. Skinner's (1953) book *Science and Human Behavior* was a significant stimulus to this growth, as were a large number of investigations, conducted during the 1950s and 1960s in the several contexts noted, all of which successfully demonstrated the behavior change effectiveness of contingency management. Much of this research sought to alter the highly aggressive or otherwise severely deviant behavior of institutionalized emotionally disturbed, autistic, or developmentally disabled children and adolescents, and did so with considerable levels of success (Ayllon & Michael, 1959; Ferster & DeMeyer, 1962; Lovaas, Schaeffer & Simmons, 1965; Wolf, Risley & Mees, 1964). In outpatient clinic and laboratory settings, successful use of contingency management was reported with such diverse behaviors as delinquency (Patterson, Ray & Shaw, 1968; Schwitzgebel, 1964), social withdrawal (Allen, Hart, Buell, Harris & Wolf, 1964; Lovaas, Koegel, Simmons & Long, 1973), fearfulness (Lazarus & Rachman, 1967; Patterson, 1965), hyperactivity (Allen, Henke, Harris, Baer & Reynolds, 1967; Hall, Lund & Jackson, 1968); depression (Wahler & Pollio, 1968); anorexia (Bachrach, Erwin & Mohr, 1965; Leitenberg, Agras & Thomson, 1968), mutism (Sherman, 1965; Straughan, 1968), and dozens of other diverse deviant behaviors involving many hundreds of youngsters and adults. As shall be made explicit throughout this chapter, the general success of this orientation to behavior change has further blossomed in the 1970s and 1980s, finding still wider application across many, many behaviors, settings, and populations.

PREPARATION FOR CONTINGENCY MANAGEMENT

The application of contingency management procedures is typically preceded by a small number of preparatory steps—deciding on the desirable goal behaviors to be sought, observing and recording the undesirable target behaviors one will seek to change in order to accomplish the behavioral goals, identifying positive reinforcers for the target person, and selecting the optimal contingency management procedure(s) to apply.

Selecting behavior change goals is usually the initial step, a step often requiring the behavior modifier to respond to several considerations in addition to the simple desirability of encouraging prosocial behavior and discouraging the antisocial. For example, in a discussion addressed to teachers regarding behavior change goal selection in classroom contexts, we observed (Goldstein, Apter & Harootunian, 1983):

> What will be the behavioral climate of your classroom? What student behaviors will be defined by you as truly disruptive and as impediments to learning, and which will be tolerated and perhaps even welcomed as normative and maybe even facilitative of the learning process? Not only should behavior change goal selection concern itself with reducing those aggressive, disruptive, acting-out behaviors which interfere with the learning process but, simultaneously, such planning of behavior modification must be acutely responsive to normal student developmental stages, conducted to the extent possible in collaboration with the students who are involved themselves, and appropriately but not overly responsive to both teacher needs and the influence on decisions about classroom decorum of overall school climate and policy.

In general, selection of behavior change goals should be done carefully, if at all possible in collaboration with the person whose behavior is to be altered, with full consideration of the range of alternative goals possible and desirable, and with recognition of the potential impact of the behavioral changes on the target person himself or herself.

The second preparatory step for effective contingency management is the specification of the undesirable or inappropriate behaviors to be altered, a step which ideally proceeds by means of systematic observation and recording. There are a number of purposes that are served by this process. Systematic observation and recording seeks to identify not only the behaviors that are undesirable, and thus possibly to be changed, but also the rate of frequency of such behaviors. This establishment of a base rate permits the behavior modifier to determine later (against the base rate) whether the behavior is remaining constant, increasing in rate or frequency or, as is hoped, actually decreasing. This monitoring of change in the behavior over time is, then, the second purpose of systematic observation and recording. Finally, the third purpose of observation and recording is to evaluate the success or failure of the completed intervention. At all three stages of this process—establishment of a base rate, monitoring, and evaluation of outcome—it is crucial that observation and recording be conducted in a systematic manner. Many authorities on classroom contingency management, for example, have commented that teacher guesses regarding the rate or frequency of a given student's aggressive, disruptive, or acting-out behavior are very often erroneously high. It is as if a small number of perhaps seriously disruptive behaviors by a student leads to a teacher's impression or label of "chronically aggressive," that may often cloud the fact that most of the time, the youngster is engaged in appropriate behaviors. Thus, for these several reasons, it is crucial to obtain an accurate accounting of how often or how long the target person engages in problematic behaviors.

The third prerequisite step necessary when preparing to apply contingency management procedures is the identification of positive reinforcers for the target person. What objects, activities or events will in fact serve as reinforcers for the particular target person involved? Four types of positive reinforcers have been identified—material, social, activity and token.

Material or tangible reinforcers are actual desirable goods or objects to be presented to the individual contingent upon his or her enactment of appropriate behaviors. One especially important subcategory of material reinforcement, primary reinforcement, occurs when the contingent event presented satisfies a basic biological need. Food is one such primary reinforcer.

Social reinforcers, most often expressed in the form of attention, praise, or approval, are particularly powerful reinforcers. In classroom contexts, for example, both teacher lore and extensive experimental research testify to the potency of teacher-dispensed social reinforcement in influencing a broad array of personal, interpersonal, and academic student behaviors.

Activity reinforcers are those events that the individual freely chooses to engage in when he or she has an opportunity to engage in several different activities. Given freedom to choose, many youngsters will watch television rather than complete their homework. The parent wishing to use this activity reinforcer information will specify to the youngster that he or she may watch television for a given time period contingent upon the prior completion of the homework. Stated otherwise, the opportunity to perform a high probability behavior (given free choice) can be used as a reinforcer for a lower probability behavior.

Token reinforcers, usually employed when more easily implemented social reinforcers prove insufficient, are symbolic items or currency (chips, stars, points, etc.) provided to the target person contingent upon the performance of appropriate or desirable behaviors. Tokens thus obtained are exchangeable for a wide range of material or activity reinforcers. The system by which specific numbers of tokens are contingently gained (or lost), and the procedures by which they may be exchanged for the backup material or activity reinforcers, is called a token economy.

Given the wide array of potential reinforcers of these several types, and the fact that almost any event may serve as a reinforcer for one individual but not another, how may the contingency manager decide which reinforcer(s) may be optimally utilized with a particular youngster or adult at a given point in time? Most simply, the target person can straightforwardly be asked which events he or she would like to earn. Often, however, this approach will not prove sufficient since people are frequently not fully aware of the range of reinforcers available to them or, when aware, may in advance discount the possibility that the given reinforcer will actually be forthcoming in a particular instance. When this is the case, other reinforcement-identification procedures must be employed. Carr (1981) and others have reported three procedures which typically have been used for this purpose.

1. *Observing effects.* The contingency manager can often make an accurate determination whether a given event is in fact functioning as a reinforcer by carefully observing its impact on the target person. It probably is if the person (a) asks that the event be repeated, (b) seems happy during its occurrence, (c) seems unhappy when the event ends, or (d) will work in order to earn the event. If one or more of these reactions is observed, the chances are good that the event is a positive reinforcer and that it can be contingently provided to strengthen appropriate, nonaggressive behaviors.

2. *Observing choices.* As we noted in connection with activity reinforcers, when a target person is free to choose among several equally available activities, the one he or she chooses and how long he or she engages in the chosen activity are both readily observed, target person-identified positive reinforcers.

3. *Questionnaires.* A small number of questionnaires exist which have been utilized effectively in identifying positive reinforcers. Tharp and Wetzel's (1969) Mediation-Reinforcer Incomplete Blank and Homme's (1971) Reinforcing Event Menu are two prominent examples. Once having chosen the desirable goal behaviors to seek, the reinforcers to provide following their occurrence, and the undesirable behaviors to be reduced or eliminated, the preparatory phase of contingency management is completed. The behavior modifier may then proceed to selecting and applying specific contingency management procedures.

PRESENTING POSITIVE REINFORCERS

A basic principle of contingency management is that the presentation of a reinforcing event contingent upon the occurrence of a given behavior will function to increase the likelihood of the recurrence of that behavior. Research has demonstrated a substantial number of considerations that influence the success of this reinforcement effort, and thus, should optimally be reflected in its presentation when seeking to increase appropriate behaviors.

Be Contingent. While this rule for reinforcer presentation may be largely obvious at this point, it is a crucial rule which is sometimes forgotten or implemented inadequately. The connection between the desirable behavior and the subsequent provision of reward should be made clear and explicit to the target person. This description, as is true for all aspects of a contingency management effort, should be behaviorally specific, that is, it is the connection between particular behavioral acts and reinforcement that is made clear, instead of using behaviorally ambiguous comments about "good behavior," "being a good person," "being well behaved," or the like.

Reinforce Immediately. Related to the communication of the behavior-reinforcement contingency, the more immediately the presentation of reinforcement occurs following the desirable behavior, the more likely is its effectiveness. Not only will rapid reinforcement augment the message that the immediately preceding behavior is desirable, but delayed reinforcer presentation runs the risk that a sequence will occur: (a) desirable behavior; (b) undesirable behavior; (c) reinforcement intended for (a) which in actuality reinforces (b).

Reinforce Consistently. The effects of positive reinforcement on altering behavior are usually gradual, not dramatic. It works to slowly strengthen behavior over a period of time. Thus, it is important that positive reinforcement be presented consistently. Consistency here means not only that the contingency manager must be consistent him/herself, but also that it is made certain that the reinforcement delivery efforts are matched by similar efforts from as many other important persons in the target person's life as possible.

Frequency of Reinforcement. When first beginning to try to establish a new, appropriate behavior, the contingency manager should seek to reinforce all or almost all instances of that behavior. This high frequency, rich reinforcement schedule is necessary initially to establish or firmly root the behavior in the individual's behavioral repertoire. Once it seems clear that the behavior has actually been acquired, it is appropriate for the contingency manager to thin the reinforcement schedule, decreasing her presentation of reinforcement so that only some of the target person's desirable behaviors are followed by reinforcement. This thinner schedule or partial reinforcement strategy is an important contributor to the continued likelihood of the appropriate behavior because such a reinforcement schedule more closely parallels the sometimes-reinforced, sometimes-not reaction the target person's appropriate behavior will elicit in other settings from other people. The contingency manager's partial reinforcement of the target person's appropriate behaviors may be on a fixed time schedule (e.g., at the end of each meeting), a fixed number of responses schedule (e.g., every fifth instance of the appropriate behavior), or (preferably) on variable time or number of response schedules. In any event, the basic strategy for reinforcement frequency should be a rich level for initial learning and partial reinforcement delivered on a variable schedule to sustain performance.

Amount of Reinforcement. In our discussion of frequency of reinforcement, we began to distinguish between learning, that is, acquiring knowledge about how to perform new behaviors, and actual performance, that is, overtly using these behaviors. The amount of reinforcement provided influences performance much more than learning. People will learn new, appropriate behaviors just about as fast for a large as for a small reward, but they are more likely to perform the behaviors on a continuing basis when large rewards are involved. Yet, rewards can be too large, causing a satiation effect in which the target person loses interest in seeking the given reinforcement because it is "too much of a good thing." Or, they can be too small—too little time on the playground, too few tokens, too thin a social reinforcement schedule. The optimal amount can be determined empirically. If a person has in the past worked energetically to obtain a particular reinforcer but gradually slacks off and seems to lose interest in obtaining it, a satiation effect has probably occurred and the amount of reinforcement should be reduced. On the other hand, if he/she seems unwilling to work for a reinforcer that you believe is desired, try giving it once or twice for free, that is, not contingent on a specific desirable behavior. If he/she seems to enjoy the reinforcer and even wishes more of the same, the amount you had been using may be too little. Increase the amount, make it contingent, and observe whether it is yielding the desired, behavior modification effect. If so, the amount of reinforcement you are offering is appropriate.

Variety of Reinforcement. We have previously mentioned a reinforcement satiation effect due to an excessive amount of reinforcement. There is a parallel type of satiation of reinforcement, occurring when the contingency manager uses the same approving phrase or other reward over and over again. The target person may perceive such reinforcement as taking on a mechanized quality, and thus lose interest in or responsiveness to it. By varying the content of the reinforcer presented, its potency can be maintained. Thus, instead of "nice job" repeated four or five times, a mix of comments—"I'm really proud of you;" "You're certainly doing fine;" "Well done"—is more likely to yield a sustained effect.

Pair with Praise. Our earlier statements about types of reinforcers emphasized that social reinforcement is most germaine to enduring behavior change, though there were circumstances under which an emphasis upon material, activity, or token reinforcers was (at least initially) more appropriate. To aid in the desired movement toward social reinforcement, the contingency manager should seek to pair all presentations of material, activity, or token reward with some expression of social reinforcement—an approving comment, a pat on the back, a wink, a smile, and so forth.

Shaping New Behaviors. Reinforcement cannot be presented contingent upon new behaviors when such behaviors are not part of the target person's behavioral repertoire. John cannot be rewarded at all for talking over his disputes with other students, much less at the proper frequency, amount, consistency, and so forth, if he never does so. Yet, the teacher is not doomed here to perpetual waiting with reinforcers at the ready, for nonemergent desirable behaviors. Approximations to such desirable negotiating behaviors, even remote approximations, can be positively reinforced. Looking at the other disputant, walking toward him, discussing an irrelevant (to the dispute) topic are all reinforceable steps in the direction of the ultimately desired behaviors. By a process of reinforcement of successively closer approximations (to the final target behavior), coupled with successive withdrawal of such reinforcement for ever-less good approximations, the behavior change process can proceed in a stepwise fashion in which the target person's behaviors are systematically shaped more closely to the final target behavior.

Contingency management operationalized by the presentation of positive reinforcers rests on a particularly substantial base of experimental support. Especially comprehensive reviews of this evidence include Bandura (1969), Gambrill (1977), Kazdin (1977), O'Leary and O'Leary (1976, 1977), and Walker (1979). Individual studies which seem to us to be particularly instructive of methods and results involving these procedures as applied to persons displaying aggressive or disruptive behavior are Adams (1973); Becker, Madsen, Arnold and Thomas (1967); Bornstein, Rychtarik, McFall, Bridgewater, Guthrie and Anton (1980); Buys (1972); Hall, Panyan, Rabon and Broden (1968); Homer and Peterson (1980); Kirschner and Levine (1975); Patterson (1982); Pinkston, Reese, LeBlanc and Baer (1973); Sewell, McCoy and Sewell (1973); and Ward and Baker (1968).

REMOVING POSITIVE
REINFORCERS

The contingency manager's behavior modification goal with persons displaying aggressive behaviors is, in a general sense, twofold. Both sides of the behavioral coin—appropriate and inappropriate, prosocial and antisocial, desirable and undesirable—must be attended to. In a proper behavior change effort, procedures are simultaneously or sequentially employed to reduce and eliminate the inappropriate, anti-social, or undesirable components of the target person's behavioral repertoire, and increase the quality and frequency of appropriate, pro-social, or desirable components. This latter task is served primarily by the contingent presentation of positive reinforcement. Conversely, the contingent removal of positive reinforcement in response to aggressive, disruptive, or similar behaviors is the major behavior modification strategy for reducing or eliminating such behaviors. Therefore, in con-junction with the procedures previously discussed for presenting posi-tive reinforcement, the contingency manager should, if possible, also simultaneously or consecutively employ one or more of the three posi-tive reinforcer removing techniques we now wish to examine.

Extinction

1. *Know when to use extinction.* Extinction is the withdrawal or removal of positive reinforcement for aggressive or other undesirable behaviors which have been either deliberately or inadvertently rein-forced in the past. Its use can be thought of prescriptively. It is the pro-cedure of choice with milder forms of aggression, such as threats, swearing, or other forms of verbal aggression, or low amplitude physi-cal aggression. More generally, extinction should be used when other individuals are not in any serious physical danger from the aggression being displayed by the target person.

2. *Provide positive reinforcement for appropriate behaviors.* We men-tioned this rule earlier, and wish to stress it here. Attempts to reduce inappropriate behavior by reinforcement withdrawal should always be accompanied by tandem efforts to increase appropriate behaviors by reinforcement provision. This combination of efforts will succeed especially well when the appropriate and inappropriate behaviors involved are opposites, or at least incompatible with one another. With aggressive youngsters in a classroom setting, for example, one can reward in-seat behavior, ignore out-of-seat behavior; reward talking at conversational level, ignore yelling.

3. *Identify the positive reinforcers maintaining inappropriate behaviors.* These are the reinforcers to be withheld. Using essentially the same observation and recording procedures described earlier in conjunction with the identification of positive reinforcers maintaining appropriate behaviors, the contingency manager should discern what the target per-son is working for, what are his or her payoffs, what are the reinforcers being sought or earned by aggression, disruptiveness, and similar behaviors. To stay with the example of aggression in a classroom con-

text, very often the answer will be attention. Being looked at, stared at, yelled at, talked to, turned toward, or laughed at are common teacher and peer reactions to a youngster's aggression. The withdrawal of such positive social reinforcement by ignoring the behaviors, by turning away, by not yelling or talking or laughing at the perpetrator are the teacher and classmate behaviors which constitute extinction.

4. *Use extinction consistently.* As was true for the provision of reinforcement, its removal must be done consistently for its intended effects to be forthcoming. This rule of consistency means that both the contingency manager and others in the target person's environment must act in concert, and that the contingency manager must be consistent with herself or himself across time.

5. *Use extinction for a long enough period of time.* Aggressive behaviors often have a long history of positive reinforcement and, especially if much of that history is one of intermittent reinforcement, efforts to undo it will have to be sustained. Carr (1981) suggests that, within a week, clear reductions in aggressive behavior should be observable. There are, however, two types of events to keep in mind when judging the effectiveness of extinction efforts. The first is what is known as the "extinction burst." When extinction is first introduced, it is not uncommon for the rate or intensity of the aggressive behavior to first increase sharply before it begins its more gradual decline toward a zero level. It is important that the contingency manager not get discouraged during this short detour in direction. Its meaning, in fact, is that the extinction is beginning to work. On occasion, inappropriate behaviors which have been successfully extinguished will reappear, for reasons that are difficult to determine. Like the extinction burst, this spontaneous recovery phenomenon is transitory, and will disappear if the contingency manager persists in the extinction effort.

The effectiveness of extinction in modifying inappropriate or undesirable behaviors has been demonstrated by many investigators, including Brown and Elliot (1965); Jones and Miller (1974); Madsen, Becker and Thomas (1968); Martin and Foxx (1973); Wahler, Winkel, Peterson and Morrison (1965); and Ward and Baker (1968).

Time Out

Time out is a procedure for removal from positive reinforcement in which a target person who engages in aggressive or other inappropriate behaviors is physically removed from all or many sources of reinforcement for a specified time period. As with extinction, its purpose is to reduce the (undesirable) behavior which immediately precedes it and on which its use is contingent. It differs from extinction in that extinction involves the removal of reinforcement from the person, while in time out, the person is usually removed from the reinforcing situation. In classroom practice with aggressive youngsters, time out has typically taken three forms. Isolation time out, the most common form, requires that the youngster be physically removed from the classroom to a time out room following specific procedures described below. Exclusion time out is somewhat less restrictive, but also involves physically removing the youngster from sources of reinforcement. Here, the youngster is required to go to a corner of the classroom, usually to sit in a "quiet chair" (Firestone, 1976), sometimes also behind a screen. There is no removal from the classroom, but there is exclusion from classroom activities for a specified time period. Nonexclusion time out (also called contingent observation), the least restrictive variant, requires young- sters to "sit and watch," on the periphery of classroom activities, observing the appropriate behaviors of other youngsters. It is a variant which, in a sense, combines time out with modeling opportunities. Its essence is to exclude youngsters from a participant role for a specified time period, while leaving their opportunity to function as an observer intact. The implementation of time out, in any of its forms, optimally employs the steps we wish to now describe.

1. *Knowing when to use time out.* Extinction, it will be recalled, was our recommended procedures for those aggressive or otherwise unde- sirable behaviors which could safely be ignored. Behaviors potentially injurious to other youngsters require a more active contingency man- agement response, one possibility of which is time out. Yet, it is also often the case that, for many youngsters at the upper junior high school and senior high school levels, physical removal of the student by the teacher is neither wise, appropriate, or even possible. For such youngsters, procedures other than extinction or time out to be dis- cussed later in this section will have to be employed. Thus, to reflect both the potential injuriousness of the youngster's behavior and the youngster's age and associated physical status, time out is recom- mended as the technique of choice for youngsters aged 2 to 12 who are displaying high rates of aggressive behavior that are potentially dangerous to other individuals. It is also the procedure to utilize for less severe forms of aggression when the combination of extinction and positive reinforcement for milder levels of aggression has been attempted and has failed.

2. *Providing positive reinforcement for appropriate behaviors.* All we have said in our earlier discussion of the implementation of this step as part of the extinction process applies with regard to time out. These procedures, providing positive reinforcement and time out, should be used in tandem. When possible, the behaviors positively reinforced

should be opposite to, or at least incompatible with, those for which the time-out procedure is instituted.

3. *Arranging an effective time out setting*. We will focus our description of the characteristics of an effective time-out setting on an isolation time-out arrangement, though its general principles readily carry over to both exclusion and nonexclusion time out environments. Essentially, two general principles are involved. The first concerns the youngster's health and safety. The physical characteristics of the time-out setting should be a small, well-lit, and well-ventilated room which provides a place for the youngster to sit. The second principle reflects the fact that the central quality of this procedure is time out from positive reinforcement. It must be a boring environment, with all reinforcers removed. There should be no attractive or distracting objects or opportunities. No toys, television, radio, books, posters, people, windows to look out, sound sources to overhear, or other obvious or not-so-obvious potential reinforcers. A barren, isolation area is the optimal time-out environment. In constructing the time-out environment, it is valuable to keep in mind that its effectiveness depends predominantly on the discrepancy in amount of reinforcement available between the pre- (i.e., timein) and post- (i.e., timeout) change environments.

4. *Placing a youngster in time out.* A number of actions may be taken by the contingency manager when initiating time out for a given youngster that serve to increase the likelihood of its effectiveness. As with the rapid presentation of positive reinforcement contingent upon appropriate behaviors, time out is optimally instituted immediately following the aggressive or other behaviors one is seeking to modify. Having earlier explained to the target person the nature of time out, as well as when and why it should be used, its initiation should be implemented in a more or less "automatic" manner following undesirable behavior, that is, in a manner which minimizes the social reinforcement of the aggression. Concretely, this means placing the youngster in time out without a lengthy explanation, but with a brief, matter-of-fact description of his or her precipitating behaviors. This placement process is best conducted without anger by the contingency manager, and without (when possible) having to use physical means for moving the youngster to the time-out room. In addition to these considerations, the effectiveness of time out is further enhanced by its consistent application when appropriate, by the same contingency manager on other occasions as well as by other contingency managers (teachers, parents, peers, etc.). Immediacy, consistency, and the several actions aimed at minimizing contingency manager presentation of reinforcement following inappropriate behavior will each function to augment the behavior change effectiveness of time out.

5. *Maintaining a youngster in time out.* The skilled contingency manager must deal with two questions during a youngster's period in time out: "What is he or she doing?" and "For how long should time out last?" The first question, dealt with by monitoring by the contingency manager, seeks to make certain that the time-out experience is not in fact functioning as a pleasant, positively reinforcing one for a given youngster. For example, rather than serve as a removal from positive reinforcement, time out may in reality be a removal from an aversive situation (negative reinforcement) if it is instituted at a time when a youngster is in an unpleasant situation from which he would prefer to escape, or if it (time out) helps him avoid such a situation. Similarly, if monitoring reveals that the youngster is singing or playing enjoyable games, the effectiveness of time out will be lessened. Unless the situation can be made essentially non-reinforcing, a different behavioral intervention may have to be used.

With regard to the duration of time out, most of its successful implementations have been from 5 to 20 minutes long, with some clear preference for the shorter levels of this range. When experimenting to find the optimal duration for any given youngster, it is best, as White, Nielsen and Johnson (1972) have shown, to begin with a short duration (e.g., 3 to 5 minutes) and lengthen the time until an effective span is identified, rather than successively shortening an initially lengthier span. This latter approach would, again, risk the danger of introducing an event experienced as positive reinforcement by the youngster when your intention was quite the opposite.

6. *Releasing a youngster from time out.* We noted earlier in connection with extinction that withdrawing of positive reinforcement leads to initial instances of an "extinction burst", when more intense or more frequent aggressiveness appears before it begins to subside. A similar response may occur with withdrawal from positive reinforcement, i.e., time out. The first few times a youngster is placed in time out, what might be called a "time out burst" or heightened aggressiveness may take place. These outbursts will usually subside, especially if the contingency manager adds the same number of minutes that the outburst lasted to the duration of the time out span.

Whether the release of the youngster was on schedule or delayed for reasons just specified, the release should be conducted in a matter-of-fact way, and the youngster should be quickly returned to regular classroom activities. Lengthy explanations or apologies by the contingency manager at this point in time are, once again, tactically erroneous provisions of positive reinforcement that communicate to the youngster that acting-out will bring a short period of removal from reinforcement and then a period of undivided attention (probably lengthier) from the contingency manager.

The effectiveness of time out in substantially reducing or eliminating aggressive or disruptive behaviors has been demonstrated by Allison and Allison (1971); Bostow and Bailey (1969); Brantner and Doherty (1983); Calhoun and Matherne (1975); Drabman and Spitalnik (1973); Patterson, Cobb and Ray (1973); Vukelich and Hake (1971); and White, Nielsen and Johnson (1972). Interestingly, as VanHouten, Nau, Mac-Kenzie-Keating, Sameoto and Colavecchia (1982) found to occur in non-targeted children in response to teacher reprimands delivered to others in the classroom, Wilson, Robertson, Herlong and Hayner (1979) report a spread of effectiveness for time out. Children observing the initiation of a classmate being sent to time out showed a concomitant reduction in their own aggressive behaviors.

Response Cost

Response cost refers to the removal of previously acquired reinforcers contingent upon, and in order to reduce future instances of the occurrence of inappropriate behaviors. The reinforcers previously acquired and herein contingently removed may have been earned, as when the use of response cost procedures is a component of a token reinforcement system, or they may have been simply provided, as is the case for a "free-standing," no token economy response cost system. In either instance, reinforcers are removed (the cost) whenever previously targeted undesirable behaviors occur (the response). The two other means we have examined for the systematic removal of positive reinforcement, extinction and time out, have frequently proven insufficient for delinquent or extremely aggressive mid- and late adolescents, even when combined with contingency manager praise or other reinforcement for appropriate behaviors. In a number of these instances, response cost procedures—especially when combined with the provision of positive reinforcement (via a token economy system) for desirable behaviors—have proven effective. Thus, not only must our selection of approach be a prescriptive function of the target youngster's characteristics, but we must also continue in implementing this approach to combine its usage with tandem procedures for providing positive reinforcement of appropriate behaviors.

We will not detail here the several rules for the effective implementation of a token economy system, because they overlap considerably with rules delineated earlier for the provision of nontoken positive reinforcers, and a description may be found in Ayllon and Azrin (1968); Christopherson, Arnold, Hill and Quilitch (1972); Kazdin (1975); Morris (1976); and Walker, Hops and Fiegenbaum, (1976). What we do wish to specify, however, are the rules for token or nontoken reinforcement removal that constitute the essence of the response cost procedure.

1. *Define inappropriate behaviors in specific terms.* As with every other contingency management procedure, it is requisite that the contingency manager think, plan, and act behaviorally. When specifying the inappropriate target behaviors whose occurrence will cost tokens, points, privileges, or other commodities or events, specific overt acts must be delineated, rather than broader behavioral characterological categories. Thus, the description "is aggressive" (a character observation) or "acts aggresively" (a broad behavioral observation) is too vague, but "swears, makes threats, raises voice, raises hands, pushes classmates" are all useful specifications.

2. *Determine the cost of specific inappropriate responses.* Just as is the case for the amount, level, or rate of positive reinforcement to be provided contingent upon desirable behaviors, the specific cost to be lost contingent upon undesirable behaviors must be determined, whether such cost is a finite number of tokens or points, a finite amount of time the television will be kept off, or otherwise. Cost setting is a crucial determinant of the success or failure of the implementations of this approach. Yet other aspects of response cost implementation will make demands on the contingency manager's skills as a creative economist. The relation of points or other reinforcers available to earn to those which can be lost, the relationship of cost to the severity of the inappropriate behavior for which that cost is levied, and a host of similar marketing, pricing, and, ultimately, motivational considerations may come into play and thus require a substantial level of contingency management expertise.

3. *Communicate contingencies.* Once the contingency manager has decided upon the specific token, point, or privilege value of the appropriate and inappropriate behaviors, it is necessary that these values be communicated to the target persons. In a classroom context, for example, a reinforcer value list indicating earnings and losses should be drawn up and posted in a readily visible area.

4. *Remove reinforcement.* Target persons must be able to not only know in advance what earnings and losses are contingent upon what desirable and undesirable behaviors, but each person must have ongoing access to his or her own earnings status. Walker (1979) has developed a simple, easily used delivery/feedback system which gives each youngster ongoing cumulative information indicating (a) when response cost (or earnings) has been applied, (b) which specific behaviors it was applied to, and (c) how many points have been lost (or earned) as a result.

As was true for the other major procedures used for the removal of

positive reinforcement (viz., extinction and time out), optimal implementation of response cost requires that the contingency manager be
(a) consistent in his or her application of it across target persons and
across time for each target person; (b) immediate in delivering contingent costs as soon as possible after the occurrence of inappropriate
behavior; and (c) impartial and inevitable, in that an instance of such
behavior leads to an instance of response cost automatically, with an
absolute minimum of special circumstances, special target persons, or
special exceptions.

A number of investigations have independently demonstrated the
behavior modification effects of response cost procedures, for example,
Burchard and Barrera (1972), Christopherson et al. (1972), Kaufman and
O'Leary (1972), O'Leary and Becker (1967), and O'Leary, Becker, Evans
and Saudargas (1969).

PRESENTATION OF AVERSIVE
STIMULI

Though the removal of positive reinforcement via extinction, time out
or response cost are typically considered punishing events, most of the
concern and controversy in the relevant literature has focused upon
forms of punishment that require the presentation of aversive stimuli,
for example, reprimands, overcorrection, and especially, corporal punishment. The effectiveness of these and similar forms of punishment in
altering targeted inappropriate behaviors such as aggression has been
shown to be a function of several factors:

1. Likelihood of punishment
2. Consistency of punishment
3. Immediacy of punishment
4. Duration of punishment
5. Severity of punishment
6. Possibility of escape or avoidance of punishment
7. Availability of alternative routes to goal
8. Level of instigation to aggression
9. Level of reward for aggression
10. Characteristics of the prohibiting agents

Punishment is more likely to lead to behavior change consequences the
more certain its application, the more consistently and rapidly it is
applied, when it is introduced at full intensity rather than gradually
increased, the longer and more intense its quality, the less likely it can
be avoided, the less available are alternative means to goal satisfaction,
the greater the level of instigation to aggression or reward for aggres-

sion, and the more potent as a contingency manager is the prohibiting agent. Thus, there are clearly several determinants of the impact of an aversive stimulus on a target person's behavior. But let us assume an instance of these several determinants combining to yield a substantial impact. What, ideally, may we hope the effect of punishment on aggression or other undesirable behavior will be? A reprimand or a paddling will not teach new behaviors. If an aggressive youngster literally is deficient in the ability to ask rather than to take, to request rather than command, or to negotiate rather than to strike out, then all the contingency manager scolding, scowling, spanking, and the like will not teach the youngster the desirable alternative behaviors. Thus, punishment, if used at all, must be combined with teacher efforts that instruct the youngster in those behaviors that are not known at all. When the youngster does possess alternative desirable behaviors, but in only approximate form, punishment may best be combined with shaping procedures. And, when high-quality appropriate behaviors are possessed by the youngster, but he or she is not displaying them, teacher use of punishment is optimally combined with any of the other procedures described earlier for the contingent presentation of positive reinforcement. In short, application of punishment techniques should always be combined with a companion procedure for strengthening appropriate alternative behaviors whether these behaviors are absent, weak, or merely unused in the youngster's behavioral repertoire.

Our urging this tandem focus on teaching desirable alternative behaviors results in particular from the fact that most investigators report that the main effect of punishment is a temporary suppression of inappropriate behaviors. While we appreciate the potential value of such a temporary suppression to the harried parent or classroom teacher seeking a more manageable home or classroom environment, it is not uncommon—because of this temporariness—for contingency managers to have to institute punishment over and over again to the same youngster for the same inappropriate behaviors. To recapitulate, we have urged thus far in this section that, if punishment is used, its use be combined with one or another means for simultaneously teaching desirable behaviors—a recommendation underscored by the common finding that when punishment does succeed in altering behavior, such effects are often temporary.

Partly because of this sometimes temporary effect, but more so for a series of even more consequential reasons, a number of contingency management researchers have essentially assumed an antipunishment stance. These researchers see little place for punishment especially in the contemporary home or classroom. Their view responds to punishment research that demonstrates undesirable side effects of punishment such as withdrawal from social contact, counteraggression toward the punisher, modeling of punishing behavior, disruption of social relationships, failure of effects to generalize, selective avoidance (refraining from inappropriate behaviors only when under surveillance), and stigmatizing labeling effects (Azrin & Holz, 1966; Bandura, 1973).

An alternative, propunishment view does exist. It is less widespread and more controversial but, as the investigators previously cited, it seeks to make its case based upon empirical evidence. Thus, it is held, there are numerous favorable effects of punishment—rapid and dependable reduction of inappropriate behaviors, the consequent opening up of new sources of positive reinforcement, the possibility of complete suppression of inappropriate behaviors, increased social and emotional behavior, imitation and discrimination learning, and other potential positive side effects (Axelrod & Apache, 1982; Newsom, Favell & Rincover, 1982; Van Houten, 1982).

The evidence is clearly not complete. Data regarding which punishment should appropriately be used with which youngsters under which circumstances is only partially available. At the present time, decisions regarding home or classroom utilization of aversive stimuli to alter inappropriate behaviors must be derived from partial data, and from each parent's and teacher's carefully considered ethical beliefs regarding the relative costs and benefits of employing punishment procedures. Our own weighing of relevant data and ethical consideration leads to our stance favoring the selective utilization at home or in the classroom of verbal punishment techniques and overcorrection, and rejecting under all circumstances the use of corporal punishment.

Verbal Reprimands

Though results are not wholly unmixed, the preponderance of research demonstrates that punishment in the form of verbal reprimands is an effective means for reducing disruptive behavior (Jones & Miller, 1974), littering (Risley, 1977), object throwing (Sajwaj, Culver, Hall & Lehr, 1972), physical aggression (Hall, Axelrod, Foundopoulos, Shellman, Campbell & Cranston, 1971) and other acting-out behaviors (O'Leary, Kaufman, Kass & Drabman, 1970). These and other relevant studies also indicate, beyond overall effectiveness, that reprimands are most potent when (a) they consistently follow each instance of the target behavior; (b) the contingency manager is physically close to the target youngster and clearly specifies in behavioral terms the inappropriate behavior being reprimanded, maintains eye contact with the youngster, uses a firm voice, firmly grasps the youngster while delivering the reprimand; (c) it is employed early in a series of offenses; and (d) it is followed by praise for behaving appropriately after the reprimand. Finally, White, Nielsen and Johnson (1972) compared reprimands to other commonly employed forms of punishment and found reprimands to be superior in effectiveness. If correct, comparative findings such as this, combined with the manner in which reprimands are so frequently negatively reinforced by the cessation of student transgression, may help explain their very heavy use by the American teacher. White (1975) found that after the second grade, the rate of teacher reprimands exceeded the rate of teacher praise and, in absolute terms, the rate of teacher reprimands was a constant one every 2 minutes across all elementary and junior high school grades. Thomas, Presland, Grant and Glynn (1978) have replicated these results. Our position favoring the selective use of reprimands rests jointly on our understanding of the foregoing research findings combined with our cost/benefit belief that such procedures not only have a high likelihood of being effective, but also have a low likelihood of being injurious—especially when combined, as we and others have repeatedly urged, with one or another means for presenting positive reinforcement for appropriate behaviors.

Overcorrection

Overcorrection, a punishment technique designed to both correct the consequences of inappropriate behaviors as well as encourage the transgressor to assume responsibility for that behavior, consists of two component procedures which have been used both alone or in combination.

The *restitution* component requires the individual who caused a disturbance, damage or other acting-out to both restore the environment or situation to its pre-disturbance quality and then improve upon it (i.e., overcorrect) beyond this pre-disturbance status. The second component, *positive practice*, requires the individual to repeatedly practice the desirable, appropriate alternative behaviors. Foxx and Bechtel (1983) comment illustratively:

> For example, an individual who overturned a table would be required first to return the table to its correct position, to dust and wax the table, and to straighten and dust all other furniture in the room . . . . The positive practice for table overturning would be to require the disruptor to perform an appropriate behavior while seated at the table. Thus, the purpose of the practice would be to teach the individual the appropriate manner in which to interact with a table. (p. 135)

The effectiveness of overcorrection is facilitated when both the restitution and positive practice are (a) topographically related to the misbehavior, (b) required immediately after the behavior, (c) extended in duration, and (d) actively performed by the person (Foxx & Azrin, 1972; Ollendick & Matson, 1978).

Since its initiation by Foxx and Azrin in 1972, certain forms of overcorrection have been developed that are directly targeted toward decelerating aggressive behavior. One form is Quiet Training or Required Relaxation (Foxx, Foxx, Jones & Kiely, 1980; Matson, Stephens & Horne, 1978), designed especially for highly agitated individuals. A second is Social Apology Training (Foxx & Azrin, 1972; Ollendick & Matson, 1976) for less aroused aggressors. The former, in some ways similar to time out, requires the person to remain quiet and relaxed on a bed until all signs of agitation have been absent for a predetermined period. Social Apology Training has been implemented by having the individual reassure everyone in the immediate environment of the earlier disturbance that the negative behaviors would not reoccur. Other uses of overcorrection that have been used with apparent effectiveness with aggressive individuals include Household Orderliness Training, Oral Hygiene Training, Personal Appearance Training, Medical Assistance Training, and Functional Movement Training (Foxx & Azrin, 1972; Foxx & Bechtel, 1983; Klinge, Thrasher & Myers, 1975).

Corporal Punishment

Though we do not know of empirical evidence bearing upon the speculation of Newsom et al. (1982) that physically painful punishment that succeeds in altering inappropriate behaviors may be less injurious and more helpful *in toto* to the target youngster than nonphysically painful but perhaps less effective alternatives, and are given pause by their speculation, we nevertheless herein take a stance opposed to corporal punishment in school or any other settings. As Axelrod and Apache (1982) urge, our guiding ethical principle is to urge "the implementation of the least drastic alternative which has a reasonable probability of success" (p. 11). Given the very substantial number of demonstrations of effective procedures involving the presentation of positive reinforcers, the similarly strong results bearing on techniques for removing such reinforcement, the just-cited evidence vis à vis verbal punishment and overcorrection, and the major paucity of research evaluating the effectiveness of corporal punishment, we see no place for it in the domain of effective contingency management.

Yet 43 of America's 50 states permit corporal punishment; and its schoolhouse and community advocates seem to be loud, numerous, and growing. Is it, as Hagebak (1979) darkly suggests, that physically punitive teachers should ask themselves "whether they tend to interpret classroom problems as a personal threat, whether they inflict punishment to protect their self-esteem, whether they retaliate rather than consider the causes of disruptive behavior objectively, and whether they derive sexual satisfaction from inflicting physical punishment?" Or, more parsimoniously, recalling our earlier definition of negative reinforcement, is parent or teacher use and reuse of corporal punishment a simple function of the fact that it intermittently succeeds in reducing or eliminating the youngster's disruptiveness, aggression, or other behavior experienced as aversive by the parent or teacher?

Whatever the motivations and reinforcements that have sustained its use, corporal punishment often fails to yield sustained suppression of inappropriate behaviors, increases the likelihood that the youngster will behave aggressively in other settings (Hyman, 1978; Maurer, 1974; Welsh, 1978), and makes no contribution at all to the development of new, appropriate behaviors. We feel quite strongly that one's behavior as a contingency manager must ethically be responsive to such accumulated empirical evidence. Ample research exists to firmly conclude that the science of behavior modification must replace the folklore of procorporal punishment beliefs.

It is appropriate, we believe, to close this discussion of punishment techniques for altering aggressive behavior with a quotation from Griffith's (1983) valuable statement on ethical considerations in the utilization of punishment. In particular, we wish to highlight the protective guidelines he promotively proposes be employed when the use of punishment is anticipated. While relevant for all forms of punishment, in our view these guidelines are especially germane to those that involve the presentation of such aversive stimuli as electric shock, aversive sounds, aversive tastes and aversive odors (Bailey, 1983; Carr & Lovaas, 1983)—all of which are punishment techniques we believe should be employed only under very special circumstances involving exhaustion of less noxious alternatives.

> Included are (a) the declaration of a policy that emphasizes a preference for positive reinforcement procedures, commits itself to using the least drastic alternative, defines abuse, and requires data collection; (b) the creation of an interdisciplinary team that serves a program planning function; (c) the requirement of a peer review process involving professionals who were not involved in the initial program plan; (d) the acquisition of properly obtained consent from the client, parent, or legal guardian; and (e) the composition of a human rights committee consisting largely of individuals outside the agency to provide advice on client rights and to monitor the results of program intervention. (Axelrod, 1983; p. 11)

Chapter 8
Prosocial Skill Training

Successful intervention in the aggressive behavior sequence, we have proposed, may occur at any point(s) in that unfolding series of events. Thus far in our presentation, we have described Anger Control Training as the intervention of choice for the usual initial trigger in the sequence, arousal-heightening self-statements; relaxation training to lower one's own and the other disputant's anger-arousal levels; communication, negotiation and contracting training to correct the malcommunicative underpinnings of the conflict; and contingency management training to seek to increase the frequency of desirable behaviors, and decrease the frequency of undesirable behaviors *already present within the individuals' behavioral repertoires*. But what of the frequent circumstance in which the prosocial behaviors that might serve as alternatives to aggression are *not* within the individual's behavioral repertoire? What if the person is literally weak or lacking in his/her ability to perform such behaviors. A contingency management approach is insufficient in this context, in that save for such often laborious procedures as shaping, it has little to offer in the circumstance of a substantial behavioral deficit. Communication Training is useful in this regard, but only with reference to the limited communication-enhancement training goals it seeks to accomplish. In the early 1970s, a valuable answer to this intervention dilemma began to emerge, as the beginning stirrings of prosocial skills training began to be heard. Bandura's (1973) research was one clear impetus to this psychoeducational perspective on the management of aggressive behavior. In his landmark book, *Aggression: A Social Learning Analysis*, he observes:

> The method that has yielded the most impressive results with diverse problems contains three major components. First, alternative modes of response are repeatedly modeled, preferably by several people who demonstrate how the new style of behavior can be used in dealing with a variety of . . . situations. Second, learners are provided with

necessary guidance and ample opportunities to practice the modeled behavior under favorable conditions until they perform it skillfully and spontaneously. The latter procedures are ideally suited for developing new social skills, but they are unlikely to be adopted unless they produce rewarding consequences. Arrangement of success experiences particularly for initial efforts at behaving differently, constitute the third component in this powerful method. . . . Given adequate demonstration, guided practice, and success experiences, this method is almost certain to produce favorable results. (Bandura, 1973, p. 253)

A second early source giving strength to this approach was the deinstitutionalization movement which began sweeping the United States, at that time, returning almost 400,000 persons to the community from long mental hospital commitments, a very great many of whom were markedly skill deficient in the capacities necessary to manage the affective, cognitive and other daily living demands to be placed upon them.

Our involvement in this movement, a prosocial skill training approach we have termed *Structured Learning*, began at that time (Goldstein, 1973). For several years thereafter, our training and research efforts were conducted in public mental hospitals with long-term, highly skill deficient, chronic patients—especially those preparing for deinstitutionalization. As our research program progressed, and demonstrated successful skill enhancement effects with regularity (Goldstein, 1982), we shifted in our focus from teaching a broad array of interpersonal and daily living skills to adult, psychiatric in-patients to a more explicit concern with skill training for aggressive individuals. Our trainee groups included spouses engaged in family disputes violent enough to warrant police intervention (Goldstein, Monti, Sardino & Green, 1978; Goldstein & Rosenbaum, 1982), child-abusing parents (Goldstein, Keller & Erne, 1985; Solomon, 1978; Sturm, 1979), and especially, overtly aggressive adolescents (Goldstein, Sherman, Gershaw, Sprafkin & Glick, 1978; Goldstein, Sprafkin, Gershaw & Klein, 1980).

A substantial body of literature has in fact directly demonstrated that delinquent and other aggressive youngsters display widespread interpersonal, planning, aggression management and other prosocial skill deficiencies. Freedman, Rosenthal, Donahoe, Schlundt and McFall (1978) examined the comparative skill competence levels of a group of juvenile delinquents and a matched group (age, IQ, socioeconomic background) of nonoffenders in response to a series of standardized role play situations. The offender sample responded in a consistently less skillful manner. Spence (1981) constituted comparable offender and nonoffender samples, and videotaped their individual interviews with a previously unknown adult. The offender group evidenced significantly less (a) eye contact, (b) appropriate head movements, and (c) speech, as well as significantly more fidgeting and gross body movement. Conger, Miller and Walsmith (1975) add to this picture of skill deficiency. They conclude from their evidence that juvenile delinquents, as compared to nondelinquent cohorts

> . . . had more difficulty in getting along with peers, both in individual one-to-one contacts and in group situations, and were less willing or able to treat others courteously and tactfully, and less able to be fair in dealing with them. In return, they were less well liked and accepted by their peers. (p. 442)

Not only are delinquents discriminable from their nondelinquent peers on a continuum of skill competence, but much the same is true for youngsters who are "merely" chronically aggressive. Patterson, Reid, Jones and Congers (1975) observe:

> The socialization process appears to be severely impeded for many aggressive youngsters. Their behavioral adjustments are often immature and they do not seem to have learned the key social skills necessary for initiating and maintaining positive social relationships with others. Peer groups often reject, avoid, and/or punish aggressive children, thereby excluding them from positive learning experiences with others. (p. 4)

It may be safely concluded that psychological skill deficiencies of diverse—especially interpersonal—types markedly characterize both predelinquent and delinquent youngsters, to a degree that significantly differentiates them from their nondelinquent or nonaggressive peers.

Since 1970, our research group has conducted a systematic research program oriented toward evaluating and improving the effectiveness of Structured Learning. Approximately 60 investigations have been conducted, at least half of which involved chronically aggressive youth or adults (Goldstein, 1982; Goldstein & Glick, 1986). The overall conclusions which may justifiably be drawn from these several empirical evaluations are twofold:

1. Skill acquisition. Across diverse aggressive trainee populations and target skills, *skill acquisition is a reliable training outcome, occurring in well over 90% of Structured Learning trainees.* While pleased with this outcome, we are acutely aware of the manner in which therapeutic gains demonstrable in the training context are rather easily accomplished—given the potency, support, encouragement, and low threat value of trainers—but that the more consequential outcome question by far pertains to trainee skill performance in real-world contexts (i.e., skill transfer).

2. Skill transfer. Across diverse trainee populations, target skills, and applied (real-world) settings, *skill transfer occurs with approximately 45–50% of Structured Learning Trainees.* Goldstein and Kanfer (1979) as

well as Karoly and Steffen (1980) have indicated that across several dozen types of psychotherapy involving many different types of psychopathology, the average transfer rate on follow-up is less than 25% of patients seen. The near 50% rate consequent to Structured Learning is a significant improvement upon this collective base rate, though it must immediately be underscored that this cumulative average transfer finding also means that the gains shown by half of our trainees were limited to in-session acquisition. Of special consequence, however, is the consistently clear manner in which skill transfer in our studies appeared to be a function of the explicit implementation of laboratory derived transfer-enhancing techniques, such as those described in chapter 10.

Concurrent with or following our development of the Structured Learning approach to prosocial skills training, a number of similar programmatic attempts to enhance social competency emerged. Those that focused at least in large part on aggressive individuals and their prosocial training include Life Skills Education (Adkins, 1970), Social Skills Training (Argyle, Trower & Bryant, 1974), AWARE: Activities for Social Development (Elardo & Cooper, 1977), Relationship Enhancement (Guerney, 1977), Teaching Conflict Resolution (Hare, 1976), Developing Human Potential (Hawley & Hawley, 1975) ASSET (Hazel, Schumaker, Sherman & Sheldon-Wildgen, 1981), Interpersonal Communication (Heiman, 1973), and Directive Teaching (Stephens, 1976). The instructional techniques which constitute each of these skills training efforts derive primarily from social learning theory and typically consist of procedures quite similar to those which constitute Structured Learning. We now wish to turn to these procedures in detail.

PREPARING FOR STRUCTURED LEARNING

Selecting Trainees

Who belongs in the Structured Learning group? As noted earlier, Structured Learning grew originally from a behavior deficit view of asocial and antisocial behavior. If such behavior is due in substantial part to a lack of ability in a variety of alternative, prosocial skills of an interpersonal, personal, aggression-management, or related nature, our selection goal is defined for us. The Structured Learning group should consist of individuals weak or deficient in one or more of the clusters of skills which constitute the Structured Learning skill curriculum (e.g., see Table 8.1 for adolescent skill curriculum). Largely or entirely irrelevant to this selection decision are most of the usual bases for treatment or training selection decisions. If the clients are skill deficient, and possess a few very basic group participation skills, we are largely unconcerned with their age, sex, race, social class or, within very broad limits, even their mental health. At times we have had to exclude persons who were severely emotionally disturbed, too hyperactive for a 30-minute session, or so developmentally disabled that they lacked the rudimentary memory and imagery abilities necessary for adequate group participation. But such persons have been relatively few in number in our training attempts. Thus, while Structured Learning is not a prescription designed for all aggressive individuals, its range of appropriate use is nevertheless quite broad. If skill deficit is the main basis for deciding whether an individual should be offered Structured Learning, how will the person's level of skill deficit be determined? We have found it useful to estimate levels of skill deficiency by employing, alone or in combination, four of the methods of assessment examined in chapters 2 and 3: interviews, direct observation, behavioral testing, and skill checklists.

Group Organization

The preparation phase of the Structured Learning group is completed by attention to those organizational details necessary for a smoothly initiated, appropriately paced, and instructionally effective group to begin. Factors to be considered in organizing the group are: number of trainees, number of trainers, number of sessions, and spacing of sessions.

Number of Trainees. Since trainee behavior in a Structured Learning group may vary greatly from person to person and from group to group, it is not appropriate that we recommend a single, specific number of trainees as optimal. Ideally, the number of trainees will permit all to role play, will lead to optimal levels of group interaction, and will provide a diverse source of performance feedback opportunities. In our experiences with delinquent adolescents, for example, these goals have most usually been met when the group's size was five to seven trainees. We have had slightly larger groups when working with abusive parents.

Number of Trainers. The role playing and feedback that make up most of each Structured Learning session are series of "action–reaction" sequences in which effective skill behaviors are first rehearsed (role played) and then critiqued (feedback). Thus, the trainer must both lead and observe. We have found that one trainer is hard pressed to do both of these tasks well at the same time, and thus, we recommend that each session be led by a team of two trainers. One trainer can usually pay special attention to the main actor, helping the actor "set the stage" and

Table 8.1. Adolescent Skill Curriculum

Group I. Beginning Social Skills

1. Listening
2. Starting a conversation
3. Having a conversation
4. Asking a question
5. Saying thank you
6. Introducing yourself
7. Introducing other people
8. Giving a compliment

Group II. Advanced Social Skills

9. Asking for help
10. Joining in
11. Giving instructions
12. Following instructions
13. Apologizing
14. Convincing others

Group III. Skills for Dealing with Feelings

15. Knowing your feelings
16. Expressing your feelings
17. Understanding the feelings of others
18. Dealing with someone else's anger
19. Expressing affection
20. Dealing with fear
21. Rewarding yourself

Group IV. Skills Alternatives to Aggression

22. Asking permission
23. Sharing something
24. Helping others
25. Negotiation
26. Using self-control
27. Standing up for your rights
28. Responding to teasing
29. Avoiding trouble with others
30. Keeping out of fights

Group V. Skills for Dealing with Stress

31. Making a complaint
32. Answering a complaint
33. Sportsmanship after the game
34. Dealing with embarrassment
35. Dealing with being left out
36. Standing up for a friend
37. Responding to persuasion
38. Responding to failure
39. Dealing with contradictory messages
40. Dealing with an accusation
41. Getting ready for a difficult conversation
42. Dealing with a group pressure

Group VI. Planning Skills

43. Deciding on something to do
44. Deciding what caused a problem
45. Setting a goal
46. Deciding on your abilities
47. Gathering information
48. Arranging problems by importance
49. Making a decision
50. Concentrating on a task

---

enact the skill's behavioral steps. While this is occurring, the other trainer can attend to the remainder of the group and help them as they observe and evaluate the unfolding role play. The two trainers can then exchange these responsibilities on the next role play.

Number of Sessions. Structured Learning groups typically seek to cover one skill in one or two sessions. The central task is to make certain that every trainee in the group role plays the given skill correctly at least once, preferably more than once. Most Structured Learning groups have met this curriculum plan by holding sessions once or twice per week. Groups have varied greatly in the total number of meetings they have held. Some have targeted only a single skill group (e.g., six skills), and thus met on a short-term, time-limited basis just to complete such a shortened curriculum. Other groups have held enough meetings to cover the full curriculum and then continued on even further to either new skills of their own creation, or repetition of just learned skills in new settings.

Spacing of Sessions. The goal of Structured Learning, as with all prosocial skill training interactions, is not merely skill learning or acquisition; much more important is skill transfer. Performance of the skill in the training setting is desired, but performance of it in the facility or community is crucial. Several aspects of Structured Learning (see p. 116) are designed to enhance the likelihood of such skill transfer; session spacing is one such aspect. As we will describe, after the trainee role plays successfully in the group and receives thorough performance feedback, he/she is assigned homework, that is, the task of carrying out in the "real world" the skill that was just correctly performed in the group. In order to ensure ample time and opportunity to carry out this very important task, Structured Learning sessions must be scheduled at least a few days apart.

Length and Location of Sessions. One-hour sessions are the typical Structured Learning format, though both briefer and longer sessions have also been successful. In general, the session goal that must be met is successful role playing and feedback for all participants, whether it takes 45 minutes, an hour, or an hour and a half.

Meeting with the Trainees Before the First Session

A final step that must be taken before holding the first session of a new Structured Learning group is to prepare the trainees for what they should expect and what will be expected of them. What this premeeting might cover is as follows.

1. *Describe what the purpose of the group will be as it relates to the trainee's specific skill deficits.* For example, with aggressive adolescent trainees, the trainer might say, "Remember when you lost privileges because you thought Henry had insulted you and you got in a shoving match with him? Well, in Structured Learning, you'll be able to learn what to do in a situation like that so you can handle it without fighting and still calmly settle whatever was going on."

2. *Describe briefly the procedure that will be used.* Although we believe that trainees typically will not have a full understanding of what Structured Learning is and what it can accomplish until after the group has begun and they have experienced it, verbal, pregroup structuring of procedures is a useful beginning. It conveys at least a part of the information necessary to help trainees know what to expect. The trainer might say, "In order to learn to handle these problem situations better, we're going to see and hear some examples of how different people handle them well. Then you will actually take turns trying some of these ways right here. We'll let you know how you did, and you'll have a chance to practice on your own."

3. *Describe some of the hoped-for benefits of active trainee participation in the group.* If the trainer has information from a trainee—for example, a completed Structured Learning skill checklist—the possible benefits described might appropriately be improved proficiency in the particular Structured Learning skills that the trainee rates as especially deficient.

4. *Describe group rules.* These rules include whatever the trainer believes the group members must adhere to in order to function smoothly and effectively with regard to attendance, punctuality, confidentiality, completion of homework assignments, and so forth. At this premeeting stage, rule structuring should be brief and tentative. Reserve a fuller discussion of this matter for the group's first session, when all members can be encouraged to participate, and when rule changes can be made by consensus if such changes are the will of the group.

CONDUCTING THE STRUCTURED LEARNING GROUP

We now wish to turn to a detailed, step-by-step, description of the procedures that constitute the Structured Learning session. The opening session will be considered first. The elements of this session that get the Structured Learning group off to a good start will be emphasized. Then we describe the procedures that constitute the bulk of most Structured Learning sessions—modeling, role playing, performance feedback, and transfer training.

The Opening Session

The opening session is designed to create a safe, nurturing, nonthreatening environment for trainees, to stimulate their interest in the group, and give more detailed information to them than was provided in their individual orientations. The trainers open the session with a brief familiarization, or warm-up period, to help participants become comfortable when interacting with the group leaders and with one another. Content for this initial phase should be interesting and nonthreatening to the trainees. Next, trainers introduce the Structured Learning program by providing trainees with a brief description of what skill training is about. Typically this introduction covers such topics as the importance of interpersonal skills for effective and satisfying living, examples of skills that will be taught, and how these skills can be useful to trainees in their everyday lives. It is often helpful to expand this discussion of everyday skill use to emphasize to the participants the importance of the undertaking and the personal relevance of learning the skill. The specific training procedures (modeling, role playing, performance feedback, and transfer training) are then described at a level that the group can easily understand. We recommend that trainers describe procedures briefly, with the expectation that trainees will understand them more fully once they have actually participated in their use.

Following introductions, the overview of Structured Learning, and the presentation of group rules, the trainers should proceed to introducing and modeling the group's first skill, conducting role plays of that skill, giving performance feedback, and encouraging transfer training. These activities make up all subsequent Structured Learning sessions.

Modeling

The modeling displays presented to trainees should depict the behavioral steps that constitute the skill being taught in a clear and unambiguous manner. All of the steps making up the skill should be modeled, in the correct sequence. Generally, the modeling will consist of live vignettes enacted by the two trainers. These modeling displays should incorporate the guidelines that follow:

1. Use at least two examples of different situations for each demonstration of a skill. If a given skill is taught in more than one group meeting, develop two more new modeling displays.

2. Select situations that are relevant to the trainees' real-life circumstances.
3. The main actor, that is, the trainer enacting the behavioral steps of
   the skill, should be portrayed as a person reasonably similar in age,
   socioeconomic background, verbal ability, and other salient characteristics to the people in the Structured Learning group.
4. Modeling displays should depict only one skill at a time. All extraneous content should be eliminated.
5. All modeling displays should depict all the behavioral steps of the
   skill being modeled in the correct sequence.
6. All displays should depict positive outcomes. Displays should
   always end with reinforcement to the model.

In order to help trainees attend to the skill enactments, skill cards that
contain the name of the skill being taught and its behavioral steps are
distributed prior to the modeling displays. Trainees are told to watch
and listen closely as the models portray the skill. Particular care should
be given to helping trainees identify the behavioral steps as they are
presented in the context of the modeling vignettes. Table 8.2 presents
the behavioral steps for those skills from the Structured Learning Adolescent Curriculum that are functionally significant alternatives to
aggressive behavior.

Role Playing

Following the modeling display, discussion should focus on relating the
modeled skill to the lives of trainees. Trainers should invite comments on
the behavioral steps and how these steps might be useful in real-life situations that trainees encounter. It is most helpful to focus on current and
future skill use rather than on past events or general issues involving the
skill. Role playing in Structured Learning is intended to serve as behavioral rehearsal or practice for future use of the skill. Role playing of past
events that have little relevance for future situations is of limited value to
trainees. However, discussion of past events involving skill use can be
relevant in stimulating trainees to think of times when a similar situation
might occur in the future. The hypothetical future situation rather than a
reenactment of the past event should be selected for role playing.

Once a trainee has described a situation in his/her own life when the
skill might be helpful, that trainee is designated the main actor. He/she
chooses a second trainee (the co-actor) to play the role of the other person (mother, peer, child, staff member, etc.) who is relevant to the situation. The trainee should be urged to pick as a co-actor someone who
resembles the real-life person in as many ways as possible—physically,
expressively, and so forth. The trainers then elicit from the main actor

any additional information needed to set the stage for role playing. To make role playing as realistic as possible, the trainers should obtain a description of the physical setting, a description of the events immediately preceding the role play, a description of the manner the co-actor should display, and any other information that would increase realism.

It is crucial that the main actor use the behavioral steps that have been modeled. This is the main purpose of the role playing. Before beginning the actual role playing, the trainer should go over each step as it applies to the particular role-play situation, thus preparing the main actor to make a successful effort. The main actor is told to refer to the skill card, where the behavioral steps are printed. The behavioral steps are also written on a chalkboard visible to the main actor as well as the rest of the group during the role playing. Before the role playing begins, trainers should remind all of the participants of their roles and responsibilities: the main actor is told to follow the behavioral steps: the co-actor, to stay in the role of the other person; and the observers, to watch carefully for the enactment of the behavioral steps. At times, feedback from other trainees is facilitated by assigning each one a single behavioral step to focus upon and provide feedback on after the role play. For the first several role plays, the observers also can be coached on kinds of cues (posture, tone of voice, content of speech, etc.) to observe.

During the role play, it is the responsibility of one of the trainers to provide the main actor with whatever help, coaching, and encouragement he/she needs to keep the role playing going according to the behavioral steps. Trainees who "break role" and begin to explain their

Table 8.2. Aggression-Relevant Structured Learning Skills

Asking for Help

1. Decide what the problem is.
2. Decide if you want help with the problem.
3. Identify the people who might help you.
4. Make a choice of helper.
5. Tell the helper about your problem.

Giving Instruction

1. Define what needs to be done and who should do it.
2. Tell the other person what you want him or her to do, and why.
3. Tell the other person exactly how to do what you want done.
4. Ask for his or her reaction.
5. Consider his or her reactions and change your direction if appropriate.

Expressing Affection

1. Decide if you have warm, caring feelings about the other person.
2. Decide whether the other person would like to know about your feelings.
3. Decide how you might best express your feelings.
4. Choose the right time and place to express your feelings.
5. Express affection in a warm and caring manner.

Expressing a Complaint

1. Define what the problem is, and who is responsible.
2. Decide how the problem might be solved.
3. Tell that person what the problem is and how it might be solved.
4. Ask for a response.
5. Show that you understand his or her feelings.
6. Come to agreement on the steps to be taken by each of you.

Persuading Others

1. Decide on your position and what the other person's is likely to be.
2. State your position clearly, completely, and in a way that is acceptable to the other person.
3. State what you think the other person's position is.
4. Restate your position, emphasizing why it is the better of the two.
5. Suggest that the other person consider your position for a while before making a decision.

Responding to the Feelings of Others (Empathy)

1. Observe the other person's words and actions.
2. Decide what the other person might be feeling, and how strong the feelings are.
3. Decide whether it would be helpful to let the other person know you understand his or her feelings.
4. Tell the other person, in a warm and sincere manner, how you think he or she is feeling.

Following Instruction

1. Listen carefully while the instructions are being given.
2. Given your reactions to the instructions.
3. Repeat the instructions to yourself.
4. Imagine yourself following the instructions and then do it.

Responding to Persuasion

1. Listen openly to the other person's position.
2. Consider the other person's possible reasons for that position.
3. Ask the other person to explain anything you don't understand about what was said.
4. Compare the other person's position with your own, identifying the pros and cons of each.
5. Decide what to do, based on what will benefit you most in the long run.

Responding to Failure

1. Decide if you have failed.
2. Think about both the personal reasons and the circumstances that have caused you to fail.
3. Decide how you might do things differently if you tried again.
4. Decide if you want to try again.
5. If it is appropriate, try again, using your revised approach.

Responding to Contradictory Messages

1. Pay attention to those body signals that help you know you are feeling trapped or confused.
2. Observe the other person's words and actions that may have caused you to have these feelings.
3. Decide whether that person's words and actions are contradictory.
4. Decide whether it would be useful to point out the contradiction.
5. Ask the other person to explain the contradiction.

Responding to a Complaint

1. Listen openly to the complaint.
2. Ask the person to explain anything you do not understand.
3. Show that you understand the other person's thoughts and feelings.
4. Tell the other person your thoughts and feelings, accepting responsibility if appropriate.
5. Summarize the steps to be taken by each of you.

Preparing for a Stressful Conversation

1. Imagine yourself in the stressful situation.
2. Think about how you will feel and why you will feel that way.
3. Imagine the other person in the stressful situation. Think about how that person will feel and why he or she will feel that way.
4. Imagine yourself telling the other person what you want to say.
5. Imagine the response that that will elicit.
6. Repeat the above steps using as many approaches as you can think of.
7. Choose the best approach.

Determining Responsibility

1. Decide what the problem is.
2. Consider possible causes of the problem.
3. Decide which are the most likely causes of the problem.
4. Take actions to test out which are the actual causes of the problem.

Responding to Anger

1. Listen openly to the other person's angry statement.
2. Show that you understand what the other person is feeling.
3. Ask the other person to explain anything you don't understand about what was said.
4. Show that you understand why the other person feels angry.
5. If it is appropriate, express your thoughts and feelings about the situation.

Setting Problem Priorities

1. List all the problems that are currently pressuring you.
2. Arrange this list in order, from most to least urgent problems.
3. Take steps (delegate, postpone, avoid) to temporarily decrease the urgency of all but the most pressing problem.
4. Concentrate on the most pressing problem.

Dealing with Being Left Out

1. Decide if you're being left out (ignored, rejected).
2. Think about why the other people might be leaving you out of something.
3. Decide how you could deal with the problem (wait, leave, tell the other people how their behavior affects you, talk with a friend about the problem).
4. Choose the best way and do it.

Dealing with an Accusation

1. Think about what the other person has accused you of (if it is accurate, inaccurate, if it was said in a mean way or in a constructive way).
2. Think about why the person might have accused you (have you infringed on his or her rights or property?).

3. Think about ways to answer the person's accusations (deny, explain your behavior, correct other person's perceptions, assert, apologize, offer to make up for what happened).
4. Choose the best way and do it.

Dealing with Group Pressure

1. Think about what the other people want you to do and why (listen to other people, decide what their real meaning is, try to understand what is being said).
2. Decide what you want to do (yield, resist, delay, negotiate).
3. Decide how to tell the other people what you want to do (give reasons, talk to one person only, delay, assert).
4. Choose the best way and do it.

---

behavior or make observer-like comments should be urged to get back into the role and explain later. If the role play is clearly going astray from the behavioral steps, the scene can be stopped, the needed instruction can be provided, and then the role play can be restarted. One trainer should be positioned near the chalkboard in order to point to each of the behavioral steps in turn as the role play unfolds, thus helping the main actor (as well as the other trainees) to follow each of the steps in order. The second trainer should sit with the observing trainees to be available as needed to keep them on task.

The role playing should be continued until all trainees have had an opportunity to participate in the role of main ator. Sometimes this will require two or three sessions for a given skill. As we suggested before, each session should begin with two new modeling vignettes for the chosen skill, even if the skill is not new to the group. It is important to note once again that while the framework (behavioral steps) of each role play in the series remains the same, the actual content can and should change from role play to role play. The problem as it actually occurs, or could occur, in each trainee's real-life environment should be the content of the given role play.

Performance Feedback

A brief feedback period follows each role play. This helps the main actor find out how well he or she followed or departed from the behavioral steps. It also examines the psychological impact of the enactment of the co-actor, and provides the main actor with encouragement to try out the role-played behaviors in real life. The trainer should ask the main actor to wait until he or she has heard everyone's comments before responding to them.

The co-actor is asked about his/her reactions first. Next, the observers comment on how well the behavioral steps were followed and other relevant aspects of the role play. Then the trainers comment in particular on how well the behavioral steps were followed and provide social reinforcement (praise, approval, encouragement) for following closely. To be most effective in their use of reinforcement, trainers should follow these guidelines:

1. Provide reinforcement only after role plays that follow the behavioral steps.
2. Provide reinforcement at the earliest appropriate opportunity after role plays that follow the behavioral steps.
3. Vary the specific content of the reinforcements offered, for example, praise particular aspects of the performance, such as tone of voice, posture, phrasing, and so forth.
4. Provide enough role-playing activity for each group member to have sufficient opportunity to be reinforced.
5. Provide reinforcement in an amount consistent with the quality of the given role play.
6. Provide no reinforcement when the role play departs significantly from the behavioral steps (except for "trying" in the first session or two).
7. Provide reinforcement for an individual trainee's improvement over previous performances.
8. Always provide reinforcement to the co-actor for being helpful, cooperative, and so forth.

In all aspects of feedback, it is crucial that the trainer maintain the behavioral focus of Structured Learning. Both trainer and trainee comments should point to the presence or absence of specific, concrete behaviors and not take the form of general evaluations or broad generalities. Feedback, of course, may be positive or negative in content. Negative comments should always be followed by a constructive comment as to how a particular fault might be improved. At minimum, a "poor" performance can be praised as "a good try" at the same time that it is being criticized for its real faults. If at all possible, trainees failing to follow the relevant behavioral steps in their role play should be given the opportunity to role play these same behavioral steps again after receiving corrective feedback. At times, as a further feedback procedure, we have audio- or videotaped entire role plays. Giving trainees post-role-play opportunities to observe themselves on tape can be an effective aid, enabling them to reflect on their own verbal and nonverbal behavior and its impact upon others.

Since a primary goal of Structured Learning is skill flexibility, role play enactments that depart somewhat from the behavioral steps may not be "wrong." That is, a different approach to the skill may in fact work in some situations. Trainers should stress that they are trying to teach effective alternatives and that the trainees would do well to have the behavioral steps being taught, or as collaboratively modified, in their repertoire of skill behaviors, available to use when appropriate.

Transfer and Maintenance Training

Several aspects of the training sessions already described have been designed primarily to make it likely that learning in the training setting will transfer to and persist in the trainees' actual real-life environments. Techniques for enhancing transfer and maintenance training as they are used in the Structured Learning sessions follow. In chapter 10, these and additional transfer-enhancing procedures will be examined in greater detail.

Provision of General Principles. It has been demonstrated that transfer of training is facilitated by providing trainees with general mediating principles governing successful or competent performance in both the training and applied real-world settings. This has been operationalized in laboratory contexts by providing subjects with the organizing concepts, principles, strategies, or rationales that explain the stimulus-response relationships operating in both the training and application settings. General principles of skill selection and utilization are provided to Structured Learning trainees verbally, visually, and in written form.

Overlearning. Overlearning involves the training of a skill beyond what is necessary to produce initial changes in behavior. The overlearning, or repetition of successful skill enactment, in the typical Structured Learning session is quite substantial. Each skill taught and its behavioral steps are:

1. Modeled several times;
2. Role played one or more times by the trainee;
3. Observed live by the trainee while every other group member role plays;
4. Read by the trainee from a chalkboard and skill card;
5. Practiced in real-life settings one or more times by the trainee as part of his formal homework assignment.

Identical Elements. Several investigators have emphasized the importance for transfer of similarity between stimulus aspects of the training and the application tasks. The greater the similarity of physical and interpersonal stimuli in the Structured Learning setting and the homework and community or other setting in which the skill is to be applied, the greater the likelihood of transfer. Structured Learning is made similar to real life in several ways. These include:

1. Designing the live modeling displays to be highly similar to what trainees face in their daily lives through the representative, relevant, and realistic portrayal of the models, protagonists, and situations;

2. Designing the role plays to be similar to real-life situations through the use of props, physical arrangement of the setting, and the choice of realistic co-actors;
3. Conducting the role play to be as responsive as possible to the real-life interpersonal stimuli to which the trainees must actually respond later with the given skill;
4. Rehearsing of each skill in role plays as the trainees actually plan to use it;
5. Assigning of homework.

Stimulus Variability. Positive transfer is greater when a variety of relevant training stimuli are employed (Callantine & Warren, 1955; Duncan 1958; Shore & Sechrest, 1961). Stimulus variability may be implemented in Structured Learning sessions by use of:

1. Rotation of group leaders across groups;
2. Rotation of trainees across groups;
3. Role playing of a given skill by trainees with several different co-actors;
4. Role playing of a given skill by trainees across several relevant settings;
5. Completion of multiple homework assignments for each given skill.

Real-life Reinforcement. Given successful implementation of both appropriate Structured Learning procedures and the transfer enhancement procedures discussed above, positive transfer—and especially maintenance over time—may still fail to occur. As Agras (1967), Gruber (1971), Patterson and Anderson (1964), Tharp and Wetzel (1969), and dozens of other investigators have shown, stable and enduring performance in application settings of newly learned skills is very much at the mercy of real-life reinforcement contingencies. We have found it useful to implement several supplemental programs outside of the Structured Learning setting that can help to provide the rewards that trainees need in order to maintain new behaviors. These programs include provisions for both external social rewards (provided by people in the trainee's real-life environments) and self-rewards (provided by the trainees themselves). A particularly useful tool for transfer enhancement that combines the possibilities of identical elements, stimulus variability, and real-life reinforcement, is the skill homework assignment.

When possible, we urge use of a homework technique we have found to be successful with most groups. In this procedure, trainees are instructed to try in their own real-life settings the behaviors they have practiced during the session. The name of the person(s) with whom they will try it, the day, the place, and so forth are all discussed. The trainee is urged to take notes on the attempt to use the skill on the

FIGURE 8.1. Homework Report Form

NAME: _____   DATE: _____

GROUP LEADERS: _____

FILL IN DURING THIS CLASS:

1. Homework assignment:
   (a) Skill:
   (b) With whom:
   (c) Use when:
   (d) Use where:

2. Steps to be followed:

FILL IN BEFORE NEXT CLASS:

3. Describe what happened when you did the homework assignment:

4. Steps you actually followed:

5. Rate yourself on how well you used the skill (check one):
   Excellent _____   Good _____   Fair _____   Poor _____

6. Describe what you feel should be your *next* homework assignment:

---

homework report form (Figure 8.1). This form requests detailed information about what happened when the trainee attempted the homework assignment, how well the relevant behavioral steps were followed, the trainee's evaluation of his/her performance, and thoughts about what the next assignment might appropriately be.

It has often proven useful to start with relatively simple homework behaviors and, as they are mastered, to work toward more complex and demanding assignments. This provides both the trainer and the people who are targets of the homework with an opportunity to reinforce each approximation to the more complex target behavior. Successful experiences at beginning-homework attempts are crucial in encouraging the trainee to make further attempts at real-life skill use.

The first part of each Structured Learning session is devoted to presenting and discussing these homework reports. When trainees have made an effort to complete their homework assignments, trainers should provide social reinforcement; failure to do homework should be met with some chagrin and expressed disappointment, followed by support and encouragement to complete the assignment. It cannot be stressed too strongly that without these or similar attempts to maximize transfer, the value of the entire training effort is in severe jeopardy.

RESEARCH ON PROSOCIAL SKILL TRAINING

In addition to our own evaluative studies of Structured Learning with aggressive populations noted earlier, a large number of other investigators have examined the efficacy of prosocial skill training with such target persons (Bornstein, Bellack & Hersen, 1980; Collingwood & Genthner, 1980; Hazel, 1981; Hollin & Courtney, 1983; Hollin & Henderson, 1981; Long & Sherer, 1985; Pentz, 1980; Sarsaon & Ganzer, 1973; Schinke, 1981; Spence, 1981; Trief, 1977). While target skills have varied across investigations, for the most part they have concerned interpersonal behaviors, prosocial alternatives to aggression and aggression-management or aggression-inhibition behaviors. As Spence (1981) correctly notes, the single case studies have tended toward micro-skill training targets—eye contact, head nods, and the like—and the multiple group studies have sought to teach more macro-skill competencies—for example; coping with criticism, negotiation, and problem solving. Results for skill acquisition have been quite consistently positive. Aggressive persons are able to learn a broad array of previously unavailable interpersonal, aggression-management, affect-relevant and related psychological competencies via the training methods examined here. Evaluation for maintenance and transfer of acquired skills yields a rather different outcome. Many studies test for neither. Those that do combine to report a mixed result. As noted earlier, our own investigative efforts in this regard (Goldstein, 1982) point to the not surprising conclusion that generalization of skill competency across settings (transfer) and time (maintenance) is very much a direct function of the degree to which the investigator/trainer implemented procedures explicitly designed to enhance transfer and/or maintenance as a part of the training effort. To summarize our view of empirical efforts to date— prosocial skills training with aggressive individuals rests on a firm investigative foundation. A variety of investigators, designs, subjects, settings and target skills is providing a healthy examination of the effectiveness of such training. Skill acquisition is a reliable outcome, but the social validity of this consistent result is tempered by the frequent failure—or at least, indeterminacy—of transfer and maintenance.

Chapter 9
Prosocial Values Training

This chapter discusses the final link in the chain of interventions we view as prescriptive for the series of behaviors that constitute the aggressive behavior sequence. The several interventions examined thus far are all designed to provide the individual with the competencies necessary to deal effectively with one or another segment of the aggressive behavior sequence, for example how to lower one's own and the other disputant's anger-arousal levels, to communicate and negotiate effectively, to employ action-promoting contracts, to use a full array of prosocial skills, and so forth. However, having such competencies in one's repertoire and actually deciding to employ them are two different matters. Especially in a societal context where aggressive behavior is often richly and reliably rewarded, persons skilled in nonaggressive alternative behaviors may still choose to utilize overt aggression. Thus, there is a need for an intervention impinging upon values that is designed to increase the chances that when such choices are being faced, the individual will be more likely to opt for the alternative that more fully considers and responds to the needs, feelings and beliefs of others, not just his or her own. That is, what is needed is a values-relevant intervention that enhances the likelihood the person will choose nonaggressive routes to resolve conflicts. Moral education appears to be just such an intervention:

> Morality involves those skills, values, and abilities that comprise (1) thinking or reasoning (problem solving, decision making) in a rational way, while (2) showing an awareness of, and consideration or caring for the needs, interests, and feelings of others as well as oneself, and (3) behaving constructively, i.e., in ways that benefit both self and others, in the problematic or conflictual social–interpersonal situations which one encounters in one's daily interactions with other people. It follows that the goal of moral education is to teach and develop, or facilitate the development of, the above skills, values, and abilities that define morality. (Edelman & Goldstein, 1981, p. 259)

A number of approaches to the enhancement of morality and allocentric values have been developed in recent years, including values clarification (Raths, Harmin & Simon, 1960), Beck's Ultimate Life Goal approach (Beck, 1971; Beck, Hersh & Sullivan, 1976; Beck & Sullivan, 1976); McPhail's Learning to Care program (McPhail, Ungoed-Thomas, & Chapman, 1975); Newman, Oliver, and Shaver's Public Issues program (Newman & Oliver, 1970; Oliver & Shaver, 1966); Wilson's Moral Components approach (Wilson, 1971, 1972, 1973); Mosher and Sprinthall's Psychological Education (Mosher & Sprinthall, 1970, 1972); Glasser's Classroom Meeting approach (Glasser, 1969); and Weinstein and Fantini's Identity Education (Weinstein & Fantini, 1970).

Of these several alternatives, we have selected Kohlberg's (1964, 1969, 1973) Moral Education as the prosocial values training method of choice in the context of aggression and its management—particularly for children, adolescents and young adults. We do so not only because of the generally firm empirical base upon which Moral Education rests, but also because (a) a considerable portion of the demonstrations of its efficacy derive from studies involving chronically aggressive individuals (e.g., Arbuthnot & Gordon, 1983; Gibbs, Arnold, Ahlborn & Chessman, 1984; Goldstein & Glick, 1986), and (b) the partial evidence that higher (e.g., postconventional) levels of moral reasoning will, under certain circumstances, relate positively to and perhaps even be promotive of such prosocial behaviors as honesty (Harris, Mussen & Rutherford, 1976; Kohlberg & Turiel, 1971; Krebs, 1976), altruism, helping others in distress, generosity (McNamee, 1977; Ugurel-Semin, 1952), and nonviolence, as reflected in refusal to inflict pain upon others (Kohlberg & Turiel, 1971).

Kohlberg's theory is typically described as a "cognitive–developmental" approach to morality. A cognitive perspective on morality emphasizes the notion that there are qualitatively different ways in which people think about, reason, and make sense of basic moral issues (e.g., value of life, truth, or justice) in their continual attempts to relate effectively to other human beings in their world. A developmental perspective on morality emphasizes the notion that these fundamentally different ways of reasoning about and making sense of basic moral issues change over time, that is, over the course of a person's growth. Central to a cognitive–developmental perspective is the notion of stages. Stages are structured or organized systems of thought. When we say that there are qualitatively different ways of thinking about moral issues over the course of a person's growth, we are saying that there are distinct stages of moral reasoning characterizing a person's development. Critical to the cognitive–developmental concept of stages are the following:

1. *The final or "highest stage" represents the theoretically "ideal" endpoint of development.* As a person develops from a young child to a mature adult, his or her ways of reasoning about moral issues progress through a series of stages toward a final or highest stage that may or may not be reached.

2. *Stages form an invariant sequence.* As a person develops, his or her ways of reasoning about moral issues progress through a series of stages (to the hypothesized final stage) in a fixed order or sequence. Although a person may progress through this sequence of stages more slowly or more rapidly than others, and although his or her development may become arrested or fixated at a particular stage (which may then become the highest stage that that person achieves); if that person does progress, it is always to the next stage up. The invariant sequence of stages is assumed to be true for all people; that is, there is a hypothesized universally invariant sequence of stages of moral development.

3. *Stages are "hierarchical integrations": higher stages are "better" than lower stages.* Each successive stage represents an increasingly integrated and effective mode of moral reasoning and problem solving than the previous stage.

4. *The motivation for stage transition is cognitive conflict.* During certain critical periods in a person's development, he or she experiences his or her current stage of moral reasoning as increasingly inadequate for understanding and resolving more complex problems and dilemmas in value–conflict situations. This induces a state of cognitive conflict, doubt, or uncertainty and dissatisfaction that in turn induces him or her to begin experimenting with modes of reasoning characteristic of the next higher stage.

According to Kohlberg, the cognitive–developmental approach to moral education is nonindoctrinative because it involves the stimulation of a natural progression of development in the direction that a person is already heading. The constituent methods and operational goals of moral education are also nonindoctrinative in the sense that at no time in its use are particular values or sets of values held to be good, or bad, or better, or worse. Instead, the goal of moral education is to enhance or raise the individual's own level of moral reasoning—to higher, more principled, less egocentric levels. The six stages of moral-reasoning demonstrated by Kohlberg (1971), are as follows:

KOHLBERG'S SIX STAGES OF
MORAL REASONING

1. *Preconventional Level.* At this level, the child is responsive to cultural rules and labels of good and bad, right or wrong, but interprets these labels in terms of either the physical or the hedonistic conse-

quences of action (punishment, reward, exchange of favors) or in terms of the physical power of those who enunciate the rules and labels. This level comprises the following two stages: (a) "Stage 1: Punishment and Obedience Orientation," when the physical consequences of action determine its goodness or badness regardless of the human meaning or value of the consequences. Avoidance of punishment and unquestioning deference to power are valued in their own right, not in terms of respect for an underlying moral order supported by punishment and authority (the later being stage 4); and (b) "Stage 2: Instrumental Relativist Orientation," when correct action consists of that which instrumentally satisfies one's own needs and, occasionally the needs of others. Human relations are viewed in terms similar to those of the market place. Elements of fairness, or reciprocity, and equal sharing are present, but they are always interpreted in a physical, pragmatic way. Reciprocity is a matter of "you scratch my back and I'll scratch yours," not of loyalty, gratitude, or justice.

2. *Conventional Level.* At this level, maintaining the expectations of the individual's family, group, or nation is perceived as valuable in its own right, regardless of immediate and obvious consequences. The attitude is one not only of *conformity* to personal expectations and social order, but of loyalty to it, of actively *maintaining*, supporting, and justifying the order and of identifying with the persons or groups involved in it. This level comprises the following two stages: (a) "Stage 3: Interpersonal Concordance or 'Good Boy–Nice Girl' Orientation," when good behavior is that which pleases or helps others and is approved of by them. There is much conformity to stereotypical images of what is majority or "natural" behavior. Behavior is frequently judged by intention; "he means well" becomes important for the first time. One earns approval by being "nice," and (b) "Stage 4: 'Law and Order' Orientation", when there is orientation toward authority, fixed rules, and the maintenance of the social order. Right behavior consists of doing one's duty, showing respect for authority, and maintaining the given social order for its own sake.

3. *Post-Conventional, Autonomous, or Principled Level.* At this level, there is a clear effort to define moral values and principles that have validity and application apart from the authority of the groups or persons holding these principles and apart from the individual's own identification with these groups. This level also has two stages: (a) "Stage 5: Social-Contract Legalistic Orientation," which has utilitarian overtones. Right action tends to be defined in terms of general individual rights and in terms of standards that have been critically examined and agreed upon by the whole society. There is a clear awareness of the relativism of personal values and opinions and a corresponding emphasis on pro-

cedural rules for teaching consensus. Aside from what is constitution-
ally and democratically agreed upon, rights are a matter of personal
"values" and "opinion." The result is an emphasis upon the "legal
point of view," but with an emphasis upon the possibility of changing
law in terms of rational considerations of social utility (rather than
freezing it in terms of Stage 4 "law and order"). Outside the legal realm,
free agreement and contract is the binding element of obligation. This is
the "official" morality of the United States government and constitu-
tion, and (b) "Stage 6: Universal Ethical-Principle Orientation," when
right is defined by the decision of conscience in accord with self-chosen
ethical principles which appeal to logical comprehensiveness, universa-
lity, and consistency. These principles are abstract and ethical (the "golden rule," the categorical imperative); however, they are not concrete
moral rules like the Ten Commandments. At heart, these are universal
principles of justice, of the reciprocity and equality of human rights,
and respect for the dignity of human beings as individual persons.

The specific contents (Kohlberg, 1976) of the moral reasoning stages
are presented in Table 9.1.

In general, the goal of enhanced moral reasoning is achieved through
peer group discussions of stimulating moral dilemmas. Through the discussion of different kinds of reasoning underlying various behavioral
choices to moral situations, youths are exposed to different ways of
thinking about moral issues. In these discussions, youths are asked to
explain the reasoning behind the position they take. In this way, group
members are exposed to different stages of moral reasoning (i.e., different rationales underlying behavioral choices). Exposure to somewhat
advanced (usually one stage higher than the youngster's own reasoning
stage) reasoning stages creates confusion for the youth. The confusion is
called *cognitive conflict* or *disequilibrium*. Exposure to somewhat more
advanced reasoning stages also provides youngsters with the opportunity to take on the role of another person (i.e., to put oneself in someone
else's shoes). In sum, there are at least three basic principles that are
necessary to enhance moral reasoning development and to form the basis
for the specific procedures used in dilemma discussion groups:

1. Exposure to the next higher stage of moral reasoning;
2. Opportunities to take on the role of another person;
3. Confusion over genuine moral dilemmas.

DILEMMA DISCUSSION GROUPS

Dilemma discussion groups can be applied to many moral issues
including the values of life, property, law, truth, affiliation, authority,
contract, conscience and punishment. As we describe fully later in this

Table 9.1. The Content of the Moral Judgment Stages

Level and Stage	What is Right	Reasons for Doing Right	Social Perspective
Level 1: Preconventional *Stage 1: Heteronomous morality*	To avoid breaking rules backed by punishment, obedience for its own sake, and avoiding physical damage to persons and property.	Avoidance of punishment and the superior power of authorities.	*Egocentric point of view.* Doesn't consider the interests of others or recognize that they differ from the actor's; doesn't relate two points of view. Actions are considered physically rather than in terms of psychological interests of others. Confusion of authority perspective with one's own.
Stage 2: Individualism, instrumental purpose, and exchange	Following rules only when it is to someone's immediate interest; action to meet one's own interests and needs and letting others do the same. Right is also what's fair, what's an equal exchange, a deal, an agreement.	To serve one's own needs or interests in a world where you have to recognize that other people have their interests, too.	*Concrete individualistic perspective.* Aware that everybody has his/her own interest to pursue and these conflict, so that right is relative (in the concrete individualistic sense).
Level 2: Conventional *Stage 3: Mutual interpersonal expectations, relationships, and interpersonal conformity*	Living up to what is expected by people close to you or what people generally expect of people in your role as son, brother, friend, etc. "Being good" is important and means having good motives, showing concern about others. It also means keeping mutual relationships, such as trust, loyalty, respect, and gratitude.	The need to be a good person in your own eyes and those of others. Your caring for others. Belief in the "golden rule". Desire to maintain rules and authority which support stereotypical good behavior.	*Perspective of the individual in relationships with other individuals.* Aware of shared feelings, agreements, and expectations which take primacy over individual interests. Relates points of view through the concrete golden rule, putting yourself in the other guy's shoes. Does not yet consider generalized system perspective.

125

Table 9.1. The Content of the Moral Judgment Stages

Level and Stage	What is Right	Reasons for Doing Right	Social Perspective
Stage 4: Social system and conscience	Fulfilling the actual duties to which you have agreed. Laws are to be upheld except in extreme cases where they conflict with other fixed social duties. Right is also contributing to society, the group, or institution.	To keep the institution going as a whole, to avoid the breakdown in the system "if everyone did it," or the imperative of conscience to meet one's defined obligations. (Easily confused with stage 3 belief in rules and authority).	*Differentiates societal point of view from interpersonal agreement or motives.* Takes the point of view of the system that defines roles and rules. Considers individual relations in terms of place in the system.
Level 3: Post-Conventional, or Principled *Stage 5: Social contract or utility and individual rights*	Being aware that people hold a variety of values and opinions, that most values and rules are relative to your group. These relative rules should usually be upheld, however, in the interest of impartiality and because they are the social contract. Some nonrelative values and rights like *life* and *liberty*, however, must be upheld in any society and regardless of majority opinion.	A sense of obligation to law because of one's social contract to make and abide by laws for the welfare of all and for the protection of all people's rights. A feeling of contractual commitment, freely enhanced upon, to family, friendship, trust and work obligations. Concern that laws and duties be based and rational calculation of overall utility, "the greatest good for the greatest number."	*Prior-to-society perspective.* Perspective of a rational individual aware of values and rights prior to social attachments and contracts. Integrate perspectives by formal mechanisms of agreement, contract objective impartiality, and due process. Considers moral and legal points of view; recognize that they sometimes conflict and finds it difficult to integrate them.
Stage 6: Universal ethical principles	Following self-chosen ethical principles. Particular laws or social agreements are usually valid because they rest on such principles. When laws violate these principles, one acts in accordance with the principle. Principles are universal principles of justice: the quality of human rights and respect for the dignity of human beings as individual persons.	The belief as a rational person in the validity of universal moral principles, and a sense of personal commitment to them.	*Perspective of a moral point of view* from which social arrangements derive. Perspective is that of any rational individual recognizing the nature of morality or the fact that persons are ends in themselves and must be treated as such.

126

chapter, what occurs in these groups consists of a six-step procedure. An overview of each step is as follows:

Step 1: Form small groups of youngsters who have achieved about 2 to 3 consecutive stages of moral reasoning (e.g., stages 1, 2, 3).

Step 2: Choose and prepare moral dilemma situations that will induce cognitive conflict and that are relevant to the youngster.

Step 3: Prepare the youngsters by explaining a rationale for dilemma discussion groups, what they will be doing and what guidelines to follow for participation in the group discussion.

Step 4: Begin the discussion by presenting the dilemma, getting initial opinions and rationales from the youngsters, and then creating a debate between the lowest and the one-stage higher reasoners (noted as +1 stage) (e.g., structure a debate between stage 1 and stage 2 reasoners).

Step 5: Guide debate through all the stages represented by group members (e.g., start with a debate between stage 1 and stage 2 reasoners, then between stage 2 and stage 3 reasoners, etc.) in order to create cognitive conflict for as many youngsters as possible; the educator then presents a +1 stage argument for the group to discuss (e.g., if the highest stage represented in the group is stage 3, then the educator would present a stage 4 argument).

Step 6: End discussion following the debate of the highest stage argument or when all the major issues and important differences of opinion have been addressed.

The assessment of moral reasoning stage and the structuring of group discussions are the major activities of the moral educator. As such, the educator must both lead, listen and observe. Typically, one leader finds it difficult to do all of these tasks successfully at the same time. Thus, it is highly recommended that each group be run by a team of two educators—a leader and a co-leader. Conducting effective dilemma discussion groups involves:

1. Knowledge of the main features of moral development theory and moral discussion group technique—its background, assumptions, procedures and goals.
2. Knowledge of moral reasoning stage assessment.
3. Ability to reason at least one stage above that of group members (+1 stage reasoning).
4. Ability to use a nondirective teaching style (e.g., ability to provide only a moderate amount of group structure).
5. Ability to maintain a "devil's advocate" position without leaving participants with the impression that there are specific ways to

behave in moral situations or right/wrong answers to the dilemma being discussed.

6. Ability to orient both group members and supporting staff to dilemma discussion groups.

7. Ability to create experiences that will promote the self-discovery of higher stage reasoning (e.g., ability to structure, initiate and sustain group discussion).

8. Ability to effectively deal with group management problems.

With such requisite group leader qualities in mind, we will examine in depth the six steps involved in running dilemma discussion groups.

Step 1: Forming Groups Based on an Initial Assessment of Stages

The first step in conducting dilemma discussion groups involves the formation of groups based on an initial assessment of moral reasoning stages. Before describing the conditions needed to form an ideal group in terms of number of participants reasoning at differing, and therefore cognitive conflict–arousing stages, it is important to stress that dilemma discussion groups can be conducted even if the ideal conditions do not exist. When ideal conditions do not exist, the educator simply takes a more active role in the moral discussion process. For example, if only one moral reasoning stage is represented in the group, the educator will always need to provide the +1 stage reasoning arguments. In fact, in most dilemma discussion groups involving antisocial youth, the educator will almost always be in the position of having to provide a +1 stage argument at least some of the time. Thus, groups can be formed even if only one stage is represented in the group. If possible, however, it is best to form an *ideal* group. To form an *ideal* group, three conditions should be met. They are:

1. *A range of consecutive moral reasoning stages must be represented by the participants* (e.g., stages 1 and 2 or stages 1, 2 and 3). Meeting this condition means that almost all group members (except the highest stage reasoners) will be exposed to +1 stage reasoning from fellow group members. It also increases the chance that participants will present different opinions. And finally, meeting this condition keeps the discussion manageable in that the educator does not have to be concerned about structuring debates across five different stages. This would not only be difficult for the educator, but would also be of little benefit to most of the participants (i.e., stage 1 reasoners, for example, are unlikely to understand the reasoning of stage 4 individuals because it is too advanced for them).

2. *The number of participants reasoning at a particular moral stage should be almost equally represented in the group* (e.g., four at stage 2, four at stage 3, and four at stage 4). Meeting this condition decreases the chances for peer rejection because it guarantees that there will be potential group support at each stage. It is often difficult for one youngster to present an argument that the rest of the group will likely disagree with because they are at a different stage.
3. *Relatively small groups should be established, consisting of about 8–12 people* (groups have, however, ranged as high as 20–30 individuals). Keeping the groups small increases the chance that everyone will have an opportunity to discuss their opinion and decrease group management problems.

In order to meet the first two of these conditions, the educator may wish to rely on such formal assessment procedures as the Moral Judgment Interview (Arbuthnot & Faust, 1981; Goldstein et al., 1986) or the Sociomoral Reflections Questionnaire (Gibbs & Widaman, 1982). Following the assessment of moral reasoning stage, youngsters should be assigned to groups in such a manner as to have in each group a range of consecutive moral reasoning stages, equal representation of each stage, and groups of about 8–12 people.

Often educators do not have the luxury of forming ideal groups either because of institutional restrictions (e.g., preformed classrooms or counseling groups) or because a range of stage reasoning is simply not available. As previously mentioned, the latter situation is often found in work with aggressive, and especially delinquent, youngsters, where moral reasoning level clearly tends to cluster at stage one. As noted earlier, under these nonideal conditions (i.e., if only one stage or two stages are represented in the group), a moral discussion program can still be conducted. In this situation, the educator will take a more active role in stimulating disagreement and in developing a variety of stage responses by either providing his/her own +1 stage arguments or by elaborating on the dilemma.

Step 2: Choosing and Preparing Dilemmas

Choosing Dilemmas. The second step in conducting dilemma discussion groups involves the selection of dilemmas for debate. Several useful compilations of moral dilemmas appropriate at diverse age levels are available (Colby & Speicher-Dubin, 1973; Fenton, 1980; Galbraith & Jones, 1976; Land & Slade, 1979; Scharf, McCoy & Rory, 1979). An often-employed dilemma, for example, is Heinz's dilemma (Gibbs et al., 1982):

In Europe, a woman was near death from a special kind of cancer. There
was one drug that the doctors thought might save her. It was a form of
radium that a druggist in the same town had recently discovered. The
drug was expensive to make, but the druggist wanted people to pay
ten times what the drug cost him to make.

   The sick woman's husband, Heinz, went to everyone he knew to bor-
row the money, but he could only get together about half of what the
druggist wanted. Heinz told the druggist that his wife was dying, and
asked him to sell it cheaper or let him pay later. But the druggist said,
"No. I discovered the drug and I'm going to make money from it." So
the only way Heinz could get the drug would be to break into the druggist's store and steal it. What should Heinz do?

In making dilemma selections, three considerations should be
reflected:

1. Select dilemmas that will generate cognitive conflict for as many participants as possible.
2. Select dilemmas that will create interesting and productive discussion.
3. Select dilemmas that clearly deal with moral issues (e.g., issues of
   life, property, affiliation, etc.)

When running groups with youngsters who reason at two or three consecutive stages, it is at times difficult to select dilemmas because the
issues that create disequilibrium for one stage of reasoners may not
create cognitive conflict for youngsters reasoning at another stage. At
the same time, different stages need to be represented in the group. To
avoid this potential problem, several guidelines can be followed.

   1. Select or construct dilemmas that generate several issues and questions, but that are open-ended so that the dilemma can be elaborated if
issues at certain stages are not automatically raised or if no counterarguments from higher stage reasoners are provided. A lack of extensive,
precise details helps maintain the open-ended quality of a dilemma so
that when higher stage counterarguments are not generated spontaneously, elaborations can be added to create these higher stage arguments or new issues can emerge. For example, suppose that in response
to the Heinz dilemma (see above), a stage 2 reasoner argues that Heinz
should steal the drug because he needs his wife. If stage 3 reasoners do
not spontaneously produce a counterargument, the educator might
elaborate on the dilemma by adding information that may change the
position of the stage 2 but not the stage 3 reasoner. Specifically, the educator might change the sick person from a wife to a friend or stranger.
This kind of elaboration is likely to create the material needed for the
development of a counterargument that is necessary for the structuring
of a debate.

2. Choose dilemmas involving situations where at least two people have differing claims (e.g., Heinz wants to save his wife's life and the druggist wants to earn money) and an individual must select one behavioral alternative or another.

3. Select dilemmas that participants will be able to understand given their intellectual abilities.

4. Select dilemmas that will most likely lead to different action alternatives for participants reasoning at different stages. With experience and some knowledge of group members, the educator's ability to correctly anticipate probable responses will increase.

5. Choose interesting dilemmas by considering their relevance to the youngsters, probability that the moral situation will actually occur in real-life, the novelty of the issue and the ability of the dilemma to stimulate challenging questions, disagreement and create cognitive conflict. It is important to stress that not all relevant issues are moral issues. For instance, many relevant dilemmas deal with controversial or personal rather than moral issues (e.g., premarital sex). It is recommended that controversial and personal issues not be selected for discussion unless it appears that the group needs to discuss these issues to maintain sustained interest in the program. If controversial issues are introduced by the group, it is best to wait until participants have met for a period of time.

Preparing Dilemmas. After selecting a number of dilemmas to be discussed, the educator must prepare the dilemmas prior to the beginning of each group. This preparation is designed to accomplish three goals:

1. To make them most useful in assessing the youngsters' moral reasoning stage;
2. To stimulate debates at different stages; and
3. To generate counterarguments at different stages, if necessary.

Such preparation is particularly important for the inexperienced educator because it is very difficult to elaborate on a dilemma or develop a counterargument on the spot. In order to adequately prepare dilemmas, the educator should follow three general guidelines. The first guideline is to try to anticipate how participants at a particular stage will respond to the dilemma by referring to the characteristics of each stage (see pp. 122–124 and Table 9.1). The second guideline involves preparing elaborations on dilemmas for those instances when it is necessary to generate disagreements between youngsters at different stages. The third guideline is that it is also important to prepare a counterargument for each of the stages represented in the group, as well as an argument that is one stage above the highest stage represented in the group.

Prior to the first dilemma discussion group, the two educators should also determine what responsibilities each will have during the group. For example, one educator may decide to take primary responsibility for asking the questions needed to get stage responses, while the other person records the responses and determines the stages. As the latter person has staged the responses, he or she may then decide to take on the primary responsibility of structuring the initial discussion while the other educator handles later debates.

Three other decisions need to be made before running a dilemma discussion group. The first involves determining how long each class should be in length. Ideally, dilemma discussion classes are held for about 1 hour. However, because the length of the class often depends on how verbal the youngsters are and on how interesting the dilemma is, sessions can range from 45–60 minutes. This raises the second question, namely how many dilemmas should be discussed in each class? During a typical 1-hour class, a complete discussion of at least one dilemma (a thorough discussion of one dilemma can take about 35–45 minutes) and the introduction and gathering of initial opinions on a second dilemma should occur. With less-verbal youngsters, it is often possible to completely discuss two different dilemmas in one session. At times, it may even be necessary to introduce a third dilemma into a session, though this is not recommended because it is difficult to completely discuss three dilemmas in 1 hour. However, given that it is a possibility, the educator must prepare three dilemmas for each class (i.e., anticipate stage responses, create elaborations and develop counterarguments). It is certainly acceptable not to complete a discussion in one session. In fact, it is sometimes desirable to leave the discussion incomplete in order to encourage participants to think about the dilemma after the class. This additional time between classes can lead to further thoughts that were not initially recognized and can facilitate moral reasoning advance. Discussion of the dilemma can be resumed in the next class if desired by the participants.

The third decision that needs to be made involves how many classes to hold. In ideal situations, dilemma discussion groups are incorporated into the ongoing activities at school, residential treatment setting, and other contexts, with sessions taking place on a continuing, open-ended basis. Yet there also exists examples of successful, that is, stage increasing use of moral education on a considerably shorter term basis—such as our own employment of it as a constituent component of Aggression Replacement Training (Goldstein et al., 1986).

Step 3: Creating the Proper Set

Once group leaders have formed their group (step 1) and have selected and prepared appropriate dilemmas (step 2), step 3, creating the proper set, marks the beginning of the actual class and is the first task the educator undertakes in the initial meeting. It is a crucial step because it establishes the foundation for the structure of the group meetings. There are four general goals that need to be accomplished during this phase of the initial session. To create proper expectations, the educator must:

Goal 1: Explain the rationale and purpose of dilemma discussion groups and some of the theory on which the class is based. The following ideas should be included in this presentation: (a) The group will meet to discuss situations when people have conflicting claims; (b) The goal of the discussion groups is to enhance everyone's ability to think or reason about these conflictual situations; (c) Although everyone may think they know how to resolve these situations, almost everybody can develop further by experimenting with different ways of thinking about conflictual situations; (d) That as people mature, they develop different ways of thinking about these situations; and (e) That discussion of conflictual situations seems to increase a person's ability to think about and solve them when they really happen.

When discussing the purpose and rationale of the group meetings, be sure to adjust the level of the presentation to the intellectual abilities of the participants, and to at least briefly include all the major ideas about the rationale underlying dilemma discussion groups. In addition, when introducing the class to youngsters, the word "moral" should be dropped as it can sometimes elicit confusion and defensiveness (this is why the class is referred to as dilemma discussion groups rather than moral education).

Goal 2: Discuss the participant's role in the group and group procedures by explaining the format of the meetings. The following ideas should be included in this presentation: (a) Conflictual situations or dilemmas will be presented by the leader to all participants; (b) These situations are not like math or similar problems because there is never one correct answer to it; (c) After presenting and reading the situation, all participants will have a chance to share their opinions and solutions; (d) Different viewpoints will then be discussed; group members will be expected to do most of the talking, which may be hard initially, but will likely become easier with time. The discussions will be something like a debate. To help everyone be actively involved we will be sitting in a circle each time we meet.

Goal 3: Explain the educator's role in the group by discussing the following points: (a) There will be no evaluations of whether your answers are right or wrong because there are no right/wrong answers; (b) The educator's role is not to present the right solution to the situation because there is none and because this is a time to use and develop ways to think and reason about these problems; (c) Although most of the talking will be done by participants, explain that the educator's role is to help everyone focus on a few ideas at a time and to help the group talk about the ideas, which are brought up in an orderly manner; (d) Although the educator will not express personal ideas and solutions, at times the educator will play "devil's advocate" when important ideas have been missed; (e) The educator will make sure that all participants have a chance to share their opinions, if desired, and that respect for each other is always maintained; and (f) The educator will help participants share their ideas clearly.

Goal 4: Explain ethical rules for group behavior and involvement by discussing the following: (a) It is important that everyone feel safe to openly share their ideas, and in order to do this all group members must respect the other person's ideas; to respect another person's opinion does not mean that you have to agree with them. It is fine to disagree because that is the best way to learn from each other. It is *not* okay to disagree by talking about unrelated issues, by not allowing someone to express an opinion even if it is different from your own, or by using personal insults. It is okay to disagree by staying on the subject, by giving everyone an equal chance to answer and by listening to what others have to say; (b) Respect participant's freedom of belief—no one should feel they have to agree with any of the positions argued by anyone else, including the educator; there are no punishments for disagreements, we simply want everyone to listen to each other and keep an open mind; (c) Respect participants' freedom of choice to share their solution to a dilemma; and (d) Respect the confidentiality of all responses made during the class (unless doing so is in some way dangerous to the individual or to others).

An example of an introduction to a dilemma discussion group is as follows: "I imagine you're wondering what this class is all about. In this class, we'll be talking about ways to resolve conflict situations, which are situations where there is more than one way to think and act. Together, we will be discussing and thinking about how you choose which way is fairer. We're really going to be focusing on how come you came up with the solution to a problem, not just what your solution is. In other words, we'll be talking about the reasons you have for coming up with a solution. I know that everybody probably thinks they know how to solve conflicts, but almost everybody can benefit by thinking about and experimenting with different ways to handle these situations. We feel that if you experiment with different ways to think about these situations now, you'll be better prepared to handle them in the future. You know, that as people get older, they naturally develop different ways of thinking about these situations. These classes often speed up this natural process by helping people develop new and better

ways to think about such situations. *Better* here does not mean *right* or
wrong. There are no right or wrong answers to these situations. However, there are better or worse solutions in the sense of helping you
learn how to get along better with people. For example, you can learn
how to make better decisions so you won't be hassled as much by
teachers, parents and peers. Also, if you respond to people differently,
they are likely to act differently to you. So the goal of the group is to
increase everyone's ability to think about conflict situations so you
might be able to avoid hassles in the future.

We're going to start these classes by having somebody, either one of
us or a group member, read a conflict situation out loud. Remember,
these situations aren't like math problems because there's never just
one correct answer to it. After reading the situation, everyone here will
have a chance to share their opinions and solutions. In fact, that's going
to be your major job in the group. That is, your job will be to discuss
with each other your differences of opinion. In other words, unlike lots
of other classes you've been in, you're expected to do most of the talking. The discussions will be something like a debate and to help everyone be involved we'll be sitting in a circle. This may be hard at first, but
with time I hope it will become easier.

While your job is to do most of the talking in here, our job will be to
help everyone focus on a few ideas at a time, to help the group talk in an
orderly way about the ideas you bring up, to help everyone share their
ideas in an understandable way, and to help make sure that everyone
who wants to will have a chance to share their ideas. Sometimes we
might take on a devil's advocate position when we think an important
idea has been missed. By 'devil's advocate,' I mean that we might take a
different position than the group to add to the discussion. However, we
won't be giving you the right solution to the situation for two reasons.
One, because there isn't one, and two, because this is a time for you to
be developing and experimenting with your own ways to think about
these problems. For the same reasons, we won't be sharing our personal
opinions about how to think about the problem. Remember, you're not
getting a grade in here, so we're not going to be judging your answers.

A couple of other points—while we want this to be a place that's
open, flexible and safe for everyone to share their ideas, there will be
some rules that we're going to follow very strictly. One rule is that all
group members will be expected to respect the other person's ideas, and
our job is to make sure that respect is maintained. This doesn't mean
that you can't disagree with each other. In fact, it's fine to disagree
because that's the best way to learn from each other. But it's not O.K. to
disagree by insulting others, by changing the subject, or by not letting
someone express an opinion just because it's different from your own.

It's O.K. to disagree by giving everyone a fair chance to answer, arguing in a fair way, staying on the subject and listening to each other. In other words, we don't want anyone to feel they have to agree with anyone else in the group, including us, just keep an open mind. There are no punishments for disagreements. I also want to mention that we expect all group members to respect each other's privacy. This means that if personal things are discussed in here, it shouldn't be discussed with others unless that person wants you to. Respecting each other's privacy doesn't mean that you can't continue to discuss the conflict problem outside the group. In fact, feel free to do this, it can often be helpful.

Does anyone have any questions about what I just said? (answer any questions) O.K., then let's get started; that's the best way to understand all this."

Step 4: Initiating Discussion

In the first group meeting, the educator initially spends some time creating a proper set (step 3 is not repeated in subsequent sessions unless necessary). This should not take longer than 10–15 minutes. Immediately following this, the educator initiates a discussion of a dilemma. The overall goal when initiating discussion involves setting up a debate between group members who have expressed the lowest reasoning stage on a dilemma and the disagreeing participants who reason one stage above the lowest stage. A discussion begins when the educator reads a dilemma to the group (if desired, one of the participants can be selected to read the dilemma). It is often helpful to provide written copies of the dilemma for participants to follow while someone reads it aloud. The educator should then make sure the dilemma is fully understood by (a) either summarizing it or asking group members to summarize the main points (these points and the characters and their roles can even be written on the board), (b) encouraging questions and (c) clarifying misperceptions about the dilemma. Following this summarizing process, the educator should provide a few minutes for participants to think about the dilemma and formulate a solution to the dilemma problem (e.g., "In a minute, everyone will have a chance to give their opinion to the problem, but let us take a few minutes to quietly think about it first"). If desired, the educator can have participants write down their responses. It is important to reiterate that in these dilemmas, a moral problem is presented in which the youngster must decide between two behavioral choices (e.g., stealing vs. not stealing). The youngster should also be thinking about why (the reasons underlying his/her decision) he/she has chosen that behavioral alternative. Following this thinking period, the educator goes around the circle (it is often helpful to start with a verbal youngster or one who appears to want to speak), having each participant express an opinion about the dilemma and reasons for choosing a particular solution (the different values presented by participants can be written on the board to aid retention and focus discussion). Inform participants that they can pass if they want to, and that they can express their opinions after the initial "go-around" if they wish. The educator will need to recall these initial statements for the subsequent discussion. For this reason, it is often helpful to take short summary notes of the initial opinions of participants. This is easily accomplished by rephrasing out loud the participant's response and, if the paraphrase is accurate, recording the major idea of the response. If possible, also record, but *do not* say aloud, the stage of the response. If the major meaning of the statement is not accurately rephrased, the educator should continue to ask probe questions. Probe questions are designed to get at the reasoning underlying the solution (e.g., "Why do you think that is the fairest solution?"). The educator should ask probe questions until he/she either understands the meaning of the response and, if possible, the stage of the response, or until the participant begins to perceive the questioning as threatening.

After getting everyone's initial opinion on the dilemma, the educator should first structure a debate between youngsters reasoning at the two lowest stages who have different positions (e.g., steal Stage 1s vs. not steal Stage 2s). Participants reasoning at other stages would not initially be included in the discussion. They would, however, be asked to listen to the debate. When initiating the discussion, the educator simply brings the attention of the group to the differing viewpoints (both solution and reasoning) by concisely restating the positions and by asking participants at the lowest stage to debate their differences with the +1 stage reasoners. The educator can choose any of the participants to begin the discussion (it is helpful to pick someone who has presented a clear and complete argument) by asking him to repeat or elaborate on his/her response. Subsequently, a +1 stage reasoner with a different solution is asked to respond. For example, the educator may initiate a discussion to the Heinz dilemma (see p. 130) by saying:

> I've heard several different viewpoints about this situation. We'll start with two of these positions. Dave, Lee and Steve don't think Heinz should steal the drug because he'll end up in jail (stage 1 response). On the other hand, Tom, Joe and Fred think Heinz should steal the drug because he needs his wife around to take care of the children (stage 2 response). Dave, how about sharing your opinion again and then, Tom, you explain to Dave and the others why you disagree with them. The rest of you can feel free to jump in and support Dave or Tom or add any other ideas.

In summary, initiating a discussion involves getting initial opinions, determining that the opinions differ across solution and stage for a subset of the group, and setting the stage for a discussion between lowest and +1 stage reasoners who hold opposite opinions. It is also important to note that the process for initiating a discussion (i.e., read and summarize the dilemma, go around the circle to get initial opinions, set up the initial discussion) is repeated every time a new dilemma is introduced into the group. Indeed, following the initial session, it is how the educator will begin every other session unless a dilemma from the prior session is being carried over into the subsequent one.

Step 5: Guiding Discussion

After an initial discussion between the lowest and +1 stage reasoners has been structured, the educator is now ready to move on to step 5, which is guiding the discussion. The educator is involved with guiding not only the initial discussion, but all subsequent debates. To effectively guide a dilemma discussion, the educator must be able to get as many youngsters as possible to experience +1 stage conflict (SC). The experience of +1 SC is achieved by (a) exposing youngsters to +1 stage reasoning, and (b) exposing participants to additional factors that promote disequilibrium. The major factor needed to elicit disequilibrium involves helping lower stage reasoners realize that their reasoning does not completely help to resolve the dilemma. It is this awareness of inadequacy that creates disequilibrium, which in combination with +1 stage reasoning, stimulates moral development. Therefore, the overall goal when guiding the initial discussion and all subsequent discussions is to have the lower stage reasoners realize the inadequacies and limitations of their reasoning. There are at least three ways that the awareness of inadequate reasoning or disequilibrium can emerge:

1. When lower stage reasoners come to realize that +1 stage reasoners are able to resolve specific aspects of the dilemma that they themselves were unable to resolve and which, therefore, initially appeared to be unresolvable;
2. When the +1 stage reasoner directly points out the limitations, flaws or contradictions of the lower stage reasoner's rationale or when the +1 stage reasoner asks questions that the lower stage reasoner cannot answer;
3. General exposure to +1 stage reasoning, even without discussion, can create disequilibrium.

Ideally, at least one of these three circumstances will emerge over the course of the +1 SC discussion without the assistance of the educator (i.e., the creation of disequilibrium and the corresponding awareness of inadequacy will result from the direct discussion between lower and +1 stage reasoners). However, even under the best of circumstances, the +1 stage reasoners will be able to accomplish this without the educator's assistance for only a portion of the time. In situations where +1 stage reasoners can point out the inadequacy of the lower stage reasoner's rationale, all the educator needs to do is encourage participants to listen to the reasoning underlying decisions and make sure participants are behaving respectfully. However, when the +1 reasoners do not state their opinion clearly or convincingly enough, the educator should first try to encourage other +1 reasoners to continue the argument and to clearly present their ideas. If this is unsuccessful, the educator should next try to clarify the +1 argument by rephrasing the position in order to help the +1 reasoners continue the discussion. If this intervention fails, it will be necessary for the educator to play "devil's advocate" by arguing for the prior +1 position or a new +1 position. The following methods can be helpful to the educator when playing the devil's advocate role to create awareness of inadequacy (i.e., disequilibrium):

1. Point out the contradictions or flaws in the lower stage argument by asking questions and/or suggesting hypothetical situations. *Example*: Using the Heinz dilemma, suppose a youngster states that everyone, including Heinz, should look out for him or herself. The educator might ask the youngster what Heinz should do if the youth needed the drug to live and it was in Heinz's best interest not to steal it. More than likely, the youngster will say Heinz should steal the drug to save his life. The educator might then respond to this contradiction and, as such, the flaws in the youngster's argument by saying, "In one situation, you said that Heinz should look out for himself, but then you said if it was your life at stake, Heinz should steal it. It sounds like you said two different things. What do you think?" If the youngster does not see the contradiction, the educator might make a more direct statement— "Are you saying that you would not want Heinz to steal the drug because it is not in his best interest even though you might die without the drug and that is not in your best interest?"

2. Present unresolvable questions to the participant. Which questions you propose, again, depends on the opinion and reasoning stage of the person. *Example*: Using the Heinz dilemma, suppose an argument is presented in which the solution is based on how much Heinz likes his wife or the druggist. The educator could then propose that both the wife and druggist are equally liked and ask, "Now how would you decide which choice to make?"

3. Point out the injustice of the decision from the perspective of

another person in the dilemma (imaginary role playing), or ask participants to imagine that an equal probability exists that they themselves
could be any person in the dilemma and to now try to arrive at a fair
solution. These role playing techniques are effective in creating awareness of inadequacy because by taking another's perspective, the injustice of a solution is somewhat easier to recognize. *Example*: In
imaginary role playing, the educator might say, "Tom, you said that
Heinz should not steal the drug for his wife. Now, pretend you are
Heinz's wife. How would you feel about your husband's refusal to steal
the drug when you will die without it because he does not want to go to
jail?" In ideal role taking, the educator might say, "Everyone pretend
there is an equal chance you might be Heinz, his wife, the druggist or
the judge. Now, try to fairly solve the situation."

4. Add hypothetical information to the dilemma or point out any
overlooked details that might increase awareness of inadequacy.
Example: Suppose a youngster states that Heinz should not steal the
drug because he would be put in jail. The educator might point out that
judges often consider the motive of the person when deciding what
sentence he will give.

5. Clarify how +1 reasoning can solve problems that lower stage reasoners cannot resolve. The clarification used will depend on the solution and reasoning stage of the response. *Example*: Consider once again
the situation of what Heinz should do if he likes his wife and the druggist equally. The educator might explain that while both people are
equally liked, being married involves a special kind of commitment, a
vow, and different responsibilities than someone has toward a friend.
So in Heinz's position, it might be fairer to uphold his vow as a husband because it would be a decision based on both contract and friend-
ship. By doing this, the educator has just demonstrated how stage 3
reasoning can be used to resolve a situation that stage 2 reasoners may
have found to be unresolvable.

6. Present a dilemma that is somewhat similar to the one being discussed, but that differs in such a way that the reasoning used in the first
dilemma would not be adequate for resolving the second dilemma.
Then demonstrate the use of +1 reasoning for the new situation.
Example: Using the Heinz dilemma as the first situation, the educator
might say "Suppose there are two men, Tom and Dick, who work in a
laboratory. It so happens that both of them are very close to discovering
a cure for cancer. In fact, Tom has half the information that is needed to
discover the cure, while Dick has the other half. Tom wants to collaborate with Dick, so that together they can discover the cure. Dick does not
want to collaborate with Tom because he wants all the credit for himself. Now Tom has to decide whether to steal this information from

Dick. In the Heinz dilemma, some of you argued that Heinz should steal because that is what a good person would do (stage 3 reasoner). Does that apply in this situation as well?" This analogous situation will often result in stage 3 reasoners realizing that their solution is inadequate. The educator might then explain that Tom could resolve the dilemma by using rules made by society that involve property rights of all people, including scientists. In this case, the rules involve respecting Dick's right to publish or share his information when he wants to.

It is important to note that the methods for playing devil's advocate are not mutually exclusive and can be used simultaneously if the opportunity arises.

With these methods for creating the awareness of inadequacy in mind, we will now return to the specific procedures to follow when guiding the discussion. Recall that the educator has already gathered initial opinions and evaluated the stage of the responses. The educator has also already initiated a discussion between the lowest stage reasoners who have taken one position on the dilemma and participants at the next stage who have taken an alternative position on the dilemma. If the +1 stage reasoner can help the lower stage reasoners recognize the inadequacy of their solution, the educator simply guides the discussion by keeping group members' attention focused on the issues and making sure respect for each other is maintained. If +1 stage reasoners cannot do this on their own, the educator guides the discussion by using one or several of the methods just described (e.g., point out contradictions, present unresolvable questions, add hypothetical information, point out overlooked details, role play, etc.). This discussion should continue until the lower stage reasoners have realized that their arguments cannot resolve the dilemma and that the +1 stage argument is more adequate, or until all major issues have been discussed and it is obvious that the lower stage reasoners will not change their rationale. The initial discussion usually takes from 10 to 20 minutes. It is important to keep in mind that it is always better to end a discussion somewhat sooner than later if you are unsure of how long to let it continue. This decreases the chance that group members who are not involved in the debate will become bored or that defensiveness or hostility will emerge between the debaters.

Following the initial discussion, the educator initiates a debate between the previous +1 stage reasoners and participants arguing from the next highest stage who make an opposite behavioral solution (e.g., if the initial discussion is between stage 1 reasoners who are against stealing, and stage 2 reasoners who advocate stealing, the next debate will be between stage 2 reasoners who are pro-stealing and stage 3 reasoners who are against stealing). Using the Heinz dilemma, the educator might introduce the second discussion by saying:

> The important differences in opinion between those who think Heinz should not steal the drug because of the negative consequences and those who think Heinz should steal the drug because of needing his wife to help around the house, have just been discussed. Some other ideas were mentioned before that we need to get back to. Joe, Bruce and Barry said that Heinz should not steal the drug, but gave a reason we have not talked about yet. If I remember it right, all three of you said that you have to consider how the druggist would feel having someone steal his property. Did I remember it correctly? Joe, could you explain to the people who feel that Heinz should steal the drug, why you think you have a fairer way of dealing with the problem?

During the second discussion, the educator's task again involves encouraging youngsters to debate their differences, to ensure continued attention on the topic, to ensure respectful treatment of each other and, if necessary, to take on the role of devil's advocate by using any of the aforementioned methods. In this debate, the previous +1 stage reasoners are provided with opportunities to discover the limitations of their reasoning and the greater adequacy of higher stage reasoning. End this debate when lower stage reasoners recognize the inadequacy of their reasoning or when all major issues have been discussed. As before, this is done by reviewing what was argued and initiating a debate between the most recent +1 stage reasoners and those at the next higher stage (e.g., if pro-stealing stage 2 reasoners and con-stealing stage 3 reasoners have just debated, the con-stealing stage 3 reasoners and pro-stealing stage 4 reasoners will debate next.) For example, the educator might say, "If I remember correctly, the three of you said . . . Can you explain to the people who have just argued why you think you have a fairer solution?" Continue using these procedures until participants at the next to the highest stage have debated those at the highest stage. In this way, the educator proceeds, stage by stage, from the lowest to the highest stage argument presented in the group. When the highest stage argument presented by any youngster is reached, the educator then presents a +1 and opposing argument in order to point out to the highest stage reasoners the inadequacy of their argument. If available, the educator should use a previously prepared argument (e.g., if the highest stage argument presented in the group is a pro-stealing stage 4 position, the educator would present a previously prepared stage 5, con-stealing position). These procedures for guiding a discussion are repeated for all sessions.

Step 6: Ending Discussion

In the sixth and final step of moral discussion, the major task required of the educator involves determining when it is appropriate to end the discussion. The discussion of a particular dilemma is stopped when the group's debate has progressed sequentially up the stages, and the educator's +1 stage argument has been discussed. In addition, the discussion is stopped when all participants have had the chance to address all relevant issues regarding the dilemma. Hopefully, all participants have experienced disequilibrium through exposure to +1 stage reasoning and have realized that their current reasoning stage is inadequate. The educator can end the discussion of a particular dilemma by summarizing the major issues addressed in the debates and by relating the discussion to situations the youngsters may have experienced or may experience in the future. Dilemma discussion meetings can be ended by following any one of several procedures. One method involves having youngsters write down the single best argument that was heard during the discussion and then reading it out loud. A second procedure involves having youngsters tell the person sitting next to them something helpful that was said during the discussion. And finally, the educator could ask several participants to say something about what was better during the current week's discussion than the prior week's debate.

To facilitate opportunities for participants to use what they have learned in the dilemma discussion group in real-life settings (i.e., transfer of training), the educator can assign homework. In the area of moral reasoning, homework assignments simply involve handing out a dilemma at the end of one class and asking participants to think about and write down their opinions and rationales in preparation for the next week's class. As part of this assignment, youngsters could be instructed to ask several different people (e.g., parents, teachers, employers, peers) what their position and reasoning is on the dilemma. Participants are asked to use, but not necessarily accept this input, in their own thinking about the dilemma. Some dilemmas are particularly amenable to the use of homework assignments. For example, in a shoplifting dilemma, youngsters could be instructed to go out and ask a store manager how he would feel if he learned a customer witnessed a shoplifting incident but did not report it to him. Since the ultimate goal of dilemma discussion groups is to prepare the youngster for real-life conflict situations, it is strongly recommended that homework assignments be used whenever possible.

Part IV
Generalization Enhancement Techniques

Chapter 10
Transfer and Maintenance

As the many citations to their respective efficacy make explicit, the several interventions focused upon in the preceding chapters—used alone, and especially in selected combinations—are a formidable array of aggression management techniques. Supportive evidence does indeed suggest that anger—arousal diminishes, communication is enhanced, compromises are negotiated, contingencies are more expertly managed, and skills and values become more prosocial. But what of the generalization of such gains to settings and people other than those involved in the original training? And what of the durability or persistence over time of whatever gains do generalize? These are, respectively, questions of transfer and maintenance, the questions that the present chapter addresses. Historically, concern with transfer and maintenance of gain from psychological intervention has passed through three phases: (a) intervention as inoculation, (b) train and hope, and (c) the development and use of transfer and maintenance enhancing procedures.

INTERVENTION AS INOCULATION

Many traditional psychological interventions—reflecting both their core belief in "personality change" as both the target and outcome in effective treatment, and their strong tendency to ignore environmental influences upon behavior—viewed successful intervention as a sort of psychological inoculation. The positive changes purported to have taken place within the individual's personality structure were supposed to arm him or her to deal effectively with problematic events wherever and whenever they occur. That is, transfer and maintenance were viewed as automatically occurring processes, following by definition from the within-therapy changes themselves. As Ford and Urban (1963) note

147

in this regard, with reference to the prevailing psychoanalytic view on this matter:

> If the patient's behavior toward the therapist is modified, the changes are expected to transfer automatically to other situations. The conflicts involved in the neurosis all became directed toward the therapist during the "transference neurosis." They are not situation-specific. They are responses looking for an object to happen to. Thus, if they are changed while they are occurring in relation to the therapist, they will be permanently changed, and can no longer attach themselves to any object in their old form. No special procedures are necessary to facilitate the transfer from the therapist to other situations if the therapist has successfully resolved the transference pattern of behavior. (p. 173)

Such purported automatic maintenance and transfer, diversely explained, also characterizes the therapeutic position of Adler (1924), Horney (1939), Rank (1945), Rogers (1951), and Sullivan (1953). In each instance, the view put forth is that when the given therapy process results in positive intrapsychic changes in the patient, the patient is assumed to be able to "take these changes with him/her" and apply them where and when needed in the real-life environment. For example, in a manner analogous to Freud, Rogers

> assumes that changes in behaviors outside of the therapy interview will follow automatically upon changes in the self-evaluative thoughts and associated emotions during the therapy hour. Changes in the self-evaluative thoughts and their emotional concomitants result in reduced anxiety, improved discrimination among situational events and responses, more accurate symbolization of them, and greater confidence in one's own decisions. These provide the conditions from which more appropriate instrumental and interpersonal responses will naturally grow. (Ford & Urban, 1963, p. 435)

This intervention as inoculation perspective was thus quite widespread among diverse approaches to psychological change through the 1950s. Since transfer and maintenance were held to inexorably occur as a consequence of within-treatment gains themselves, no call emerged for the development of purposeful means for their enhancement.

TRAIN AND HOPE

In the 1960s and 1970s, first intuitively, and then based on a wealth of empirical follow-up evidence, it became increasingly clear that psychological inoculation was far more myth than reality. In fact, we held, much of what constituted traditional psychotherapy was *anti*-transfer and maintenance in its design and impact:

> If we wish to minimize the transfer of psychotherapy learning to extra-

therapy situations, a number of things may be done. First, a single therapist should provide some rather distinctive personal cues, such as appearance, dress, and manner, that would mark him as a rather special person, different from others. Second, an unvarying and powerful stimulus pattern should provide a context for the therapy, thus ensuring that whatever responses may be developed would become very strongly attached to the unique therapy stimuli. For example, the therapist would use one office for every situation. The furniture in the office would be distinctive and it would not vary from session to session. There should be some stimuli which would identify the office as such and mark it off from other places; for example, diplomas on the wall, bookshelves, and filing cabinets. And, not to belabor the point unduly, the therapy would be conducted on the same day of every week, at the same time of day, and for some standard length of time, say 50 minutes.

Although the picture we have just drawn may seem exaggerated, we are convinced that it is substantially justified. It is evident to us that the field of psychotherapy can profit greatly from a more intent look at its practices and possibilities from the standpoint of the concept of transfer of training. (Goldstein, Heller & Sechrest, 1966, p. 226)

Psychotherapy research as a viable enterprise was initiated in the 1950s and became quite substantial in both quantity and scope during the 1960s and 1970s. Much of the outcome research conducted included systematic follow-up probes, seeking to ascertain whether gains evident at the termination of formal intervention had generalized across settings and/or time. Stokes and Baer (1977), describing this phase as one in which transfer and maintenance were hoped for, and noted but not pursued, comment:

Studies that are examples of Train and Hope across time are those in which there was a change from the intervention procedures, either to a less intensive but procedurally different program, or to no program or no specifically defined program. Data or anecdotal observations were reported concerning the maintenance of the original behavior change over the specified time intervening between the termination of the formal program and the postchecks. (p. 351)

The overwhelming result of these many investigations was that much more often than not, transfer and maintenance of intervention gains did not occur. Treatment did not often serve as an inoculation; gains did not persist automatically; transfer and maintenance did not necessarily follow from the initial training and the hoped-for generalization of its effects (Goldstein & Kanfer, 1979; Hayes, Rincover & Solnick, 1980; Karoly & Steffen, 1980; Kaufman, Nussen & McGee, 1977; Kazdin, 1975; Keeley, Shemberg & Carbonell, 1976). Furthermore, as Marlatt and Gordon (1980) demonstrated, relapse was not only a common follow-up outcome (especially with addictive disorders), but—highlighting the potency of the environment in determining whether transfer or maintenance occur—76% of the relapse episodes could be accounted for by environmental demands requiring coping with social pressures, coping with interpersonal conflict, and coping with the negatively emotional states subsequently engendered. If such be the case, then—these several writers chorused—transfer and maintenance must be actively sought. And, in fact, the failure of inoculation thinking, as revealed by the evidence accumulated during the train and hope phase, indeed led to the third, current phase of concern with generalization, the energetic development, evaluation and clinical use of a number of procedures explicitly designed to enhance transfer and maintenance of intervention gains.

THE DEVELOPMENT OF
TRANSFER AND MAINTENANCE
ENHANCERS

The early call by ourselves and others for this developmental effort also made the belief explicit that the technology of transfer and maintenance enhancement that would hopefully result would have its roots in the empirical literature on learning and its transfer in nonclinical contexts:

> A different assumption regarding response maintenance and transfer of therapeutic gains has in recent years begun to emerge in the psychotherapy research literature, especially that devoted to the outcome of behavior modification intervention. This assumption also rests on the belief that maintenance and transfer of therapeutic gain are not common events but, instead of positing that they should occur via an automatic process whose instigation lies within the procedures of the therapy itself, the position taken is that new maintenance-enhancing and transfer-enhancing techniques must be developed and purposefully and systematically incorporated into the ongoing treatment process. Thus, not satisfied that "behaviors usually extinguish when a program is withdrawn (Kazdin, 1975, p. 213)" or that "removal of the contingencies usually result in a decline of performance to or near baseline levels (Kazdin, 1975, p. 215)," a number of therapy practitioners and researchers are actively seeking to identify, evaluate, and incorporate into ongoing treatment a series of procedures explicitly designed to enhance the level of transfer which ensues. As we have stated elsewhere, the starting point in this search for effective gain maintenance and transfer-enhancers is clear: We need specific knowledge of the conditions under which learning or other changes that take place in therapy will be carried over into extra-therapy situations. . . . We cannot assume that a behavior acquired in the therapy situation, however well learned, will carry over into other situations. Unquestionably the phenomena of therapy are orderly and lawful; they follow definite rules. We must, then, understand the rules that

determine what responses will be generalized, or transferred, to other situations and what responses will not. As a first approximation to the rules obtaining in psychotherapy, we suggest the knowledge gained from study of transfer of other habits (Goldstein, Heller, & Sechrest, 1966, p. 244). [Goldstein & Kanfer, 1979, p. 6]

The effort to develop effective and reliable means for maximizing transfer and maintenance, while clearly still ongoing, has been a largely successful one. A variety of useful techniques have been developed, evaluated and incorporated, into clinical practice. These several procedures, which collectively constitute the current technology of transfer and maintenance enhancement, are listed in Table 10.1, and are examined in detail in the remainder of this chapter.

TRANSFER ENHANCING
PROCEDURES

Sequential Modification

Sequential modification refers to the utilization of an intervention in one setting, testing for transfer in a second setting and, if found not to occur, then implementing the same intervention in that second (or third, fourth, etc.) setting. Epps, Thompson and Lane (1985) comment:

> Stokes and Baer (1977) refer to generalization as the occurrence of behavior under different, *nontraining* conditions without implementing the same behavior-change program in these conditions as was used in the original training environment. Technically, then, sequential modification is not really an example of programming for generalization because what was originally a nontreatment setting . . . becomes a treatment setting when the intervention is implemented there. . . . It is a frequently used technique that may help students demonstrate appropriate behavior under a variety of conditions. (p. 100)

We will not dwell at length on this approach to enhancing appropriate behaviors in real-world contexts, since we agree that formally, it is not a transfer-enhancing technique. We merely identify it here because of both its frequency of use and because its behavior-spread goals are identical to those sought by the transfer-enhancing techniques we will now consider.

Provision of General Principles

Transfer of training has been shown to be facilitated by providing the trainee with the general mediating principles that govern satisfactory performance on both the original and transfer tasks. He or she can be

Table 10.1. Transfer and Maintenance Enhancing Procedures

Transfer

1. Sequential modification
2. Provision of general principles (a.k.a. general case programming)
3. Overlearning (a.k.a. maximizing response availability)
4. Stimulus variability (a.k.a. train sufficient exemplars, train loosely)
5. Identical elements (a.k.a. programming common stimuli)
6. Mediated generalization (a.k.a. self-recording, self-reinforcement, self-instruction)

Maintenance

1. Thin reinforcement (increase intermittency, unpredictableness)
2. Delay reinforcement
3. Fade prompts
4. Booster sessions
5. Prepare for real-life nonreinforcement: (a) Teach self-reinforcement; (b) Teach relapse and failure management skills; (c) Use graduated homework assignments
6. Program reinforcement
7. Use natural reinforcers: (a) Observe real-life settings; (b) Identify easily reinforced behaviors; (c) Teach reinforcement recruitment; (d) Teach reinforcement recognition

given the rules, strategies, or organizing principles that lead to successful performance. This general finding, that mediating principles for successful performance can enhance transfer to new tasks and contexts, has been reported in a number of domains of psychological research. These include studies of labeling, rules, advance organizers, learning sets, and deutero-learning. It is a robust finding indeed, with empirical support in both laboratory (Duncan, 1958; Goldbeck, Bernstein, Hellix & Marx, 1957; Hendrickson & Schroeder, 1941; Ulmer, 1939) and clinical settings, the latter including the scripted roles in Kelly's (1955) fixed-role therapy, directives in Haley's (1976) problem-solving therapy, strategies in Phillips' (1956) assertion-structured therapy, principles in MacGregor, Ritchie, Serrano and Schuster's (1964) multiple-impact therapy, problem-solving skills in Steiner, Wyckoff and Marcus' (1975) radical therapy, cognitive maps in Watkin's (1972) transductive learning therapy, and in many of the self-regulatory, mediational interventions which lie at the heart of cognitive behavior therapy (Kanfer & Karoly, 1972; Kendall & Braswell, 1985).

Overlearning

Transfer of training has been shown to be enhanced by procedures that maximize overlearning or response availability. The likelihood that a response will be available is very clearly a function of its prior usage. We repeat and repeat foreign language phrases we are trying to learn, insist that our child spend an hour per day in piano practice, and devote considerable time practicing to make a golf swing smooth and "automatic." These are simply expressions of the response availability notion, that is, the more we have practiced (especially *correct*) responses, the easier it will be to use them in other contexts or at later times. We need not rely solely on every day experience. It has been well-established empirically that, other things being equal, the response that has been emitted most frequently in the past is more likely to be emitted on subsequent occasions. This finding is derived from studies of the frequency of evocation hypothesis (Underwood & Schulz, 1960), the spew hypothesis (Underwood & Schulz, 1960), preliminary response pretraining (Atwater, 1953; Cantor, 1955; Gagne & Foster, 1949) and overlearning (Mandler, 1954; Mandler & Heinemann, 1956). In all of these related research domains, real-life or laboratory-induced prior familiarization with given responses increased the likelihood of their occurrence on later trials. Mandler (1954) summarizes much of this research as it bears upon transfer by noting that "learning to make an old response to a new stimulus showed increasing positive transfer as the degree of original training was increased (p. 412)." Mandler's own studies in this domain, that is, studies of overlearning, are especially relevant to our present theme, because it is not sheer practice of attempts at prosocial effective behaviors that is of most benefit to transfer. It is practice of *successful* attempts.

Overlearning is a procedure whereby learning is extended over more trials than are necessary merely to produce initial changes in the individual's behavior. In all too many instances of near-successful therapy, one or two successes at a given task are taken as evidence to move on to the next task or the next level of the original task. To maximize transfer via overlearning, the foregoing is a therapeutic technique error. Mandler's (1954) subjects were trained on the study task until they were able to perform it without error (either 0, 10, 30, 50, or 100 consecutive times). As noted earlier, transfer varied with the degree of original learning. To maximize transfer through the use of this principle, the guiding rule should not be "practice *makes* perfect" (implying to simply practice until one gets it right, and then move on), but practice *of* perfect (implying numerous overlearning trials of correct responses after the initial success).

Stimulus Variability

In the previous section, we addressed enhancement of transfer by means of practice and repetition, that is, the sheer number of correct responses that the trainee makes to a given stimulus. Transfer is also enhanced by the variability or range of stimuli to which the individual responds. For example, Duncan (1958) has shown that on a paired-associates task, transfer is markedly enhanced by varied training. Training on even only two stimuli is better than training on a single stimulus. Other investigators have obtained similar results in concept attainment tasks, showing more rapid attainment when a variety of examples is presented (Callantine & Warren, 1955; Shore & Sechrest, 1961). As we have noted elsewhere in response to studies such as these: "The implication is clear that in order to maximize positive transfer, training should provide for some sampling of the population of stimuli to which the response must ultimately be given (Goldstein et al., 1966, p. 220)." Kazdin (1975) comments:

> One way to program response maintenance and transfer of training is to develop the target behavior in a variety of situations and in the presence of several individuals. If the response is associated with a range of settings, individuals, and other cues, it is less likely to be lost when the situations change. (p. 211)

Epps et al. (1985) discuss stimulus variability for transfer enhancement purposes under the rubrics "training sufficient examples" and "train loosely". They observe:

> Generalization of new skills or behaviors can also be facilitated by training students under a wide variety of conditions. Manipulating the numbers of trainers, settings, and response classes involved in the intervention promotes generalization by exposing the student to a variety of situations. (p. 26)

Stimulus variability has only a modest history of use in clinical contexts thus far, for example, multiple impact therapy by MacGregor et al. (1964); in the use of multiple therapists by Dreikurs, Schulman, and Mosak (1952), Hayward, Peters, and Taylor (1952), and Whitaker, Malone, and Warkentin (1966); in round-robin therapy (Holmes, 1971); in rotational therapy (Slavin, 1967); and in rotational group therapy (Frank, 1973). In the clinical realm of anger management, Feindler and Ecton (1986) urge the employment of stimulus variability ("varied task training") for transfer enhancement purposes through the use of diverse role-play stimulus situations. In their anger control training, chronically aggressive youngsters respond to such provocation as:

- *Peer conflict* over property, money, relationships, trust, teasing, drugs, sex and pressure to conform. Family conflict over curfew, household responsibilities, money, friends, personal property, other restrictions, personal hygiene and habits.
- *Conflict with authority figures* such as teachers, counselors, probation officers, policemen, bus drivers, lifeguards, salespeople, and so

forth. These conflicts usually revolve around rule violation and punishment.

- *Conflict with unknown peers* such as members of other groups (those
  in class, a gang, a ward, etc.) who the adolescent does not know.
  These conflicts usually involve some sort of provoking act such as
  stealing, teasing, ignoring.

Identical Elements

In perhaps the earliest experimental concern with transfer-enhance-
ment, Thorndike and Woodworth (1901) concluded that when there was
a facilitative effect of one habit on another, it was to the extent that and
because they shared identical elements. Ellis (1965) and Osgood (1953)
have more recently emphasized the importance for transfer of similarity
between characteristics of the training and application tasks. As
Osgood (1953) notes, "the greater the similarity between practice and
test stimuli, the greater the amount of positive transfer (p. 213)." This
conclusion rests on a particularly solid base of experimental support,
involving studies of both motor (Crafts, 1935; Duncan, 1953; Gagne,
Baker & Foster, 1950) and verbal (Osgood, 1949, 1953; Underwood, 1951;
Young & Underwood, 1954) behaviors.

In the contexts of psychotherapy and training, the principle of identical elements could be implemented by procedures that function to
increase the "real-lifeness" of the stimuli (people, behaviors, places,
events, etc.) to which the therapist or trainer is helping the target person learn to respond with effective, satisfying responses. There exist
two broad strategies for attaining such high levels of veridicality
between intherapy and extratherapy stimuli. The first is to move the
therapy out of the typical office setting and into the very interpersonal
and physical context in which the person's real-life difficulties are being
experienced. Such in vivo therapies are in fact a growing reality, as the
locus of at least some treatments shifts to homes, planes, bars, elevators,
and other problem sites (Sherman, 1979; Sherman & Levine, 1979). And,
to be sure, the several marital and family therapies are all examples of
identical elements in the interpersonal sense, as the persons treated and
the persons to whom they must apply their therapeutic learnings are
one and the same.

The second broad approach to maximizing identical elements or, as
Epps et al. (1985) put it, programming common stimuli, is to remain in a
training setting but to enhance its physical and/or interpersonal "real-
lifeness". We regularly follow this strategy in our prosocial skills training with aggressive adults and youth, by creating role play contexts
(with each trainee's help) that appear like and feel like "the real thing"

(Goldstein et al., 1986). Transitional living centers, the systematic use of "barbs" (Epps et al., 1985) or "red flags" (McGinnis & Goldstein, 1984) are other diverse operationalizations of transfer enhancement achieved by maximizing identical elements.

Mediated Generalization

The one certain commonality, by definition present in both training and application settings, is the target trainee himself or herself. Mediated generalization—mediated by the trainee, not others—is an approach to transfer enhancement which relies upon training the trainee in a series of context-bridging, self-regulation competencies (Kanfer & Karoly, 1972; Neilans & Israel, 1981). Operationally, it consists of instructing the trainee in self-recording, self-reinforcement, self-punishment, and self-instruction. Epps et al. (1985) working in a special education setting, have structured these generalization mediating steps as follows:

Self-Recording

1. The teacher sets up the data collection system, that is, selects a target behavior, defines it in measurable terms, and decides on an appropriate recording technique.
2. The teacher tries out the data collection system.
3. The teacher teaches the trainee how to use the data collection system.
4. The trainee is reinforced by the teacher for taking accurate data.

Self-Reinforcement

1. The teacher determines how many points a trainee has earned, and the trainee simply records these.
2. The teacher tells the trainee to decide how many points should be awarded for appropriate behavior.
3. The trainee practices self–reinforcement under teacher supervision.
4. The trainee employs self–reinforcement without teacher supervision.

Self-Punishment

Self-punishment, operationalized in this example by response cost (taking away points) is trained in a fading-of-the-teacher manner directly parallel to that just described for self-reinforcement.

Self-Instruction

1. The teacher models the appropriate behavior while talking himself or herself through the task out loud so that the trainee can hear.
2. The trainee performs the task with overt instructions from the teacher.
3. The trainee performs the task with overt self-instructions.
4. The trainee performs the task with covert self-instructions.

As the cognitive behavior modification therapies have grown in popularity in recent years, especially those relying heavily on self-instructional processes, self-mediated approaches to generalization have correspondingly grown in frequency of use.

MAINTENANCE ENHANCING TECHNIQUES

The persistence, durability or maintenance of behaviors developed by means such as those presented earlier in this book is primarily a matter of the manipulation of reinforcement—both during the original training and in the post-intervention, real-world context. In the remaining sections of this chapter, we will offer the several specific means by which such maintenance-enhancing manipulation of reinforcement may proceed.

Thinning of Reinforcement

A rich, continuous reinforcement schedule is optimal for the establishment of new behaviors. Maintenance of such behaviors will be enhanced if the reinforcement schedule is gradually thinned. Thinning of reinforcement optimally will proceed from a continuous (all trials) schedule, to one or another form of intermittent schedule, to the level of sparse and infrequent reinforcement characteristic of the natural environment. In fact, the maintenance-enhancing goal of such a thinning process is make the trainer-offered reinforcement schedule indiscriminable from that typically offered in real-world contexts.

Delay of Reinforcement

Resistance to extinction is also enhanced by delay of reinforcement. As Epps et al. (1985) note:

> During the early stages of an intervention, reinforcement should be immediate and continuously presented contingent on the desired response. . . . After the behavior becomes firmly established in the

student's repertoire, it is important to introduce a delay in presenting
the reinforcement. Delayed reinforcement is a closer approximation to
reinforcement conditions in the natural environment. . . . (p. 21)

Delay of reinforcement may be implemented, according to Sulzer-
Azaroff and Mayer (1977) by (a) increasing the size or complexity of the
response required before reinforcement is provided, (b) adding a time
delay between the response and the delivery of reinforcement, and (c)
in token systems, increasing the time interval between receiving tokens
and the opportunity to spend them, and/or requiring more tokens in
exchange for a given reinforcer.

Fading of Prompts

Maintenance may be enhanced by the gradual removal of suggestions, reminders, prompts or similar coaching or instruction. Fading of
prompts is a means for moving away from artificial control (the
trainer's) to more natural (self) control of desirable behaviors. As with
all the enhancement techniques examined herein, fading of prompts
should be carefully planned and systematically implemented.

Booster Sessions

The importance of fading of prompts not withstanding, instruction in
the specifics of given appropriate behaviors, and their reinforcement,
may have to be reinstated periodically in order for them to continue in
the natural environment. Booster sessions between trainer and trainee,
either on a pre-planned schedule or as-needed, have often proven quite
valuable in this regard (Feindler & Ecton, 1986; Karoly & Steffan, 1980).

Prepare for Natural Environment
Nonreinforcement

Though both trainer and trainee may energetically take several steps
(see p. 160) to maximize the likelihood that reinforcement for appropriate behaviors will in fact occur in the natural environment, on a number
of occasions, it will not be forthcoming. It is important for maintenance
purposes that the trainee be prepared for this eventuality. Skill in
self-reinforcement, described in our earlier examination of mediated
generalization, is one means of responding in a maintenance-promoting
manner when the desirable behaviors are performed correctly, but are
unrewarded by external sources. When the trainee performs the behaviors incorrectly, or inappropriately in the natural environment, the
trainee will respond optimally to the environment's nonreinforcement if

he or she has earlier learned skills and cognitive interpretations for dealing with relapse and failure experiences. Kendall and Braswell (1985) have proposed means for implementing this suggestion. A third way in which the trainee may be prepared for nonreinforcement in the natural environment, at least in the context of prosocial skills training and similar interventions, is the use of graduated homework assignments. In our approach to prosocial skills training, for example, skills role-played successfully within group sessions are assigned as homework, to be completed before the next session with the real-life father, wife, child, employer, who was portrayed by the role player's co-actor in the role play. However, as homework assignments are discussed, on occasion it becomes clear that the real-life figure is too difficult an application setting target, too harsh, too unresponsive, or simply too unlikely to provide reinforcement for competent skill use. Under this circumstance, with the newly learned skill still fragile, and the potential homework environment looming as nonrewarding, we have recast the homework assignment toward two or three more benevolent and more responsive target figures. When the trainee finally does utilize the skill correctly with the originally skipped-over target figure, and receives no contingent reinforcement, his or her string of previously reinforced trials help minimize the likelihood that the behavior will extinguish.

Program Reinforcement in the Natural Environment

The maintenance-enhancing techniques examined thus far are targeted toward the trainee himself or herself—his or her reinforcement schedule, instruction, booster sessions, and preparation for nonreinforcing consequences. But maintenance of appropriate behaviors may be enhanced by efforts directed toward others, especially those others in the trainee's natural environment who function as the main providers of the trainee's reinforcement. Galassi and Galassi (1984) comment:

> Significant others can be trained to deliver the same or similar contingencies in the natural environment as occurred during treatment. Parents, peers, and teachers can be taught to apply reinforcement for appropriate behavior. . . . Perhaps even better than individuals being taught new behaviors in a treatment setting by professionals and later having significant others trained to insure transfer to the natural environment, is training significant others initially to conduct the entire training process in the natural environment. (p. 12)

Patterson and Brodsky (1966), Nay (1979), Tharp and Wetzel (1969) and Walker, Hops and Johnson (1975) are among the several investigators who have repeatedly demonstrated the efficacy of this now generally employed approach to maintenance enhancement.

Use Natural Reinforcers

A final and especially valuable approach to the enhancement of maintenance is the use of reinforcers that naturally and readily exist in the trainee's real-world environment. Stokes and Baer (1977) observe:

> Perhaps the most dependable of all generalization programming mechanisms is the one that hardly deserves the name: the transfer of behavioral control from the teacher-experimenter to stable, natural contingencies that can be trusted to operate in the environment to which the subject will return, or already occupies. To a considerable extent, this goal is accomplished by choosing behaviors to teach that normally will meet maintaining reinforcement after the teaching. (p. 353)

Galassi and Galassi (1984) similarly comment:

> We need to target those behaviors for changes that are most likely to be seen as acceptable, desirable, and positive by others. Ayllon and Azrin (1968) refer to this as the 'Relevance of Behavior Rule'. 'Teach only those behaviors that will continue to be reinforced after training'. (p. 10)

Alberto and Troutman (1982) suggest a four-step process that facilitates effective use of natural reinforcers: (a) observe which specific behaviors are regularly reinforced, and how they are reinforced, in the major settings that constitute the trainee's natural environment, (b) train the trainee in a selected number of such naturally reinforced behaviors (e.g., certain social skills, grooming behaviors), (c) teach the trainee how to recruit or request reinforcement, for example, by tactfully asking peers or others for approval or recognition, and (d) teach the trainee how to recognize reinforcement when it is offered, for example, its presence in certain gestures or facial expressions may be quite subtle for many trainees.

The call in the 1960s for a technology of transfer and maintenance enhancement has been vigorously and effectively answered. That technology, examined in this chapter, is substantial and still growing. Its full employment in the context of the aggression management interventions examined in this book is most strongly recommended.

Chapter 11
Summary

Aggressive encounters between husbands and wives, parents and children, people who know each other, and people who do not, fill our mass media and our lives daily. The need to identify persons, events and environments in which such behavior has a high probability of occurrence, as well as effective means for reducing the frequency and intensity of such behavior remains great. We have sought in this book to present in concrete detail the state-of-the-art technology for the assessment and modification of aggressive behavior. Means for its prediction and identification, as well as a sequence of empirically supported interventions for its reduction, the training of alternative prosocial behaviors and values, and procedures for maximizing the likelihood that such gains will both transfer and maintain have each been presented and examined.

Our clinical recommendation is a prescriptive one, urging upon the practitioner confronted with aggressive persons a treatment strategy which most fully tries to tie diagnosis to intervention, assessment to modification procedures employed. It is our hope that the array of effective assessment and modification techniques examined in chapters 2–9 will maximize the opportunity to implement such a prescriptive strategy.

As is optimally true for all other types of target behaviors, the number and quality of interventions aimed at reducing aggression and promoting its alternatives is never complete. We have constructed and recommended a sequence of interventions which rests on at least adequate empirical support, and which are parallel in their targets for change to the aggressive behavior sequence. But many other interventions— some of long standing, some quite new—also exist as potentially valuable means of intervening in aggressive behavior. These include assertiveness training (Fehrenbach & Thelen, 1981; Rimm, Hill, Brown & Stuart, 1974), participant modeling (Goodwin & Mahoney, 1975), participant monitoring (Price & Haynes, 1980), problem-solving training (Grant, 1986; Kennedy, 1982), empathy training (Goldstein & Michaels, 1985), the use of humor (Baron & Ball, 1974; Smith, 1973), basic education programs (Roundtree & Faily, 1980), contingent exercise (Luce, Delquadri & Hall, 1980), and organized games (Murphy, Hutchison & Bailey, 1983). Clearly, while the problem of aggression and its impact in modern society is most serious, the existing and potential technology for its modification is most promising.

References

Abramovitch, R., Konstantareas, M. & Homan, L. (1980). An observational assessment of change in two groups of behaviourally disturbed boys. *Journal of Child Psychology and Psychiatry, 21,* 133–141.

Achenbach, T. M., & Edelbrock, C. (1983). *Manual for the Child Behavior Checklist and Revised Child Behavior Profile.* Burlington, VT: University of Vermont Department of Psychiatry.

Adams, G. R. (1973). Classroom aggression: Determinants, controlling mechanisms, and guidelines for the implementation of a behavior modification program. *Psychology in the Schools, 10,* 155–168.

Adkins, W. R. (1970). Life skills: Structured counseling for the disadvantaged. *Personnel and Guidance Journal, 49,* 108–116.

Adler, A. (1924). *The practice and theory of individual psychology.* New York: Harcourt Brace.

Agras, W. S. (1967). Behavior therapy in the management of chronic schizophrenia. *American Journal of Psychiatry, 124,* 240–243.

Alberto, P. A., & Troutman, A. C. (1982). *Applied behavior analysis for teachers: Influencing student performance.* Columbus, OH: Charles E. Merrill.

Allen, K. E., Hart, B., Buell, J. S., Harris, F. R., & Wolf, M. (1964). Effects of social reinforcement on isolated behaviors of a nursery school child. *Child Development, 35,* 511–518.

Allen, K. E., Henke, L. B., Harris, F. R., Baer, D. M., & Reynolds, N. J. (1967). Control of hyperactivity by social reinforcement of attending behavior. *Journal of Educational Psychology, 58,* 231–237.

Allison, T. S., & Allison, S. L. (1971). Time out from reinforcement: Effect on sibling aggression. *Psychological Record, 21,* 81–85.

Allport, F. H. (1924). *Social psychology.* Boston: Houghton Mifflin.

Allred, G. (1977). *Husband and wife communication training: An experimental study.* Unpublished doctoral dissertation, Florida State University.

Apter, S. J. (1982). *Troubled children—troubled systems.* New York: Pergamon Press.

Apter, S. J., & Propper, C. A. (1986). Ecological perspectives on youth violence. In S. J. Apter and A. P. Goldstein (Eds.), *Youth violence: Programs & prospects.* New York: Pergamon.

Arbuthnot, J., & Faust, A. (1981). *Teaching moral reasoning: Theory and practice.* New York: Harper & Row.

Arbuthnot, J., & Gordon, D. A. (1983). Moral reasoning development in correctional intervention. *Journal of Correctional Education, 34,* 133–138.

Argyle, M., Trower, P., & Bryant, B. (1974). Explorations in the treatment of personality disorders and neuroses by social skill training. *British Journal of Medical Psychology, 47,* 63–72.

Atrops, M. (1978). *Behavioral plus cognitive skills for coping with provocation in male offenders.* Unpublished doctoral dissertation, Fuller Theological Seminary.

Atwater, S. K. (1953). Proactive inhibition and associative facilitation as affected by degree of prior learning. *Journal of Experimental Psychology, 46,* 400–404.

Axelrod, S. & Apache, J. (Eds.) (1982). *The effects of punishment on human behavior.* New York: Academic Press.

Ayllon, T., & Azrin, N. H. (1968). *The token economy: A motivational system for therapy and rehabilitation.* New York: Appleton-Century-Crofts.

Ayllon, T., & Michael, J. (1959). The psychiatric nurse as a behavioral engineer. *Journal of the Experimental Analysis of Behavior, 2,* 323–334.

Azrin, N. H., & Holz, W. C. (1966). Punishment. In W. K. Honig (Ed.), *Operant behavior: Areas of research and application.* New York: Appleton-Century-Crofts.

Azrin, N. H., Naster, B. J., & Jones, R. (1973). Reciprocity counseling: A rapid learning-based procedure for marital counseling. *Behavior Research and Therapy, 11,* 365–382.

Bachrach, A. J., Erwin, W. J., & Mohr, J. P. (1965). The control of eating behavior in an anorexic by operant conditioning techniques. In L. P. Ullmann and L. Krasner (Eds.), *Case studies in behavior modification.* New York: Holt, Rinehart & Winston.

Bailey, S. L. (1983). Extraneous aversives. In S. Axelrod and J. Apache (Eds.), *The effects of punishment on human behavior,* 247–284. New York: Academic Press.

Bandura, A. (1973). *Aggression: A social learning analysis.* Englewood Cliffs, NJ: Prentice-Hall.

Bandura, A. (1977). *Social learning theory.* Englewood Cliffs, NJ: Prentice-Hall.

Bandura, A., Ross, D., & Ross, S. A. (1963). Imitation of film—mediated aggressive models. *Journal of Abnormal and Social Psychology, 66,* 3–11.

Barlow, D. H., Hayes, S. C., & Nelson, R. (1984). *The scientist practitioner: Research and accountability in clinical and educational settings.* New York: Pergamon Press.

Barnes, H. J., & Olson, D. H. (1982). Parent-adolescent communication scale. In D. H. Olson, *Family inventories: Inventories used in a national survey of families across the family life cycle.* St. Paul: Family Social Science, University of Minnesota.

Baron, R. A. (1977). *Human aggression.* New York: Plenum Press.

Baron, R. A., & Ball, R. L. (1974). The aggression-inhibiting influence of nonhostile humor. *Journal of Experimental Social Psychology, 10,* 23–33.

Beck, C. (1971). *Moral education in the schools: Some practical suggestions.* Toronto: Ontario Institute for Studies in Education.

Beck, C., Hersh, R., & Sullivan, E. (1976). *The moral education project (year 4): Annual report, 1975–1976.* Toronto: Ontario Institute for Studies in Education.

Beck, C., & Sullivan, E. (1976). *The reflective approach in values education: The moral education project, year 3.* Toronto: Ontario Institute for Studies in Education.

Becker, W. C., Madsen, C. H., Arnold, C. R., & Thomas, D. R. (1967). The contingent use of teacher attention and praise in reducing classroom behavior problems. *The Journal of Special Education, 1,* 287–307.

Bem, S. L. (1967). Verbal self control: The establishment of effective self-instruction. *Journal of Experimental Psychology, 74,* 485–491.

Bender, N. N. (1976). Self-verbalization versus tutor verbalization in modifying impulsivity. *Journal of Educational Psychology, 68,* 347–354.

Berkowitz, L. (1962). *Aggression: A social psychological analysis.* New York: McGraw-Hill.

Berkowitz, L. (1974). Some determinants of impulsive aggression: Role of mediated associations with reinforcement for aggression. *Psychological Review, 81,* 165–176.

Biaggio, M. K. (1980). Assessment of anger arousal. *Journal of Personality Assessment, 44,* 289–298.

Biaggio, M. K., Supplee, K., & Curtis, N. (1981). Reliability and validity of four anger scales. *Journal of Personality Assessment, 45,* 639–648.

Boike, M. F., Gesten, E. L., Cowen, E. L., Felner, R. D., & Francis, R. (1978). Relationships between family background problems and school problems and competencies of young children. *Psychology in the Schools, 15,* 283–290.

Borkovec, T. D., Grayson, J. B., & Cooper, K. M. (1978). Treatment of general tension: Subjective and physiological effects of progressive relaxation. *Journal of Consulting and Clinical Psychology, 46,* 518–528.

Borkovec, T. D., Grayson, J. B., O'Brien, G. T. & Weerts, T. C. (1979). Relaxation treatment of pseudoinsomnia and idiopathic insomnia: An electroencephaloraphic evaluation. *Journal of Applied Behavior Analysis, 12,* 37–54.

Bornstein, M., Bellack, A. S., & Hersen, M. (1980). Social skills training for highly aggressive children. *Behavior Modification, 4,* 173–186.

Bornstein, P. H., Anton, B., Harowski, K. H., Weltzein, R. T., McIntyre, T. J., & Hocker-Wilmot, J. (1981). Behavioral-communications treatment of marital discord: Positive behaviors. *Behavioral Counseling Quarterly, 1,* 189–199.

Bornstein, P. H., Hamilton, S. B., & McFall, M. E. (1981). Modification of adult aggression: A critical review of theory, research, and practice. In M. Hersen, R. M. Eisler, and P. M. Miller (Eds.), *Progress in behavior modification* (vol. 12). New York: Academic Press.

Bornstein, P. H., & Quevillon, R. P. (1976). The effects of a self-instructional package on overactive preschool boys. *Journal of Applied Behavior Analysis, 9,* 179–188.

Bornstein, P. H., Rychtarik, R. G., McFall, M. E., Bridgewater, C. A., Guthrie, L., & Anton, B. (1980). Behaviorally-specific report cards and self-determined reinforcements. *Behavior Modification, 4,* 71–81.

Bosco, A. (1973). *Marriage encounter: Rediscovery of love.* St. Meinrad, IN: Abbey Press.

Bostow, D. E., & Bailey, J. B. (1969). Modification of severe disruptive and aggressive behavior using brief time-out and reinforcement procedures. *Journal of Applied Behavior Analysis, 2,* 31–37.

Brantner, J. P. & Doherty, M. A. (1983) A review of timeout: A conceptual and methodoligical analysis. In S. Apelrod & J. Apache (Eds.). The effect of punishment on human behavior. New York: Academic Press.

Braswell, L., Kendall, P. C., & Urbain, E. S. (1982). A multistudy analysis of the role of socioeconomic status (SES) in cognitive behavioral treatments with children. *Journal of Abnormal Child Psychology, 10,* 443–449.

Bright, P. D., & Robin, A. L. (1981). Ameliorating parent-adolescent conflict with problem-solving communication training. *Journal of Behavior Therapy & Experimental Psychiatry, 12,* 275–280.

Brock, G. W. (1978). *Unilateral marital intervention. Training spouses to train their partners in communication skills.* Unpublished doctoral dissertation, Pennsylvania State University.

Brown, P., & Elliott, R. (1965). Control of aggression in a nursery school class. *Journal of Experimental Child Psychology, 2,* 103–107.

Burba, J., Hubbell, R., Preble, M., Spinelli, R. & Winter, N. (1972). *Communication skills workshop manual.* Fort Collins, Colorado: University of Colorado Counselling Center.

Burgess, R. L. (1979). Child abuse: A social interactional analysis. In B. B. Fahey & A. E. Kazden (Eds.), *Advances in child clinical psychology.* (Vol. 2). New York: Plenum.

Burchard, J. D., & Barrera, F. (1972). An analysis of timeout and response cost in a programmed environment. *Journal of Applied Behavior Analysis, 5,* 271–282.

Buss, A. H. (1961). *The psychology of aggression.* New York: Wiley.

Buss, A. H., & Durkee, A. (1957). An inventory for assessing different kinds of hostility. *Journal of Consulting Psychology, 21,* 343–349.

Buys, C. J. (1972). Effects of teacher reinforcement on elementary pupils' behavior and attitudes. *Psychology in the Schools, 9*, 278–288.

Calhoun, K. S., & Matherne, P. (1975). The effects of varying schedules of timeout on aggressive behavior of a retarded girl. *Journal of Behavior Therapy & Experimental Psychiatry, 6*, 139–143.

Callantine, M. F., & Warren, J. M. (1955). Learning sets in human concept formation. *Psychological Reports, 1*, 363–367.

Camp, B. W. (1977). Verbal mediation in young aggressive boys. *Journal of Abnormal Psychology, 86*, 145–153.

Camp, B. W., Blom, G., Herbert, F. & VanDoormick, W. (1977). "Think aloud": A program for developing self-control in young aggressive boys. *Journal of Abnormal Child Psychology, 5*, 157–169.

Cantor, J. H. (1955). Amount of pretraining as a factor in stimulus pre-differentiation and performance set. *Journal of Experimental Psychology, 50*, 188–184.

Carkhuff, R. R. (1971). Training as a preferred mode of treatment. *Journal of Consulting Psychology, 18*, 121–131.

Carr, E. G. (1981). Contingency management. In A. P. Goldstein, E. G. Carr, W. Davidson, and P. Wehr. *In response to aggression.* New York: Pergamon Press.

Carr, E. G., & Lovaas, O. I. (1983). Contingent electric shock as a treatment for severe behavior problems. In S. Axelrod and J. Apache (Eds.), *The effects of punishment on human behavior,* New York: Academic Press.

Carroll, J. L., & Rest, J. R. (1981). Development in moral judgment as indicated by rejection of lower-stage statements. *Journal of Research in Personality, 15*, 538–544.

Christopherson, E. R., Arnold, C. M., Hill, D. W., & Quilitch, H. R. (1972). The home point system: Token reinforcement procedures for application by parents of children with behavior problems. *Journal of Applied Behavior Analysis, 5*, 485–497.

Coats, K. I. (1979). Cognitive self-instructional training approach for reducing disruptive behavior of young children. *Psychological Reports, 44*, 127–134.

Colby, A., & Speicher-Dubin, B. (1973). *Dilemmas for applied use.* Unpublished manuscript, Harvard University, Cambridge, MA.

Collingwood, T. R., & Genthner, R. W. (1980). Skills training as treatment for juvenile delinquents. *Professional Psychology, 11*, 591–598.

Cone, J. D. (1978). The behavioral assessment grid (BAG): A conceptual framework and a taxonomy. *Behavior therapy, 9*, 882–888.

Conger, J. J., Miller, W. C., & Walsmith, C. R. (1975). Antecedents of delinquency: Personality, social class, and intelligence. In P. H. Mussen, J. J. Conger, and J. Kagen (Eds.) *Readings in child development and personality.* New York: Harper & Row.

Connor, W. H. (1974). Effects of brief relaxation training on automatic response and electromyogram biofeedback treatments for muscle contraction headaches. *Psychophysiology, 11*, 591–599.

Cook, W., & Medley, D. (1954). Proposed hostility and pharasic-virtue scales for the MMPI. *Journal of Applied Psychology, 38*, 414–418.

Copeland, A. P. (1981). The relevance of subject variables in cognitive self-instructional programs for impulsive children. *Behavior Therapy, 12*, 520–529.

Copeland, A. P. (1982). Individual differences factors in children's self-management: Toward individualized treatments. In P. Karoly and F. H. Kanfer (Eds.), *Self-management and behavior change: From theory to practice.* New York: Pergamon Press.

Crafts, L. W. (1935). Transfer as related to number of common elements. *Journal of General Psychology, 13*, 147–158.

Crain, D. (1977). *Awareness and the modification of anger problems.* Unpublished doctoral dissertation, University of California at Los Angeles.

Curran, J. P. (1977). Skills training as an approach to the treatment of heterosexual-social anxiety: A review. *Psychological Bulletin, 84*, 140–157.

Delprato, D. J., & Dekraker, T. (1976). Metronome-conditioned hypnotic-relaxation in the treatment of test anxiety. *Behavior Therapy, 7*, 379–381.

Deluty, R. H. (1979). Children's Action Tendency Scale: A self-report measure of aggressiveness, assertiveness, and submissiveness in children. *Journal of Consulting and Clinical Psychology, 47*, 1061–1071.

Deluty, R. H. (1981). Alternative thinking ability of aggressive, assertive, and submissive children. *Cognitive Therapy and Research, 5*, 309–312.

Deluty, R. H. (1983). Children's evaluations of aggressive, assertive, and submissive responses. *Journal of Clinical Child Psychology, 12*, 124–129.

Deluty, R. H. (1984). Behavioral validation of the Children's Action Tendency Scale. *Journal of Behavioral Assessment, 6*, 115–130.

Dickie, J. (1973). *Private speech: The effect of presence of others, task and interpersonal variables*. Unpublished doctoral dissertation, Michigan State University.

Diener, E., Dinnen, J., & Endressen, K. (1975). Effects of altered responsibility, cognitive set, and modeling on physical aggression and deindividuation. *Journal of Personality and Social Psychology, 31*, 328–337.

Dishion, T. J., Loeber, R., Stouthamer-Loeber, M., & Patterson, G. R. (1984). Skill deficits and male adolescent delinquency. *Journal of Abnormal Child Psychology, 12*, 37–54.

Dodge, K. A., McClaskey, C. L., & Feldman, E. (1985). Situational approach to the assessment of social competence in children. *Journal of Consulting and Clinical Psychology, 53*, 344–353.

Dodge, K. A., & Murphy, R. R. (1984). The assessment of social competence in adolescents. In P. Karoly & J. J. Steffan (Eds.), *Adolescent behavior disorders: Foundations and contemporary concerns*. Lexington, MA: Lexington Books.

Dollard, J., Doob, L. W., Miller, N. E., Mowrer, O. H., & Sears, R. R. (1939). *Frustration and aggression*. New Haven, CT: Yale University.

Douglas, V. I., Parry, P., Marton, P., & Garson, C. (1976). Assessment of a cognitive training program for hyperactive children. *Journal of Abnormal Child Psychology, 4*, 389–410.

Drabman, R. S., Hammer, D., & Rosenbaum, M. S. (1979). Assessing generalization in behavior modification with children: The generalization map. *Behavioral Assessment, 1*, 203–219.

Drabman, R., & Spitalnik, R. (1973). Social isolation as a punishment procedure: A controlled study. *Journal of Experimental Child Psychology, 16*, 236–249.

Driekurs, R., Schulman, B. H., & Mosak, H. (1952). Patient-therapist in multiple psychotherapy: Its advantages to the therapist. *Psychiatric Quarterly, 26*, 219–227.

Duncan, C. P. (1953). Transfer in motor learning as a function of degree of first-task learning and inter-task similarity. *Journal of Experimental Psychology, 45*, 1–11.

Duncan, C. P. (1958). Recent research on human problem solving. *Psychological Bulletin, 56*, 397–429.

Edelman, E. M., & Goldstein, A. P. (1981). Moral education. In A. P. Goldstein, E. G. Carr, W. S. Davidson & P. Wehr (Eds.), *In response to aggression*. New York: Pergamon Press.

Edmunds, G., & Kendrick, D. C. (1980). *The measurement of human aggressiveness*. Chicester: Ellis Horwood.

Eisler, R. M., & Hersen, M. (1973). Behavior techniques in family-oriented crisis intervention. *Archives of General Psychiatry, 28*, 111–116.

Elardo, P., & Cooper, M. (1977). *AWARE: Activities for social development*. Reading, MA.: Addison-Wesley.

Elitzur, B. (1976). Self-relaxation program for acting-out adolescents. *Adolescence, 44*, 569–572.

Ellis, H. (1965). *The transfer of learning*. New York: Macmillan.

Ely, A. L., & Guerney, B. C. (1973). Efficacy of the training phase of conjugal therapy. *Psychotherapy: Theory, Research & Practice, 10*, 201–207.

Epps, S., Thompson, B. J., & Lane, M. P. (1985). *Procedures for incorporating generalization programming into interventions for behaviorally disordered students.* Ames, Iowa: Unpublished manuscript.

Evans, D. R. (1971). Specific aggression, arousal, and reciprocal inhibition therapy. *Western Psychologist, 1*, 125–130.

Evans, D. R., Hearn, M. T., & Saklofake, D. (1973). Anger, arousal and systematic desensitization. *Psychological Reports, 32*, 625–626.

Evans, D., & Strangeland, M. (1971). Development of the reaction inventory to measure anger. *Psychological Reports, 29*, 412–414.

Ewart, C. K., Taylor, C. B., Kraemer, H. C., & Agras, W. S. (1984). Reducing blood pressure reactivity during interpersonal conflict: Effects of marital communication training. *Behavior Therapy, 15*, 473–484.

Farrell, A. D., Curran, J. P., Zwick, W. R., & Monti, P. M. (1983). Generalizability and discriminant validity of anxiety and social skills ratings in two populations. *Behavioral Assessment, 6*, 1–14.

Fee, R. A., & Girdano, D. A. (1978). The relative effectiveness of three techniques to induce the trophotropic response. *Biofeedback and Self-regulation, 3*, 145–157.

Fehrenbach, P. A., & Thelen, M. H. (1981). Assertive-skills training for inappropriately aggressive college males: Effects on assertive and aggressive behaviors. *Journal of Behavior Therapy & Experimental Psychiatry, 12*, 213–217.

Feindler, E. L. (1979). *Cognitive and behavioral approaches to anger control training in explosive adolescents.* Unpublished doctoral dissertation, West Virginia University.

Feindler, E., & Ecton, R. (1986). *Anger control training.* New York: Pergamon Press.

Feindler, E. L., & Fremouw, W. J. (1983). Stress inoculation training for adolescent anger problems. In D. Meichenbaum and M. E. Jaremko (Eds.), *Stress reduction and prevention.* New York: Plenum Press.

Feindler, E. L., Latini, J., Nape, K., Romano, J., & Doyle, J. (1980). *Anger reduction methods for child-care workers at a residential delinquent facility.* Presented at Association for the Advancement of Behavior Therapy, New York City.

Feindler, E. L., Marriott, S. A., & Iwata, M. (1984). Group anger control training for junior high school delinquents. *Cognitive Therapy and Research, 8*, 299–311.

Fensterheim, H. (1972). Assertive methods and marital problems. In R. D. Rubin, J. Henderson, and L. P. Ullman (Eds.), *Advances in behavior therapy.* New York: Academic Press.

Fenton, E. (1980). *Leading dilemma discussions: A workshop.* Unpublished manuscript, Carnegie-Mellon University, Pittsburgh, PA.

Ferster, C. B., & DeMeyer, M. K. (1962). A method for the experimental analysis of the behavior of autistic children. *American Journal of Orthopsychiatry, 32*, 89–98.

Filley, A. C. (1974). *Interpersonal conflict resolution.* Glenview, IL: Scott, Foresman.

Filsinger, E. E. (Ed.) (1983). *Marriage and family assessment.* Beverly Hills, CA: Sage.

Finch, A. J., & Eastman, E. S. (1983). A multimethod approach to measuring anger in children. *Journal of Psychology, 115*, 55–60.

Finch, A. J., Saylor, C. F., & Nelson, W. M. (1983). *The Children's Inventory of Anger: A self-report measure.* Paper presented at the 91st annual meeting of the American Psychological Association, Anaheim, CA.

Firestone, P. (1976). The effects of side effects of timeout on an aggressive nursery school child. *Journal of Behavior Therapy & Experimental Psychiatry, 6*, 79–81.

Ford, D. H., & Urban, H. B. (1963). *Systems of psychotherapy.* New York: Wiley.

Foster, S. L., Prinz, R. J., & O'Leary, K. D. (1983). Impact of problem solving communication training and generalization procedures on family conflict. *Child & Family Behavior Therapy, 5,* 1–23.

Foxx, C. L., Foxx, R. M., Jones, J. R. & Kiely, D. (1980). Twenty-four hour social isolation. *Behavior Modification, 4,* 130–144.

Foxx, R. M., & Azrin, N. H. (1972). Restitution: A method of eliminating aggressive-disruptive behavior of retarded and brain damaged patients. *Behavior Research and Therapy, 10,* 15–27.

Foxx, R. M., & Bechtel, D. R. (1983). Overcorrection: A review and analysis. In S. Axelrod and J. Apache (Eds.), *The effects of punishment on human behavior.* New York: Academic Press.

Frank, R. (1973). Rotating leadership in a group therapy setting. *Psychotherapy: Theory, Research and Practice, 10,* 337–338.

Freedman, B. J., Rosenthal, L., Donahoe, C. P., Schlundt, D. G., & McFall, R. M. (1978). A social-behavioral analysis of skill deficits in delinquent and nondelinquent adolescent boys. *Journal of Consulting and Clinical Psychology, 46,* 1448–1462.

Freud, S. (1955). Beyond the pleasure principle. *Standard edition* (vol. 18). (J. Strachey, Ed. & trans.) London: Hogarth. (Originally published in 1920.)

Freud, S. (1964). Why war? *Standard edition* (vol 22). (J. Strachey, Ed. & trans.) London: Hogarth. (Originally published in 1933.)

Friedman, P. M. (1972). Personalistic family and marital therapy. In A. A. Lazarus (Ed.), *Clinical behavior therapy.* New York: Brunner/Mazel.

Gaffney, L. R., & McFall, R. M. (1981). A comparison of social skills in delinquent and nondelinquent adolescent girls using a behavioral role-playing inventory. *Journal of Consulting and Clinical Psychology, 49,* 959–967.

Gagne, R. M., Baker, K. E., & Foster, H. (1950). On the relation between similarity and transfer of training in the learning of discriminative motor tasks. *Psychological Review, 57,* 67–79.

Gagne, R. M., & Foster, H. (1949). Transfer to a motor skill from practice on a pictured representation. *Journal of Experimental Psychology, 39,* 342–354.

Galassi, J. P., & Galassi, M. D. (1984). Promoting transfer and maintenance of counseling outcomes. In S. D. Brown and R. W. Lent (Eds.), *Handbook of counseling psychology.* New York: Wiley.

Galbraith, R. B., & Jones, T. M. (1976). *Moral reasoning: A teaching handbook for adapting Kohlberg to the classroom.* Anoka, MN: Greenhaven Press.

Gambrill, E. D. (1977). *Behavior modification.* San Francisco: Jossey-Bass.

Garrison, S. R., & Stolberg, A. L. (1983). Modification of anger in children by affective imagery training. *Journal of Abnormal Child Psychology, 11,* 115–130.

Genshaft, J. L. (1980). Personality characteristics of delinquent subtypes. *Journal of Abnormal Child Psychology, 8,* 279–283.

Gibbs, J. C., Arnold, K. D., Ahlborn, H. H., & Cheesman, F. L. (1984). Facilitation of sociomoral reasoning in delinquents. *Journal of Consulting and Clinical Psychology, 52,* 37–45.

Gibbs, J. C., & Widaman, K. F. (1982). *Social intelligence.* Englewood Cliffs, NJ: Prentice-Hall.

Glasser, W. (1969). *Schools without failure.* New York: Harper & Row.

Goldbeck, R. A., Bernstein, B. B., Hellix, W. A., & Marx, M. H. (1957). Application of the half-split technique to problem-solving tasks. *Journal of Experimental Psychology, 53,* 330–338.

Goldfried, M., & D'Zurilla, T. J. (1969). A behavioral-analytic model for assessing competance. In C. D. Spielberger (Ed.), *Current topics in clinical and community psychology* (vol. 1). New York: Academic Press.

Goldfried, M. R., & Trier, C. S. (1974). Effectiveness of relaxation as an active coping skill. *Journal of Abnormal Psychology, 83,* 348–355.

Goldstein, A. P. (1973). *Structured learning therapy: Toward a psychotherapy for the poor.* New York: Academic Press.

Goldstein, A. P. (1978). *Prescriptions for child mental health and education.* New York: Pergamon Press.

Goldstein, A. P. (1982). *Psychological skills training.* New York: Pergamon Press.

Goldstein, A. P., Apter, S., & Harootunian, B. (1983). *School violence.* Englewood Cliffs, NJ: Prentice-Hall.

Goldstein, A. P., & Glick, B. (1986). *Aggression replacement training: A comprehensive intervention for aggressive youth.* Champaign, IL: Research Press.

Goldstein, A. P., Glick, B., Reiner, S., Zimmerman, D., Coultry, T., & Gold, D. (1986). Aggression replacement training: A comprehensive intervention for juvenile delinquents. *Journal of Correctional Education, 37,* 120–126.

Goldstein, A. P., Heller, K., & Sechrest, L. B. (1966). *Psychotherapy and the psychology of behavior change.* New York: Wiley.

Goldstein, A. P., & Kanfer, F. (Eds.) (1979). *Maximizing treatment gains.* New York: Academic Press.

Goldstein, A. P., & Keller, H. R. (1983). Aggression prevention and control: Multi-targeted, multi-channel, multi-process, multi-disciplinary. In Center for Research on Aggression (Ed.), *Prevention and control of aggression* (pp. 338–350). New York: Pergamon Press.

Goldstein, A. P., Keller, H. R. & Erne, D. (1985). *Changing the abusive parent.* Champaign, Ill.: Research Press.

Goldstein, A. P., & Michaels, G. (1985). *Empathy: Development, training and consequences.* Hillsdale, NJ: Erlbaum.

Goldstein, A. P., Monti, P. J., Sardino, T. J., & Green, D. J. (1978). *Police crisis intervention.* New York: Pergamon Press.

Goldstein, A. P., & Rosenbaum, A. (1982). *Aggress-less.* Englewood Cliffs, NJ: Prentice-Hall.

Goldstein, A. P., Sherman, M., Gershaw, N. J., Sprafkin, R. P., & Glick, B. (1978). Training aggressive adolescents in prosocial behavior. *Journal of Youth and Adolescence, 7,* 73–92.

Goldstein, A. P., Sprafkin, R. P., & Gershaw, N. J. (1976). *Skill training for community living.* New York: Pergamon Press.

Goldstein, A. P., Sprafkin, R. P., Gershaw, N. J., & Klein, P. (1980). *Skillstreaming the adolescent.* Champaign, IL: Research Press.

Goldstein, A. P., & Stein, N. (1976). *Prescriptive psychotherapies.* New York: Pergamon Press.

Goldstein, R. (1974). Brain research and violent behavior. *Archives of Neurology, 30,* 1–18.

Goodwin, S. E., & Mahoney, M. J. (1975). Modification of aggression through modeling: An experimental probe. *Journal of Behavior Therapy and Experimental Psychiatry, 6,* 200–202.

Gottman, J. M., & Levenson, R. W. (1986). Assessing the role of emotion in marriage. *Behavioral Assessment, 8,* 31–48.

Gottman, J., Markman, H., Notarius, C., & Gonso, J. (1976). *The couples guide to communication.* Champaign, IL: Research Press.

Gottman, J., Notarius, C., Markman, H., Bank, S., Yoppi, B., & Rubin, M. E. (1976). Behavior exchange theory and marital decision making. *Journal of Personality and Social Psychology, 34,* 14–23.

Grant, J. (1986). *Problem solving training for delinquent youth.* Unpublished doctoral dissertation, Syracuse University.

Green, R., & Murray, E. (1973). Instigation to aggression as a function of self-disclosure and threat to self-esteem. *Journal of Consulting and Clinical Psychology, 40,* 440–443.

Griffith, R. G. (1983). The administrative issues: An ethical and legal perspective. In S. Axelrod and J. Apache (Eds.), *The effects of punishment on human behavior* (pp. 317–338). New York: Academic Press.

Grimm, L. G. (1980). The evidence for cue-controlled relaxation. *Behavior Therapy, 11,* 283–293.

Gruber, R. P. (1971). Behavior therapy: Problems in generalization. *Behavior Therapy, 2,* 361–368.

Guerney, B. G. (1964). Filial therapy: Description and rationale. *Journal of Consulting Psychology, 28,* 304–310.

Guerney, B. G. (1977). *Relationship enhancement.* San Francisco: Jossey-Bass.

Hagebak, R. (1979). Disciplinary practices in Dallas. In D. G. Gil (Ed.), *Child abuse and violence.* New York: AMS Press.

Haley, J. (1976). *Problem solving therapy.* San Francisco: Jossey-Bass.

Hall, R. V., Axelrod, S., Foundopoulos, M., Shellman, J., Campbell, R. S., & Cranston, S. S. (1971). The effective use of punishment to modify behavior in the classroom. *Educational Technology, 11,* 24–26.

Hall, R. V., Lund, D., & Jackson, D. (1968). Effects of teacher attention on study behavior. *Journal of Applied Behavior Analysis, 1,* 1–12.

Hall, R. V., Panyan, M., Rabon, D., & Broden, M. (1968). Instructing beginning teachers in reinforcement procedures which improve classroom control. *Journal of Applied Behavior Analysis, 1,* 315–22.

Hanson, R. W. (1971). *Assertion training program.* Unpublished manuscript. Palo Alto, CA: Veterans Administration Hospital.

Hare, M. A. (1976). Teaching conflict resolution simulations. Presented at Eastern Community Association, Philadelphia.

Harris, S., Mussen, P., & Rutherford, E. (1976). Some cognitive, behavioral and personality correlates of maturity of moral development. *Journal of Genetic Psychology, 128,* 123–185.

Hartig, M., & Kanfer, F. H. (1973). The role of verbal self-instruction in children's resistance to temptation. *Journal of Personality and Social Psychology, 25,* 259–267.

Hartwig, W. H., Dickson, A. L., & Anderson, H. N. (1980). Conflict Resolution Inventory: Factor analytic data. *Psychological Reports, 46,* 1009–1010.

Hawley, R. C., & Hawley, I. L. (1975). *Developing human potential: A handbook of activities for personal and social growth.* Amhurst, MA: Educational Research Associates.

Hayes, S. C., Rincover, A., & Solnick, J. V. (1980). The technical drift of applied behavior analysis. *Journal of Applied Behavior Analysis, 13,* 275–285.

Hayward, M. L., Peters, J. J., & Taylor, J. E. (1952). Some values of the use of multiple therapists in the treatment of psychoses. *Psychiatric Quarterly, 26,* 244–249.

Hazel, J. S., Schumaker, J. B., Sherman, J. A., Sheldon-Wildgen, J. (1981). *ASSET: A social skills program for adolescents.* Champaign, IL: Research Press.

Hazel, J. S., Sherman, J. A., Schumaker, J. B., & Sheldon, J. (1985). *Group social skills training with adolescents: A critical review.* Unpublished manuscript, University of Kansas.

Heath, B. L. (1978). *Application of verbal self-instructional training procedures to classroom behavior management.* Unpublished doctoral dissertation, University of Minnesota.

Hedlund, B. L., & Lindquist, C. U. (1984). The development of an inventory for distinguishing among passive, aggressive, and assertive behavior. *Behavioral Assessment, 6,* 379–390.

Heiman, H. (1973). Teaching interpersonal communications. *N. Dakota Speech & Theatre Association Bulletin, 2,* 7–29.

Hellman, D., & Blackman, N. (1966). Enuresis, firesetting, and cruelty to animals: A triad predictive of adult crime. *American Journal of Psychiatry, 122,* 1431–1435.

Hendrickson, G., & Schroeder, W. H. (1941). Transfer of training in learning to hit a submerged target. *Journal of Educational Pychology, 32,* 205–213.

Herrell, J. M. (1971). Use of systematic desensitization to eliminate inappropriate anger. Presented at American Psychological Association, Washington, D.C.

Hersen, M., & Barlow, D. H. (1976). *Single case experimental designs: Strategies for studying behavior change.* New York: Pergamon Press.

Hickman, M. E., & Baldwin, B. A. (1971). The use of programmed instruction to improve communication in marriage. *Family Coordinator, 20,* 121–125.

Higa, W. R. (1973). *Self-instructional versus direct training in modifying children's impulsive behavior.* Unpublished doctoral dissertation, University of Hawaii.

Hollin, C. R., & Courtney, S. A. (1983). A skills training approach to the reduction of institutional offending. *Personality and Individual Differences, 4,* 257–264.

Hollin, C. R., & Henderson, M. (1981). The effects of social skills training on incarcerated delinquent adolescents. *Social Work, 1,* 145–155.

Holmes, D. S. (1971). Round robin therapy: A technique for implementing the effects of psychotherapy. *Journal of Consulting and Clinical Psychology, 37,* 324–331.

Homer, A. L., & Peterson, L. (1980). Differential reinforcement of other behavior: A preferred response elimination procedure. *Behavior Therapy, 11,* 449–471.

Homme, L. (1971). *How to use contingency contracting in the classroom.* Champaign, IL: Research Press.

Horney, K. (1939). *New ways in psychoanalysis.* New York: Norton.

Hyman, I. A. (1978). Is the hickory stick out of tune? *Today's Education, 2,* 30–32.

Jacobson, E. (1929). *Progressive relaxation.* Chicago: University of Chicago Press.

Jacobson, E. (1939). Variation in blood pressure with skeletal muscle tension and relaxation. *Annals of Internal Medicine, 12,* 1194–1212.

Jacobson, E. (1964). *Anxiety and tension control.* Philadelphia, Pennsylvania: Lippincott.

Jacobson, N. S. (1977). Problem solving and contingency contracting in the treatment of marital discord. *Journal of Consulting and Clinical Psychology, 45,* 92–100.

Jacobson, N. S., & Margolin, G. (1979). *Marital therapy: strategies based on social learning and behavioral exchange principles.* New York: Brunner/Mazel.

Jacobson, N. S., & Martin, B. (1976). Behavioral marriage therapy: Current status. *Psychological Bulletin, 83,* 540–556.

Jones, F. H., & Miller, W. H. (1974). The effective use of negative attention for reducing group disruption in special elementary school classrooms. *The Psychological Record, 24,* 435–448.

Kagan, J. (1966). Reflection-implusivity: The generality and dynamics of conceptual tempo. *Journal of Abnormal Psychology, 71,* 17–24.

Kanfer, F., & Karoly, P. (1972). Self-control: A behavioristic excursion into the lion's den. *Behavior Therapy, 3,* 398–416.

Karoly, P., & Steffen, J. (1980). *Improving the long term effects of psychotherapy.* New York: Guilford Press.

Kauffman, J. M., Nussen , J. L., & McGee, C. S. (1977). Follow-up in classroom behavior modification: Survey and discussion. *Journal of School Psychology, 15,* 343–348.

Kaufman, H., & Feshbach, S. (1963). The influence of anti-aggressive communications upon the response to provocation. *Journal of Personality, 31,* 428–444.

Kaufman, K. F., & O'Leary, K. D. (1972). Reward, cost and self-evaluation procedures for disruptive adolescents in a psychiatric hospital school. *Journal of Applied Behavior Analysis, 5,* 293–310.

Kazdin, A. E. (1975). *Behavior modification in applied settings.* Homewood, IL: Dorsey Press.

Kazdin, A. E. (1977). Assessing the clinical or applied significance of behavior change through social validation. *Behavior Modification, 1,* 427–452.

Kazdin, A. E. (1980). *Research design in clinical psychology.* New York: Harper & Row.

Kazdin, A. E., Esveldt-Dawson, K., Unis, A. S., & Rancurrello, M. D. (1983). Child and parent evaluations of depression and aggression in psychiatric inpatient children. *Journal of Abnormal Child Psychology, 11,* 401–413.

Kazdin, A. E., & Frame, C. (1983). Aggressive behavior and conduct disorder. In R. J. Morris & T. R. Krathochwill (Eds.), *The practice of child therapy.* New York: Pergamon Press.

Kazdin, A. E., Matson, J. L., & Esveldt-Dawson, K. (1984). The relationship of role-playing assessment of children's social skills to multiple measures of social competence. *Behavior Research and Therapy*, *23*, 129–139.

Keeley, S. M., Shemberg, K. M., & Carbonell, J. (1976). Operant clinical intervention: Behavior management or beyond? Where are the data? *Behavior Therapy*, *7*, 292–305.

Keller, H. R. (1981). Behavioral consultation. In J. C. Conoley (Ed.), *Consultation in schools: Theory, research, technology* (pp. 59–99). New York: Academic Press.

Keller, H. R. (1986). Behavioral observation approaches to assessment of personality. In H. M. Knoff (Ed.), *The psychological assessment of child and adolescent personality*. New York: Guilford.

Kelly, G. A. (1955). *The psychology of personal constructs*. New York: Norton.

Kendall, P. C. (1977). On the efficacious use of verbal self-instruction procedures with children. *Cognitive Therapy and Research*, *1*, 331–341.

Kendall, P. C., & Braswell, L. (1985). *Cognitive-behavioral therapy for impulsive children*. New York: Guilford Press.

Kendall, P. C., & Korgeski, G. P. (1979). Assessment and cognitive-behavioral interventions. *Cognitive Therapy and Research*, *3*, 1–21.

Kennedy, R. E. (1982). Cognitive-behavioral approaches to the modification of aggressive behavior in children. *School Psychology Review*, *11*, 47–55.

Kifer, R. E., Lewis, M. A., Green, D. R., & Phillips, E. L. (1974). Training predelinquent youths and their parents to negotiate conflict situations. *Journal of Applied Behavior Analysis*, *7*, 357–364.

King, N. J. (1980). The therapeutic utility of abbreviated progressive relaxation: A critical review with implications for clinical progress. In M. Hersen and A. Bellack (Eds.), *Progress in behavior modification*. New York: Academic Press.

Kirschner, N. M., & Levine, L. (1975). A direct school intervention program for the modification of aggressive behavior. *Psychology in the Schools*, *12*, 202–208.

Kleiman, A. (1974). *The use of private speech in young children and its relation to social speech*. Unpublished doctoral dissertation, University of Chicago.

Klinge, V., Thrasher, P., & Myers, S. (1975). Use of bedrest overcorrection in a chronic schizophrenic. *Journal of Behavior Therapy and Experimental Psychiatry*, *6*, 69–73.

Knox, D. (1971). *Marriage happiness*. Champaign, IL: Research Press.

Kohlberg, L. (1969). Stage and sequence: The cognitive-development approach to socialization. In D. A. Goslin (Ed.), *Handbook of socialization theory and research*. Chicago: Rand McNally.

Kohlberg, L. (1971). Stages of moral development as a basis for moral education. In C. M. Beck, B. S. Crittendon, and E. V. Sullivan (Eds.), *Moral education: Interdisciplinary approaches*. New York: Newman Press.

Kohlberg, L. (1976). Moral stages and moralization: The cognitive-development approach. In T. Lickona (Ed.), *Moral development and behavior: Theory, research and social issues*. New York: Holt, Rinehart & Winston.

Kohlberg, L., & Turiel, E. (1971). Moral development and moral education. In G. S. Lesser (Ed.), *Psychology and educational practice*. Chicago: Scott Foresman.

Kopel, S., & Arkowitz, H. (1975). The role of attribution and self-perception in behavior change: Implications for behavior therapy. *Genetic Psychology Monographs*, *92*, 175–212.

Kratochwill, T. R. (Ed.) (1978). *Single subject research: Strategies for evaluating change*. New York: Academic Press.

Krebs, R. L. (1967). *Some relationships between attention and resistance to temptation*. Unpublished doctoral dissertation, University of Chicago.

L'Abate, L. (1975). A positive approach to marital and familial intervention. In L. R. Wolberg and M. L. Aronson (Eds.), *Group therapy 1975: An overview*. New York: Stratton Intercontinental Medical Book Corp.

Land, N., & Slade, A. (1979). Stages. *Understanding how you make moral decisions.* New York: Holt and Rinehart.

Lazarus, A. A., & Rachman, S. (1967). The use of systematic desensitization in psychotherapy. *South African Medical Journal, 31,* 934–937.

Lederer, W., & Jackson, D. D. (1968). *The mirage of marriage.* New York: Norton.

Ledingham, J. E. (1981). Developmental patterns of aggressive and withdrawn behavior in childhood: A possible method for identifying preschizophrenics. *Journal of Abnormal Child Psychology, 9,* 1–22.

Ledingham, J. E., & Schwartzman, A. E. (1984). A 3-year follow-up of aggressive and withdrawn behavior in childhood: Preliminary findings. *Journal of Abnormal Child Psychology, 12,* 157–168.

Lefkowitz, M., Eron, L., Walder, L., & Huesman, L. (1977). *Growing up to be violent.* New York: Pergamon Press.

Leitenberg, H., Agras, W. S., & Thomson, L. E. (1968). A sequential analysis of the effect of selective positive reinforcement in modifying anorexia nervosa. *Behaviour Research and Therapy, 6,* 211–218.

Liberman, R. P., King, L. W., DeRisi, W. J., & McCann, M. (1975). *Personal effectiveness.* Champaign, IL: Research Press.

Liberman, R. P., Levine, J., Wheeler, E., Sanders, N., & Wallace, C. (1976). Experimental evaluation of marital group therapy, Behavioral vs. interaction-insight formation. *Acta Psychiatrica Scandinavia, 17,* 10–16.

Little, V. L., & Kendall, P. C. (1979). Cognitive-behavioral interventions with delinquents: Problem solving, role-taking, and self-control. In P. C. Kendall and S. D. Hollan (Eds.), *Cognitive-behavioral interventions.* New York: Academic Press.

Loeber, R., & Schmaling, K. B. (1985a). Empirical evidence for overt and covert patterns of antisocial conduct problems: A meta-analysis. *Journal of Abnormal Child Psychology, 13,* 337–352.

Loeber, R., & Schmaling, K. B. (1985b). The utility of differentiating between mixed and pure forms of antisocial child behavior. *Journal of Abnormal Child Psychology, 13,* 315–336.

Long, S. J., & Sherer, M. (1985). Social skills training with juvenile offenders. *Child & Family Behavior Therapy, 6,* 1–11.

Lorenz, K. (1966). *On aggression.* New York: Harcourt Brace.

Lorien, R. P., Cowen, E. L, & Caldwell, R. A. (1975). Normative and parametric analyses of school maladjustment. *American Journal of Community Psychology, 3,* 291–301.

Lovaas, O. I., Koegel, R., Simmons, J. Q., & Long, J. S. (1973). Some generalization and follow-up measures on autistic children in behavior therapy. *Journal of Applied Behavior Analysis, 6,* 131–166.

Lovaas, O. I., Schaeffer, B., & Simmons, J. (1965). Building social behavior in autistic children by use of electric shock. *Journal of Experimental Research in Personality, 1,* 99–109.

Lowe, M. R., & Cautela, J. R. (1978). A self-report measure of social skills. *Behavior Therapy, 9,* 535–544.

Luce, S. C., Delquadri, J., & Hall, R. V. (1980). Contingent exercise: A mild but powerful procedure for suppressing inappropriate verbal and aggressive behavior. *Journal of Applied Behavior Analysis, 13,* 583–594.

Luiselli, J. K., Marholin, D., Steinman, D. L., & Steinman, W. M. (1979). Assessing the effects of relaxation training. *Behavior Therapy, 10,* 663–668.

Luria, A. R. (1961). *The role of speech in the regulation of normal and abnormal behavior.* New York: Liveright.

Luther, E. R. (1971). Treatment of migraine headache by conditioned relaxation: A case study. *Behavior Therapy, 2,* 592–593.

Mace, D., & Mace, V. (1976). Marriage enrichment: A preventive group approach for couples. In D. H. L. Olson (Ed.), *Treating Relationships* (pp. 321–336). Lake Mills, IA: Graphic Publishing.

MacGregor, R., Rithchie, A. M., Serrano, A. C., & Schuster, F. P. (1964). *Multiple impact therapy with families.* New York: McGraw-Hill.

Madsen, C. J., Becker, W. C., & Thomas, D. R. (1968). Rules, praise, and ignoring: Elements of elementary classrooms control. *Journal of Applied Behavior Analysis, 1,* 139–150.

Mallick, S. K., & McCandless, B. R. (1966). A study of catharsis of aggression. *Journal of Personality and Social Psychology, 4,* 591–596.

Mandler, G. (1954). Transfer of training as a function of degree of response overlearning. *Journal of Experimental Psychology, 47,* 411–417.

Mandler, G., & Heinemann, S. H. (1956). Effect of overlearning of a verbal response on transfer of training. *Journal of Experimental Psychology, 52,* 39–46.

Marlatt, G. A., & Gordon, J. R. (1980). Determinants of relapse: Implications for the maintenance of behavior change. In P. O. Davidson (Ed.), *Behavioral medicine: Changing health lifestyles.* New York: Brunner/Mazel.

Martens, B. K., & Keller, H. R. (in press). Training school psychologists in the scientific tradition. *School Psychology Review.*

Martin, P. L., & Foxx, R. M. (1973). Victim control of the aggression of an institutionalized retardate. *Journal of Behavior Therapy and Experimental Psychiatry, 4,* 161–165.

Martin, R. P., Hooper, S., & Snow, J. (1986). Behavior rating scale approaches to personality assessment in children and adolescents. In H. M. Knoff (Ed.), *The psychological assessment of child and adolescent personality.* New York: Guilford.

Matson, J. L., Rotatori, A. F., & Helsel, W. J. (1983). Development of a rating scale to measure social skills in children: The Matson Evaluation of Social Skills with Youngsters (MESSY). *Behavior Research and Therapy, 21,* 335–340.

Matson, J. L., Stephens, R. M., & Horne, A. M. (1978). Overcorrection and extinction-reinforcement as rapid methods of eliminating the disruptive behaviors of relatively normal children. *Behavioral Engineering, 4,* 89–94.

Maurer, A. (1974). Corporal punishment. *American Psychologist, 29,* 614–626.

May, J. R., & Johnson, H. J. (1973). Physiological activity to internally elicited arousal and inhibitory thoughts. *Journal of Abnormal Psychology, 82,* 239–245.

McCord, J. (1979). Some child rearing antecedents to criminal behavior in adult men. *Journal of Personality and Social Psychology, 37,* 1477–1486.

McCullough, J. P., Huntsinger, G. M., & Nay, W. R. (1977). Self-control treatment of aggression in a sixteen year old male. *Journal of Consulting Psychology, 45,* 322–331.

McFall, R. M., & Twentyman, C. T. (1973). Four experiments on the relative contributions of rehearsal, modeling and coaching to assertion training. *Journal of Abnormal Psychology, 81,* 199–218.

McGinnis, E., & Goldstein, A. P. (1984). *Skillstreaming the elementary school child.* Champaign, IL: Research Press.

McNamee, S. (1977). Moral behavior, moral development and motivation. *Journal of Moral Education, 7,* 27–31.

McPhail, P., Ungoed-Thomas, J. R., & Chapman, H. (1975). *Learning to care: rationale and method of the lifeline program.* Niles, IL: Argus Communications.

Meichenbaum, D. (1977). *Cognitive behavior modification.* New York: Plenum Press.

Meichenbaum, D., Gilmore, B., & Fedoravicius, A. (1971). Group insight vs. group desensitization in treating speech anxiety. *Journal of Consulting and Clinical Psychology, 36,* 410–421.

Meichenbaum, D. H., & Goodman, J. (1969). The developmental control by verbal operants. *Journal of Experimental Child Psychology, 7,* 533–565.

Meichenbaum, D. H., & Goodman, J. (1971). Training impulsive children to talk to themselves: A means of developing self-control. *Journal of Abnormal Psychology, 77,* 113–126.

Miller, L. S., & Funabiki, D. (1983). Predictive validity of the Social Performance Survey Schedule for component interpersonal behaviors. *Behavioral Assessment, 6,* 33–44.

Miller, N. E. (1941). The frustration-aggression hypothesis. *Psychological Review, 48,* 337–342.

Miller, S. L. (1971). *The effects of communication training in small groups upon self-disclosure and openness in engaged couples' systems of interaction: A field experiment.* Unpublished dissertation, University of Minnesota.

Miller, S., Nunnally, E. W., & Wackman, D. B. (1975). *Alive and aware: Improving communication in relationships.* Minneapolis: Interpersonal Communications Programs.

Monahan, J. (1981). *The clinical prediction of violent behavior.* Rockville, MD: National Institute of Mental Health.

Monahan, J., & O'Leary, K. D. (1971). Effects of self-instruction on rule-breaking behavior. *Psychology Reports, 29,* 1059–1066.

Monti, P. M. (1983). The Social Skills Intake Interview: Reliability and convergent validity assessment. *Journal of Behavior Therapy and Experimental Psychiatry, 14,* 305–310.

Monti, P. M., Wallander, J. L., Ahern D. K., Abrams, D. B., & Munroe, S. M. (1983). Multimodal measurement of anxiety and social skills in a behavioral role-play test: Generalizability and discriminant validity. *Behavioral Assessment, 6,* 15–25.

Moon, J. R., & Eisler, R. M. (1983). Anger control: An experimental comparison of three behavioral treatments. *Behavior Therapy, 14,* 493–505.

Morris, R. J. (1976). *Behavior modification with children.* Cambridge, MA: Winthrop.

Mosher, R., & Sprinthall, N. (1970). Psychological education in the secondary schools. *American Psychologist, 25,* 911–916.

Mosher, R., & Sprinthall, N. (1972). Psychological education: A means to promote personal development during adolescence. In R. E. Purpel and M. Belanger (Eds.), *Curriculum and the cultural revolution* (pp. 117–132). Berkeley, CA: McCutchan.

Mowrer, O. H., & Mowrer, W. A. (1938). Enuresis: A method for its study and treatment. *American Journal of Orthopsychiatry, 8,* 436–447.

Murphy, H. A., Hutchison, J. M., & Bailey, J. S. (1983). *Journal of Applied Behavior Analysis, 16,* 29–35.

Mussen, P. H. (1963). *The psychological development of the child.* Englewood Cliffs, NJ: Prentice-Hall.

Nay, W. R. (1979). Parents as real life reinforcers: The enhancement of parent-training effects across conditions other than training. In A. P. Goldstein and F. H. Kanfer (Eds.), *Maximizing treatment gains.* New York: Academic Press.

Neilans, T. H., & Israel, A. C. (1981). Towards maintenance and generalization of behavior change: Teaching children self-regulation and self-instructional skills. *Cognitive Therapy and Research, 5,* 189–195.

Nelson, W. M., & Finch, A. J. (1978). *The Children's Inventory of Anger (CIA).* Unpublished manuscript, Medical University of South Carolina.

Newman, F., & Oliver, D. (1970). *Clarifying public issues: An approach to teaching social studies.* Boston: Little Brown.

Newsom, C., Favell, J. E., Rincover, A. (1982). The side effects of punishment. In S. Axelrod & J. Apsche (Eds.) *The effects and side effects of punishment on human behavior.* New York: Academic Press.

Novaco, R. W. (1975). *Anger control: The development and evaluation of an experimental treatment.* Lexington, MA: Lexington.

Novaco, R. W. (1978). Anger and coping with stress. In J. Foreyt and D. Rathjen (Eds.), *Cognitive behavior therapy: Therapy, research and practice.* New York: Plenum Press.

Nunnally, E. W. (1971). *Effects of communication training upon interaction awareness and empathic accuracy of engaged couples: A field experiment.* Unpublished doctoral dissertation, University of Minnesota.

O'Donnell, C. R., & Worell, L. (1973). Motor and cognitive relaxation in the desensitization of anger. *Behavior Research and Therapy, 11*, 473–481.

O'Leary, K. D., & Becker, W. C. (1967). Behavior modification of an adjustment class: A token reinforcement program. *Exceptional Children, 33*, 637–642.

O'Leary, K. D., Becker, W. C., Evans, M. B., & Saudargas, R. A. (1969). A token reinforcement program in a public school: A replication and systematic analysis. *Journal of Applied Behavior Analysis, 2*, 3–13.

O'Leary, K. D., Kaufman, K. F., Kass, R. E., & Drabman, R. S. (1970). The effects of loud and soft reprimands on the behavior of disruptive students. *Exceptional Children, 37*, 145–155.

O'Leary, K. D., & O'Leary, S. G. (1977). *Classroom management.* New York: Pergamon Press.

O'Leary, K. D., & Turkewitz, H. (1978). The treatment of marital disorders from a behavioral perspective. In T. J. Paolino and S. McCrady (Eds.), *Marriage and the treatment of marital disorders from three perspectives: Psychoanalytic, behavioral, and systems theory.* New York: Brunner/Mazel.

O'Leary S. G., & O'Leary K. D. (1976). Behavior modification in the school. In H. Leitenberg (Ed.), *Handbook of behavior modification and behavior therapy.* Englewood Cliffs, NJ: Prentice-Hall.

Oliver, D., & Shaver, J. (1966). *Teaching public issues in the high school.* Boston: Houghton Mifflin.

Ollendick, T. H., & Matson, J. L. (1976). An initial investigation into the parameters of overcorrection. *Psychological Reports, 39*, 1139–1142.

Ollendick, T. H., & Matson, J. L. (1978). Overcorrection: An overview. *Behavior Therapy, 9*, 830–842.

Osgood, C. E. (1949). The similarity paradox in human learning: A resolution. *Psychological Review, 56*, 132–143.

Osgood, C. E. (1953). *Method and theory in experimental psychology.* New York: Oxford University Press.

Ostrov, E., Marohn, R. C., Offer, D., Curtiss, G., & Feczko, M. (1980). The Adolescent Antisocial Behavior Check List. *Journal of Clinical Psychology, 36*, 594–601.

Palkes, H., Stewart, M., & Kahana, B. (1968). Porteus Maze performance of hyperactive boys after training in self-directed verbal commands. *Child Development, 39*, 817–826.

Parker, J. C., Gilbert, G. S., & Thoreson, R. W. (1978). Reduction of autonomic arousal in alcoholics: A comparison of relaxation and mediation techniques. *Journal of Consulting and Clinical Psychology, 46*, 879–86.

Parsons, B. V., & Alexander, J. F. (1973). Short-term family intervention: A therapy outcome study. *Journal of Consulting and Clinical Psychology, 41*, 195–201.

Patterson, G. R. (1965). A learning theory approach to the treatment of the school phobic child. In L. P. Ullman and L. Krasner (Eds.), *Case studies in behavior modification.* New York: Holt, Rinehart & Winston.

Patterson, G. R. (1982). *Coercive family process.* Eugene, OR: Castalia Publishing Co.

Patterson, G. R., & Anderson, D. (1964). Peers as social reinforcers. *Child Development, 35*, 951–960.

Patterson, G. R., & Bank, L. (1986). Bootstrapping your way in the nomological thicket. *Behavioral Assessment, 8*, 49–73.

Patterson, G. R., & Brodsky, G. A. (1966). A behavior modification program for a child with multiple problem behaviors. *Journal of Child Psychology and Psychiatry, 7*, 277–295.

Patterson, G. R., Cobb, J. A., & Ray, R. S. (1973). A social engineering technology for retraining the families of aggressive boys. In H. E. Adams and I. P. Unikel (Eds.), *Issues and trends in behavior therapy*. Springfield, IL: C. C. Thomas.

Patterson, G. R., & Hops, H. (1972). Coercion, a game for two: Intervention techniques for mental conflict. In R. E. Ulrich and P. Mountjoy (Eds.), *The experimental analysis of social behavior*. New York: Appleton-Century-Crofts.

Patterson, G. R., Ray, R., & Shaw, D. (1968). *Direct intervention in families of deviant children*. Unpublished manuscript, University of Oregon.

Patterson, G. R., Reid, J. G., Jones, R. R., & Conger, R. E. (1975). *A social learning approach to family intervention*. Vol. 1, Eugene, OR: Castalia Publishing Co.

Patterson, G. R., & Stouthamer-Loeber, M. (1984). The correlation of family management practices and delinquency. *Child Development, 55*, 1299–1307.

Paul, G. L. (1969). Chronic mental patients: Current status-future directions. *Psychological Bulletin, 71*, 81–94.

Pendleton, L. R., & Tasto, D. L. (1976). Effects of metronome-conditioned relaxation, metronome-induced relaxation, and progressive muscle relaxation on insomnia. *Behavior Research and Therapy, 14*, 165–166.

Pentz, M. A. (1980). Assertion training and trainer effects on unassertive and aggressive adolescents. *Journal of Counseling Psychology, 27*, 76–83.

Pierce, R. M. (1973). Training in interpersonal communication skills with partners of deteriorating marriages. *Family Coordinator, 22*, 223–27.

Pinkston, E. M., Reese, N. M., LeBlanc, J. M., & Baer, D. M. (1973). Independent control of a preschool child's aggression and peer interaction by contingent teacher attention. *Journal of Applied Behavior Analysis, 6*, 115–24.

Pitkanen-Pulkkinen, L. (1981). Concurrent and predictive validity of self-reported aggressiveness. *Aggressive Behavior, 7*, 97–110.

Posey, C. D., & Hess, A. K. (1985). Aggressive response sets and subtle-obvious MMPI scale distinctions in male offenders. *Journal of Personality Assessment, 49*, 235–239.

Pressley, M. (1979). Increasing children's self-control through cognitive interventions. *Review of Educational Research, 49*, 319–370.

Price, M. G., & Haynes, S. N. (1980). The effects of participant monitoring and feedback on marital interaction and satisfaction. *Behavior Therapy, 11*, 134–139.

Prinz, R. J., Foster, S., Kent, R. N., & O'Leary, K. D. (1979). Multivariate assessment of conflict in distressed and non-distressed mother-adolescent dyads. *Journal of Applied Behavior Analysis, 12*, 691–700.

Rachman, S. (1968). The role of muscular relaxation in desensitization therapy. *Behavior Research & Therapy, 6*, 159–166.

Rank, O. (1945). *Will therapy and truth and reality*. New York: Knopf.

Rappaport, A. F. (1971). *The effects of an intensive conjugal relationship modification program*. Unpublished doctoral dissertation, Pennysylvania State University.

Rappaport, A. F., & Harrell, J. (1972). A behavior exchange model for marital counseling. *Family Coordinator, 21*, 203–212.

Raths, L. E., Harmin, M., & Simon, S. B. (1966). *Values and teaching: Working with values in the classroom*. Columbus, OH: Charles Merrill.

Rhode, N., Rasmussen, D., & Heaps, R. S. (1971). *Let's communicate: A program designed for effective communication*. Presented at American Personnel and Guidance Association.

Rimm, D. C., DeGroot, J. D., Boord, P., Heiman, J., & Dillow, P. V. (1971). Systematic desensitization of an anger response. *Behavior Research & Therapy, 9*, 273–280.

Rimm, D. C., Hill, G. A., Brown, N. N., & Stuart, J. E. (1974). Group assertive training in treatment of expression of inappropriate anger. *Psychological Reports, 34*, 791–798.

Rimm, D. C., & Litvak, S. B. (1969). Self-verbalization and emotional arousal. *Journal of Abnormal Psychology, 74*, 181–187.

Risley, T. R. (1977). The social context of self-control. In R. Stuart (Ed.), *Behavioral self management*. New York: Brunner/Mazel.

Robertson, K. R., & Milner, J. S. (1985). Convergent and discriminant validity of the Child Abuse Potential Inventory. *Journal of Personality Assessment, 49*, 86–88.

Robin, A. L., Armel, S., & O'Leary, K. D. (1975). The effects of self-instruction on writing deficiencies. *Behavior Therapy, 6*, 178–187.

Robin, A. L., Kent, R., O'Leary, K. D., Foster, S., & Prinz, R. (1977). An approach to teaching parents and adolescents problem-solving communication skills: A preliminary report. *Behavior Therapy, 8*, 639–43.

Robin, A., Schneider, M., & Dolnick, M. (1976). The turtle technique: An extended case study of self-control in the classroom. *Psychology in the Schools, 13*, 449–453.

Robinson, E. H., & Eyberg, S. M. (1981). The dyadic parent–child interaction coding system: Standardization and validation. *Journal of Consulting and Clinical Psychology, 49*, 245–250.

Rogers, C. R. (1951). *Client-centered therapy*. Boston: Houghton Mifflin.

Rose, S. D. (1977). *Group therapy: A behavioral approach*. Englewood Cliffs, NJ: Prentice-Hall.

Rosenzweig, S. (1976). Aggressive behavior and the Rosenzweig Picture-Frustration (P-F) Study. *Journal of Clinical Psychology, 32*, 885–891.

Roundtree, G. A., & Faily, A. (1980). The impact of educational programs on acts of aggression and rule violations in a female prison population. *Corrective and Social Psychiatry, 26*, 144–145.

Russell, J. A., & Mehrabian, A. (1974). Distinguishing anger and anxiety in terms of emotional response factors. *Journal of Consulting and Clinical Psychology, 42*, 79–83.

Russell, P. L., & Brandsma, J. M. (1974). A theoretical and empirical integration of the rational-emotive and classical conditioning theories. *Journal of Consulting and Clinical Psychology, 42*, 389–397.

Russell, R. K., & Sipich, J. F. (1974). Treatment of test anxiety by cue-controlled relaxation. *Behavior Therapy, 5*, 673–676.

Sajwaj, T., Culver, P., Hall, C., & Lehr, L. (1972). Three simple punishment techniques for the control of classroom disruptions. In G. Semb (Ed.), *Behavior analysis and education*. Lawrence, Kansas: University of Kansas Press.

Sanders, R. W. (1978). Systematic desensitization in the treatment of child abuse. *American Journal of Psychiatry, 135*, 483–484.

Sarason, I. J., & Ganzer, V. J. (1973). Modeling and group discussion in the rehabilitation of juvenile delinquents. *Journal of Counseling Psychology, 20*, 442–449.

Scharf, P., McCoy, W., & Rory, D. (1979). *Growing up moral: Dilemmas for the intermediate grades*. Minneapolis, MN: Winston Press.

Schinke, S. P. (1981). Interpersonal skills training with adolescents. In M. Hersen, R. M. Eisler, and P. M. Miller (Eds.), *Progress in Behavior Modification* (vol. 11) (pp. 65–111). New York: Academic Press.

Schlichter, K. J., & Horan, J. J. (1981). Effects of stress inoculation on the anger and aggression management skills of institutionalized juvenile delinquents. *Cognitive Therapy and Research, 5*, 359–365.

Schneider, M. (1974). Turtle technique in the classroom. *Teaching Exceptional Children, 7*, 22–24.

Schrader, C., Long, J., Panzer, C., Gillet, D., & Kornblath, R. (1979). *An anger control package for adolescent drug abusers*. Presented at Association for the Advancement of Behavior Therapy, Atlanta.

Schwartz, G. E. (1971). Cardiac responses to self-induced thoughts. *Psychophysiology, 8,* 462–467.

Schwitzgebel, R. (1964). *Street corner research: An experimental approach to the juvenile delinquent.* Cambridge, MA: Harvard University Press.

Selby, M. J. (1984). Assessment of violence potential using measures of anger, hostility, and social desirability. *Journal of Personality Assessment, 48,* 531–544.

Sewell, E., McCoy, J. F. & Sewell, W. R. (1973). Modification of an antagonistic social behavior using positive reinforcement for other behavior. *Psychological Record, 23,* 499–504.

Shapiro, E. S., Santz, F. E. & Hofman, R. (1985). Validity of rating scales in assessing agressive behavior in classroom settings. *Journal of School Psychology, 23,* 69–80.

Sherman, A. R. (1979). In vivo therapies for phobic reactions, instrumental behavior problems, and interpersonal communication problems. In A. P. Goldstein and F. H. Kanfer (Eds.), *Maximizing treatment gains.* New York: Academic Press.

Sherman, A. R., & Levine, M. P. (1979). In vivo therapies for compulsive habits, sexual difficulties, and severe adjustment problems. In A. P. Goldstein and F. H. Kanfer (Eds.), *Maximizing treatment gains.* New York: Academic Press.

Sherman, A. R., & Plummer, I. L. (1973). Training in relaxation as a behavioral self-management skill: An exploratory investigation. *Behavior Therapy, 4,* 543–550.

Sherman, J. A. (1965). Use of reinforcement and imitation to reinstate verbal behavior in mute psychotics. *Journal of Abnormal Psychology, 70,* 155–164.

Shore, E., & Sechrest, L. (1961). Concept attainment as a function of number of positive instances presented. *Journal of Educational Psychology, 52,* 303–307.

Skinner, B. F. (1938). *The behavior of organisms: An experimental analysis.* New York: Appleton-Century-Crofts.

Skinner, B. F. (1953). *Science and human behavior.* New York: Macmillan.

Slavin, D. R. (1967). *Response transfer of conditional affective responses as a function of an experimental analogue of rotational psychotherapy.* Unpublished doctoral dissertation, Northwestern University.

Smith, R. E. (1973). The use of humor in the counterconditioning of anger responses: A case study. *Behavior Therapy, 4,* 576–580.

Solomon, E. (1978). Structured learning therapy with abusive parents: Training in self-control. Unpublished doctoral dissertation, Syracuse University.

Spence, S. H. (1981). Differences in social skills performance between institutionalized juvenile male offenders and a comparable group of boys without offense records. *British Journal of Clinical Psychology, 20,* 163–171.

Spielberger, C. D., Jacobs, G., Russell, S., & Crane, R. S. (1983). Assessment of anger: The state-trait anger scale. In J. N. Butcher and C. D. Spielberger (Eds.), *Advances in personality assessment* (vol. 2). Hillsdale, NJ: Lawrence Erlbaum.

Steen, P. L., & Zuriff, G. E. (1977). The use of relaxation in the treatment of self-injurious behavior. *Journal of Behavior Therapy and Experimental Psychiatry, 8,* 447–448.

Stein, M., & Davis, J. K. (1982). *Therapies for adolescents: Current treatment for problem behaviors.* San Francisco: Jossey-Bass.

Steiner, C., Wyckoff, H. & Marcus, J. (1975). *Readings in radical psychiatry.* New York: Grove Press.

Stephens, T. M. (1979). *Directive teaching of children with learning and behavioral handicaps.* Columbus: Charles E. Merrill.

Stokes, T. F., & Baer, D. M. (1977). An implicit technology of generalization. *Journal of Applied Behavior Analysis, 10,* 349–367.

Straughan, J. (1968). The applications of operant conditioning to the treatment of elective mutism. In H. N. Sloane, Jr., and B. A. MacAulay (Eds.), *Operant procedures in remedial speech and language training.* Boston: Houghton Mifflin.

Straus, M. A. (1979). Measuring intrafamily conflict and violence: The Conflict Tactics (CT) Scales. *Journal of Marriage and the Family, 41,* 75–88.

Stuart, R. B. (1969). Operant-interpersonal treatment for marital discord. *Journal of Consulting and Clinical Psychology, 33,* 675–680.

Stuart, R. B. (1971). Behavioral contracting within the families of delinquents. *Journal of Behavior Therapy and Experimental Psychiatry, 2,* 1–11.

Sturm, D. (1979). *Therapist aggression tolerance and dependency tolerance under standardized client conditions of hostility and dependency.* Unpublished masters thesis, Syracuse University.

Sullivan, H. S. (1953). *Conceptions of modern psychiatry.* New York: Norton.

Sulzer-Azaroff, B., & Mayer, G. R. (1977). *Applying behavior analysis procedures with children and youth.* New York: Holt, Rinehart & Winston.

Taylor, C. B., Farquhar, J. W., Nelson, E., & Agras, S. (1977). Relaxation therapy and high blood pressure. *Archives of General Psychiatry, 34,* 339–342.

Taylor, S. P. (1967). Aggressive behavior and physiological arousal as a function of provocation and the tendency to inhibit aggression. *Journal of Personality, 35,* 297–310.

Terkelson, C. (1976). Making contact: Parent–child communication skill program. *Elementary School Guidance and Counseling, 11,* 89–99.

Tharp, R. G., & Wetzel, R. J. (1969). *Behavior modification in the natural environment.* New York: Academic Press.

Thomas, J. D., Presland, I. E., Grant, M. D., & Glynn, T. L. (1978). Natural rates of teacher approval and disapproval in grade 7 classrooms. *Journal of Applied Behavior Analysis, 11,* 91–94.

Thorndike, E. L., & Woodworth, R. S. (1901). The influence of improvement in one mental function upon the efficiency of other functions. *Psychological Review, 8,* 247–61.

Tinbergen, N. (1968). On war and peace in animals and man. *Science, 160,* 1411–1418.

Tower, R. B., & Singer, J. L. (1981). The measurement of imagery: How can it be clinically useful? In P. C. Kendall and S. D. Hollon (Eds.), *Assessment strategies for cognitive-behavioral interventions.* New York: Academic Press.

Travis, P., & Travis, R. (1975). The pairing enrichment program: Actualizing the marriage. *The Family Coordinator, 24,* 161–165.

Trief, P. (1976). *The reduction of egocentrism in acting-out adolescents by structured learning therapy.* Unpublished doctoral dissertation, Syracuse University.

Turk, D. (1976). *An expanded skills training approach for the treatment of experimentally induced pain.* Unpublished doctoral dissertation, University of Waterloo.

Ugurel-Semin, R. (1952). Moral behavior and moral judgment of children. *Journal of Abnormal and Social Psychology, 47,* 463–475.

Ulmer, G. (1939). Teaching geometry to cultivate reflective thinking: An experimental study with 1239 high school pupils. *Journal of Experimental Education, 8,* 18–25.

Underwood, B. J. (1951). Associative transfer in verbal learning as a function of response similarity and degree of first-list learning. *Journal of Experimental Psychology, 42,* 44–53.

Underwood, B. J., & Schultz, R. W. (1960). *Meaningfulness and verbal behavior.* New York: Lippincott.

Urbain, E. S., & Kendall, P. C. (1981). *Interpersonal problem-solving, social perspective-taking and behavioral contingencies: A comparison of group approaches with impulsive-aggressive children.* Unpublished manuscript, University of Minnesota.

VanHouton, R. (1982). Punishment: From the animal laboratory to the applied setting. In S. Axelrod and J. Apsche (Eds.), *The effects and side effects of punishment on human behavior.* New York: Academic Press.

VanHouten, R., Nau, P. A., MacKenzie-Keating, S., Sameota, D., & Colavecchia, B. (1982). An analysis of some variables influencing the effectiveness of reprimands. *Journal of Applied Behavioral Analysis, 15,* 65–83.

Von Benken, E.A. (1977). *Clinical reduction of anger and aggression by systematic desensitiza-tion*. Unpublished doctoral dissertation, University of Cincinnati.

Vondracek, F. W., Stein, A. H., & Friedrich, L. K. (1973). A non-verbal technique for assessing frustration response in pre-school children. *Journal of Personality Assessment, 37*, 355–362.

Vukelich, R., & Hake, D. F. (1971). Reduction of dangerously aggressive behavior in a severely retarded resident through a combination of positive reinforcement procedures. *Journal of Applied Behavior Analysis, 4*, 215–225.

Vygotsky, L. S. (1962). *Thought and language*. Cambridge, MA: M.I.T. Press.

Wahler, R. G., & Pollio, H. R. (1968). Behavior and insight: A case study in behavior ther-apy. *Journal of Experimental Research in Personality, 3*, 45–56.

Wahler, R. G., Winkel, G. H., Peterson, R. F., & Morrison, D. C. (1965). Mothers as behav-ior therapists for their own children. *Behavior Research and Therapy, 3*, 113–124.

Walker, H. M. (1979). *The acting-out child: Coping with classroom disruption*. Boston: Allyn & Bacon.

Walker, H. M., Hops, H., & Fiegenbaum, E. (1976). Deviant classroom behavior as a func-tion of combinations of social and token reinforcement and cost contingency. *Behavior Therapy, 7*, 76–88.

Walker, H. M., Hops, H., & Johnson, S. M. (1975). Generalization and maintenance of classroom treatment effects. *Behavior Therapy, 6*, 188–200.

Ward, M. H., & Baker, B. L. (1968). Reinforcement therapy in the classroom. *Journal of Applied Behavior Analysis, 1*, 323–28.

Warner, G., & Lance, J. W. (1975). Relaxation therapy in migraine and chronic tension headache. *Medical Journal of Australia, 1*, 298–301.

Watkins, B. R. (1972). The development and evolution of a transductive learning technique for the treatment of social incompetence. *Dissertation Abstracts International, 33*, 2361.

Watson, J. B., & Rayner, R. (1920). Conditioned emotional reactions. *Journal of Experimen-tal Psychology, 3*, 1–114.

Watzlawick, P., Beavin, J. H., & Jackson, D. D. (1967). *Pragmatics of human communica-tion—A study of interactional patterns, pathologies, and paradox*. New York: Norton.

Webster, C. D., Ben-Aron, M. H., & Hucker, S. J. (1985). *Dangerousness: Probability and pre-diction psychiatry and public policy*. New York: Cambridge University.

Webster-Stratton, C. (1985). Comparisons of behavior transactions between conduct-dis-ordered children and their mothers in the clinic and at home. *Journal of Abnormal Child Psychology, 13*, 169–184.

Weinreich, R. J. (1975). *Inducing reflective thinking in impulsive, emotionally disturbed chil-dren*. Unpublished masters thesis, Virginia Commonwealth University.

Weinstein, G., & Fantini, M. (1970). *Toward humanistic education: A curriculum effect*. New York: Praeger.

Weiss, R. L., Birchler, S. R. & Vincent, J. P. (1974). Contractual models for negotiation training in marital dyads. *Journal of Marriage and the Family*, May, 321–330.

Weiss, R. L., Hops, H., & Patterson, G. R. (1973). A framework for conceptualizing marital conflict. In F. W. Clark and L. A. Hamerlynck (Eds.), *Critical issues in research and prac-tice*. Champaign, IL: Research Press.

Weissberg, M. (1975). Anxiety-inhibiting statements and relaxation combined in two cases of speech anxiety. *Journal of Behavior Therapy and Experimental Psychiatry, 6*, 163–164.

Wells, R. A., Figurel, J. A., & McNamee, P. (1975). Group facilitative training with con-flicted marital couples. In A. G. Gurman and D. G. Rice (Eds.), *Couples in conflict*. New York: Jason Aronson.

Welsh, R. S. (1978). Delinquency, corporal punishment and the schools. *Crime & Delin-quency*, 336–354.

Wheeler, L., & Caggiula, A. R. (1966). The contagion of aggression. *Journal of Experimental Social Psychology, 2*, 1–10.

Whitaker, C. A., Malone, T. P., & Warkentin, J. (1966). Multiple therapy and psychotherapy. In F. Fromm-Reichmann & M. Moreno (Eds.), *Progress in psychotherapy*. New York: Grune and Stratton.

White, G. D., Nielson, G., & Johnson, S. M. (1972). Timeout duration and the suppression of deviant behavior in children. *Journal of Applied Behavior Analysis, 5*, 111–120.

White, M. A. (1975). Natural rates of teacher approval and disapproval in the classroom. *Journal of Applied Behavior Analysis, 8*, 367–372.

Williams, D. Y., & Akamatsu, T. J. (1978). Cognitive self-guidance training with juvenile delinquents. *Cognitive Therapy and Research, 2*, 285–288.

Wilson, C., Robertson, S., Herlong, L., & Haynes, S. (1979). Vicarious effects of time-out in the modification of aggression in the classroom. *Behavior Modification, 3*, 97–111.

Wilson, J. (1971). *Education in religion and the emotions*. London: Heinemann Educational Books.

Wilson, J. (1972). *Practical methods of moral education*. London: Heinemann Educational Books.

Wolf, M., Risley, T., & Mees, H. (1964). Application of operant conditioning procedures to the behavior problems of an autistic child. *Behavior Research & Therapy, 1*, 305–312.

Wolfgang, M., Figlio, R., & Sellin, T. (1972). *Delinquency in a birth cohort*. Chicago: University of Chicago.

Wolpe, J. (1969). *The practice of behavior therapy*. New York. Pergamon Press.

Wolpin, M., & Raines, J. (1966). Visual imagery, expected roles and extinction as possible factors in reducing fear and avoidance behavior. *Behavior Research and Therapy, 4*, 25–38.

Wyckoff, P. J. (1978). *Communication skills training: A treatment of marital discord*. Unpublished doctoral dissertation, Brigham Young University.

Young, R. K., & Underwood, B. J. (1954). Transfer in verbal materials with dissimilar stimuli and response similarity varied. *Journal of Experimental Psychology, 47*, 153–159.

Yudofsky, S. C., Silver, J. M., Jackson, W., Endicott, J., & Williams, D. (1986). The Overt Aggressive Scale for the objective rating of verbal and physical aggression. *American Journal of Psychiatry, 143*, 35–39.

Zelin, M. L., Alder, G., & Myerson, P. G. (1972). Anger self-report: An objective questionnaire for the measurement of aggression. *Journal of Consulting and Clinical Psychology, 39*, 340.

Zimmerman, A. R. (1978). *The effects and effectiveness of a communication-oriented workshop in marital conflict resolution*. Unpublished doctoral dissertation, University of Minnesota.

Author Index

185

Subject Index

About the Authors

Arnold P. Goldstein (PhD, Pennsylvania State University, 1959) has spent his career as researcher and practitioner in a diversity of applied psychological settings—clinical, educational, industrial, and correctional. He joined the Clinical Psychology section of Syracuse University's Psychology Department in 1963, and taught there and directed its Psychotherapy Center until 1980. In 1981, he founded the Center for Research on Aggression, which he currently directs, and in 1985 moved to Syracuse University's Division of Special Education. Professor Goldstein has a career-long interest in difficult-to-reach clients. Since 1980, his main research and psychoeducational focus has been on incarcerated juvenile offenders and child-abusing parents. He is the developer of Structured Learning, a psychoeducational program and curriculum designed to teach prosocial behaviors to chronically antisocial persons. Professor Goldstein's books include *Psychotherapy and the Psychology of Behavior Change, Psychotherapeutic Attraction, Changing Supervisor Behavior, Structured Learning Therapy: Toward a Psychotherapy for the Poor, Skill Training for Community Living, Skillstreaming the Adolescent, School Violence, Agress-less, Police Crisis Intervention, Hostage, Prevention and Control of Aggression, Aggression in Global Perspective, In Response to Aggression,* and *Aggression Replacement Training.*

Harold R. Keller (PhD, Florida State, 1968) is Associate Professor of Psychology and Education at Syracuse University. He was formerly a member of the faculty at the University of South Carolina. Professor Keller is Director of the Syracuse University School Psychology Program and a member of the Center for Research on Aggression. His research interests concern alternative assessment and programming strategies with socioculturally different and handicapped children, and children's interactions with peers and adults (teachers, parents). In addition to

197

journal articles on these topics, he has written chapters on child abuse, behavioral assessment and consultation, and behavioral observation. With Arnold P. Goldstein and Diane Erne, he wrote *Changing the Abusive Parent.*

Psychology Practitioner Guidebooks

Editors
Arnold P. Goldstein, Syracuse University
Leonard Krasner, Stanford University & SUNY at Stony Brook
Sol L. Garfield, Washington University

Elsie M. Pinkston & Natham L. Linsk—CARE OF THE ELDERLY: A Family Approach

Donald Meichenbaum—STRESS INOCULATION TRAINING

Sebastiano Santostefano—COGNITIVE CONTROL THERAPY WITH CHILDREN AND ADOLESCENTS

Lillie Weiss, Melanie Katzman & Sharlene Wolchik—TREATING BULIMIA: A Psychoeducational Approach

Edward B. Blanchard & Frank Andrasik—MANAGEMENT OF CHRONIC HEADACHES: A Psychological Approach

Raymond G. Romanczyk—CLINICAL UTILIZATION OF MICRO-COMPUTER TECHNOLOGY

Philip H. Bornstein & Marcy T. Bornstein—MARITAL THERAPY: A Behavioral-Communications Approach

Michael T. Nietzel & Ronald C. Dillehay—PSYCHOLOGICAL CONSULTATION IN THE COURTROOM

Elizabeth B. Yost, Larry E. Beutler, M. Anne Corbishley & James R.

Allender—GROUP COGNITIVE THERAPY: A Treatment Method for Depressed Older Adults

Lillie Weiss—DREAM ANALYSIS IN PSYCHOTHERAPY

Edward A. Kirby & Liam K. Grimley—UNDERSTANDING AND TREATING ATTENTION DEFICIT DISORDER

Jon Eisenson—LANGUAGE AND SPEECH DISORDERS IN CHILDREN

Eva L. Feindler & Randolph B. Ecton—ADOLESCENT ANGER CONTROL: Cognitive-Behavioral Techniques

Michael C. Roberts—PEDIATRIC PSYCHOLOGY: Psychological Interventions and Strategies for Pediatric Problems

Daniel S. Kirschenbaum, William G. Johnson & Peter M. Stalonas, Jr.—TREATING CHILDHOOD AND ADOLESCENT OBESITY

W. Stewart Agras—EATING DISORDERS: Management of Obesity, Bulimia and Anorexia Nervosa

Ian H. Gotlib—TREATMENT OF DEPRESSION—An Interpersonal Systems Approach

Walter B. Pryzwansky & Robert N. Wendt—PSYCHOLOGY AS A PROFESSION: Foundations of Practice

Cynthia D. Belar, William W. Deardorff & Karen E. Kelly—THE PRACTICE OF CLINICAL HEALTH PSYCHOLOGY

Paul Karoly & Mark P. Jensen—MULTIMETHOD ASSESSMENT OF CHRONIC PAIN

William L. Golden, E. Thomas Dowd & Fred Friedberg—HYPNO-THERAPY: A Modern Approach

Patricia Lacks—BEHAVIORAL TREATMENT FOR PERSISTENT INSOMNIA

Arnold P. Goldstein & Harold Keller—AGGRESSIVE BEHAVIOR: Assessment and Intervention

C. Eugene Walker, Barbara L. Bonner & Keith L. Kaufman—THE PHY-SICALLY AND SEXUALLY ABUSED CHILD: Evaluation and Treatment

Robert E. Becker, Richard G. Heimberg & Alan S. Bellack—SOCIAL SKILLS TRAINING TREATMENT FOR DEPRESSION